People and Nature

Blackwell Primers in Anthropology

Each volume in this series offers a lively take on a traditional area of anthropological study. Written explicitly for nonspecialists by top scholars, these concise books provide theoretically sophisticated yet accessible and engaging introductions. They will be invaluable to students and all those who seek pithy overviews on central topics.

Published

1. People and Nature: An Introduction to Human Ecological Relations
   Emilio F. Moran

Forthcoming

2. Anthropology of Politics: An Introduction
   Linda Green
3. Medical Anthropology: An Introduction
   Margaret Lock and Vinh Kim Nguyen
4. Linguistic Anthropology: An Introduction
   Laura M. Ahearn

People and Nature

An Introduction to Human Ecological Relations

Emilio F. Moran

BLACKWELL PUBLISHING
350 Main Street, Malden, MA 02148-5020, USA
9600 Garsington Road, Oxford OX4 2DQ, UK
550 Swanston Street, Carlton, Victoria 3053, Australia

First published 2006 by Blackwell Publishing Ltd

1   2006

Library of Congress Cataloging-in-Publication Data

Moran, Emilio F.
  People and nature : an introduction to human ecological relations / Emilio F. Moran.
    p. cm. — (Blackwell primers in anthropology)
  Includes bibliographical references and index.
  ISBN-13: 978-1-4051-0571-2 (hardcover : alk. paper)
  ISBN-10: 1-4051-0571-2 (hardcover : alk. paper)
  ISBN-13: 978-1-4051-0572-9 (pbk. : alk. paper)
  ISBN-10: 1-4051-0572-0 (pbk. : alk. paper)
   1. Nature—Effect of human beings on.   2. Human beings—Effect of environment
on.   3. Environmental degradation.   4. Environmental policy.   I. Title.   II. Series.

GF75.M67 2006
304.2—dc22

                                                                      2005021020

A catalogue record for this title is available from the British Library.

Set in 11.5/13.5pt Bembo
by Graphicraft Limited, Hong Kong
Printed and bound in the United Kingdom
by TJ International Ltd, Padstow, Cornwall

The publisher's policy is to use permanent paper from mills that operate
a sustainable forestry policy, and which has been manufactured from pulp
processed using acid-free and elementary chlorine-free practices. Furthermore,
the publisher ensures that the text paper and cover board used have met
acceptable environmental accreditation standards.

For further information on
Blackwell Publishing, visit our website:
www.blackwellpublishing.com

This book is dedicated to
EMILY VICTORIA MORAN

Your mantra, "No thanks, I have plenty,"
your love of plants and animals,
your quiet but rich appreciation of the environment
have been an inspiration to me in life, and in writing this book.

Contents

Figures

Preface

My goal in this book is to introduce the reader to the evidence, both historical and contemporary, for how the reciprocal interactions between people and nature have developed, the urgency for action now to prevent truly disastrous consequences, and to make suggestions as to how we might go about doing so. While the book does not follow the usual organization for an introduction to human ecology, cultural ecology, or ecological anthropology text, the book covers much of this material in what I hope is a more engaging organization. Therefore, I give priority to recognizing why this subject is not only academic, but has to do with our very existence on this planet as biological entities. That having been said, the solutions must come from people as cultural and historical entities, and the solutions will vary across the planet as a result. There are no truly global solutions to the contemporary global environmental problem but, rather, a diversity of pathways to achieve sustainability.

Because the book is written to engage the reader from the outset, I hope it is of interest to the lay reader who wishes to be up-to-date on the evidence for our current crisis, and who is looking for possible ways to think and to act about this urgent problem. One of the important messages in the book is that changing business-as-usual (which has gotten us in this current environmental crisis) begins with the individual making choices to change their priorities. This means changing consumption behavior (i.e., needs not wants); changing behavioral patterns (e.g., turn off the TV, walking instead of driving); and sending a message to government and industry that one wants a very different set of goods and services more attuned with the value of our natural world – of which we are an integral part.

I have tried to minimize the use of jargon, although in the interest of accuracy I have sometimes left technical terms in the text, but tried to provide a clear sense of the meaning. Throughout the book I use the term "we", in many cases referring to those of us who live in urban-industrial societies of the West. Sometimes it is used to refer to us as members of the human species. I trust the difference will be clear in the context in which it is used. Because of the language in which this is written originally (i.e., English), and its distributor (i.e., Blackwell), the text is written with a Euro-American audience in mind primarily. I do not see why it might not communicate clearly to readers in other languages, but there would surely be some changes I would make if it were, for example, translated into Japanese or Chinese. For example, the discussion in chapter 2 and thereafter with regards to the Western dichotomy between people and nature, or nature and society, addresses a particular problem in Western philosophy, which many other societies would find peculiar and interesting but less central to how they might go about addressing the current environmental crisis.

This book owes a debt of gratitude to many, many people. If I were to name each and every one I am grateful to I am afraid this section would run for many pages. My thoughts have been influenced by many professors over the years, many colleagues who have read and commented on my work, many students whose ideas have inspired me and make me happier each year that I chose the academic path that I did. I have been particularly influenced by many colleagues in the global environmental change community with whom I have worked over the past decade, whether in scientific steering committees such as the Land Use and Land Cover Change Programme and the Large Scale Biosphere Atmosphere Experiment in Amazonia, or in the National Research Council's Committee on the Human Dimensions of Global Change. Service on these committees brought me in close contact with some of the finest scholars in the world, and they have inspired and encouraged me in this book to be not just academic but passionately engaged. I want to thank the many friends who provided encouragement, and family members who were not only patient with me, but gave me the love and sense of community that I see as fundamental to our future as a species on this planet. In particular, I want to thank my daughter Emily. Over the years she has taught me that we do not need more things, but that we have plenty already. That enjoying nature – plants, animals, bugs, the sun, the rain, the air we breathe, everything – makes us richer than anything we could possibly buy. I thank her for teaching me this by word and by example, and I dedicate this book to her in appreciation of this powerful lesson, and with much love.

Acknowledgments

In addition to the broad thanks I extended above, I want to thank my Blackwell editors, Jane Huber and Emily Martin, who were supportive of this project from the very beginning, and who provided just the right amount of push to ensure that the book made its way into print in a timely manner. The staff at my research center, Anthropological Center for Training and Research on Global Environmental Change (ACT), at Indiana University, provided wonderful support from the outset to the completion of this book project – typing and correcting the manuscript, finding sources, finding illustrations, seeking permissions to use materials printed elsewhere, and being as excited about the book as I was. In particular, I want to thank Vonnie Peischl and Tracie Hase who were there for me and the book each step of the way. Other staff helped generate some figures from original data sources so that readers could enjoy fresh material, whether from our own center's data, or from major databases, such as the UN data on population. I want to thank Angela Martin, Scott Hetrick, Sarah Mullin, Paula Dias, and Alvaro D'Antona in particular. I want to thank Indiana University, which has over the years supported my scholarly endeavors, and my colleagues in anthropology, geography, political science, sociology, history, and environmental sciences who were valuable sounding boards for many of these ideas.

I welcome the thoughts from each of you, readers. Every book, and every idea, is a work in progress. I welcome you to send me your thoughts on how we might better meet the challenge that we all face as members of a species on this beautiful planet.

Emilio F. Moran
Bloomington, Indiana

1

Human Agency and the
State of the Earth

Introduction

Each year, a well-known non-governmental organization publishes a State-of-the-Earth report. The story told in this report has not changed much in the past 20 years: the Earth continues to be treated with little thought for the future. More and more species are going extinct. Wetlands are disappearing at a rapid rate, endangering the migration routes of birds. Unprecedented levels of CO_2 threaten our climate system, coral reefs, and the Antarctic ice sheets. Even our closest ape relatives are finding less and less of their habitat left standing to ensure their survival. The story goes on, giving cause for considerable alarm. Even with the rise of a discourse about sustainability in recent years, there is very little evidence that governments are succeeding in implementing concrete strategic policies which ensure a sustainable Earth system as a practical objective. Yet, that is exactly what must be done. Without a conscious objective of ensuring the sustainability of the world's ecological systems, our days on this planet may be counted.

What is not widely recognized, is that we have in the past 50 years, changed nearly every aspect of our relationship with nature. Yes, the Industrial Revolution began some 300 years ago and we have been gradually increasing our impacts on the Earth over that period (Turner et al. 1990). In the past 10,000 years, in various times and places, we have had impacts that were considerable *at local scale* (Redman 1999; Redman et al. 2004). But never before has our impact been at *planetary* scale, and that is what we are having trouble understanding. As a species we think and act locally. That has been our hallmark and the reason for our success spreading over the face of the Earth – except that we have for the first time in human evolution begun to have a cumulative impact that is not just local but global.

Our impact in the past 50 years has no analogue. We have no equivalent experience in our entire history or prehistory as a species, for what we are currently doing to the Earth. Throughout the manuscript I use the term "we" most often in referring to our species. However, in terms of current impact, this "we" does not apply evenly across all members of the human family. Many ethnic populations throughout the world have a much lighter impact on the planet than members of urban–industrial societies, and have very different conceptualizations of how to treat nature. I trust readers will be able to distinguish what I mean throughout the manuscript. Clearly, the burden on the planet today is coming from urban–industrial societies and this "we" has to step forward now and take responsibility for solving the problem it has created. We must lead by example.

We have now data and information at global scale that has begun to alert us to the magnitude and seriousness of the processes we have unleashed. This evidence tells us of exponential increase in carbon dioxide, exponential rates of ozone depletion and nitrous oxide concentrations in the atmosphere, rapid losses in tropical rainforests, increases in the frequency of natural disasters, and in the rate of species extinctions. The same can be said for fertilizer consumption, damming of rivers, water use, paper consumption, the number of people living in cities, and the number of motor vehicles. There has also been a steady increase in the last 50 years in the incidence of armed conflict worldwide (Kates and Parris 2003:8062). In 1992, one third of the world's countries were involved in such conflicts, and in that year 40 million refugees and displaced persons were affected by armed conflicts (ibid.). These figures do not include the growing globalization of both terror and crime beyond state borders. Some have described this growing conflict in terms of "the coming anarchy" and as a "clash of civilizations" (ibid.).

The exponential increase in all these measurable phenomena is tied most fundamentally to two factors: the increase in the human

Figure 1.1   Highway gridlock. © CORBIS

population, and our consumption habits. Indeed, one must think of these two factors in tandem. One Euroamerican citizen consumes 25 times the resources than one average citizen from India, Guatemala, or another less-developed country does (Redclift 1996; Wernick 1997). Dependence on fossil fuels is but a reflection of these differences (see Figure 1.1). While birth rates have steadily declined to replacement level or even below in developed countries, these populations continue to impact the Earth's resources far more than the larger populations in developing countries. Both "the North" (i.e., developed countries) and "the South" (i.e., developing countries) have a huge impact on nature, the former through consumption, and the latter through population increases. If we want to leave an Earth worth living in to our children, both the North and South will need to change how they go about their business. Yet, changing business-as-usual, i.e., our "culture," world-view, and values, is easier said than done.

Whether in the North or South, specific societies have deeply held cultural and historical traditions that have both positive and negative elements that facilitate and hinder our capacity to respond to the current crisis in the Earth system. Looking to our own societies in North America and Europe, we can point positively to democratic institutions that provide effective mechanisms for citizens to respond to information provided to them whether about the effectiveness of schools in educating children, political priorities, or the state of the local environment. Yet, if democratic institutions are among the best mechanisms available to societies to respond to information, how do we explain the lack of responsiveness in the United States to the growing evidence for a global environmental crisis? Side by side with democratic institutions, the United States has (unlike Europe) a culture of individualism (Bellah et al. 1986) and a much greater value given to capital accumulation as a measure of a person's worth than in almost any other society. This pair of cultural values tends to sway a great portion of the citizenry against environmental regulations – seeing them as costly and thus likely to increase taxes on individuals, and to raise the cost of environmental goods and services. Even the promotion of public transportation as a response to reducing fossil fuel emissions is opposed by many in the United States on the grounds that it limits personal freedom to go about as one pleases, despite the costs to the country (in terms of dependence on foreign oil supplies), and the globe (in terms of emission of earth-warming gases). So, while the great majority of Americans see themselves as "environmentalists" (Kempton et al. 1995), they do not make a connection between this identity and the need to restrain their use of the personal car, as the latter infringes on their individual freedom.

In all societies one sees conflicting cultural values as well as partisan lobbies to benefit a segment of society without regard for the benefit accruing to others or to the condition of the environment. Europe has similar traditions to the United States in a number of regards (democratic institutions, capitalism) but it does not value individualism above the common good. This has made it possible for them to more quickly accept reduction of carbon dioxide in the atmosphere to 1992 levels, than for the United States and thus to support the Kyoto Protocol on the emission of greenhouse gases. A profound rift between the more advanced nations of Western Europe and the USA has developed over the willingness of the former to set limits on carbon dioxide emissions, and the unwillingness of the

USA to do so. The use, and misuse, of the Earth's resources is at the very center of international negotiations, the global political economy, and the fate of nations.

Each country will have a slightly different twist to its story: a product of the historically contingent nature of human affairs. Other countries may lack, for example, the democratic institutions' capacity to mobilize the populace in its own interest, but they may have rulers who respond quickly to evidence for environmental crisis: witness the rapid reforestation of China in the past 20 years, following decades of rapid deforestation (Fang et al. 2001). The pace of the reforestation has been without equal in the world, despite the many economic constraints faced by China and its vast population. It is not being suggested here that authoritarian regimes are a solution to environmental problems but, rather, that each nation faces different sets of challenges, based upon their political, economic and cultural situation. In short, there is no single solution to the current global environmental crisis. Human agents in specific places will need to work within the constraints and opportunities provided by their physical, social, economic, and cultural setting. This is why in solving environmental problems we must see human agents not just as "the problem" but also as the source of the solutions (Gupta comments, in Agrawal 2005:181). There are no ready-made solutions for all nations but only a challenge to be faced by groups of nations in addressing problems that cut across national boundaries and that affect people at a variety of scales from local to regional to national to global.

People concerned with the current environmental crisis, whether environmentalists or not, face a fundamental divergence in values, even if they agree on objectives. This divergence has been characterized in a variety of ways: as a divergence between a biocentric view of nature and one that is anthropocentric; or as a "deep" vis-à-vis a "shallow" ecology; and as the rift between Moralists and Aggregators (Norton 1991). Moralists, deep ecologists and biocentrists view nature and its creatures as having as many rights as humans do (e.g., John Muir, one of the founders and first President of the Sierra Club), whereas Aggregators, shallow ecologists and anthropocentrists tend to give humans a higher place and seek to balance the goals of conservation and development (e.g., Gifford Pinchot, who brought scientific forestry from Europe to the USA and created the field we now know as "conservation" with the support of Teddy Roosevelt). John Muir, who traveled with Gifford Pinchot in 1896 to the Grand Canyon, comments in his writings that he stopped Pinchot from killing a tarantula they came across "because it has as much right there as we did" (quoted in Norton 1991:17). Pinchot equated happiness in utilitarian terms and thus saw no conflict between timber production and grazing as legitimate and even desirable uses of national forests. By contrast, Muir fought him when these economic uses came at the expense of aesthetic considerations and other less obvious goals such as watershed protection. Muir represented a scientific tradition associated with older naturalists who combined aesthetic, moral, and scientific ideas – what Norton (1991:34) calls an "ecstatic science." His legacy provided preservationists with a deep respect for holistic explanations, and a longing for a science that did not banish values and awe from the process of observing and protecting nature. He differed from Pinchot largely in wanting to see the aesthetic goals as important as those of economics. Pinchot, by contrast, thought that forestry science should be value-free, a notion that Muir scoffed at. Despite their differences, they co-created the environmentalist movement in the United States and they laid the ground for debates that rage still today, between using nature for human ends, and valuing nature for itself.

These polarized views found a degree of synthesis in Aldo Leopold's 1948 classic, *A Sand County Almanac.* Leopold accepted and elaborated on Muir's views of ecstatic science, rejected the value-free scientific model of Pinchot, and pointed to an organic synthesis based upon a cultural conception of the good life. Thus, the resource manager's role was that of helping the public develop an ecological conscience – a conscience that had to grow from one's own history as a nation deeply entwined with nature. His views swung between an anthropocentric and a biocentric focus, because both are needed, and environmentalists on the whole since then manifest different degrees of this organic synthesis. The debate will never be fully resolved because human choices are always contingent, and people will make use of resources. The question is how to set restraints on such resource use, when, where, and for what purpose.

The nature–culture dichotomy has been central to Western thinking since time immemorial. It allowed some progress to be made in
developing both materialist and symbolic approaches to human–
environment interactions – but it also impeded progress by keeping
these two valid perspectives apart, rather than seeking a synthesis as
Leopold sought to do (Descola and Palsson 1996). Evidence has
accumulated that the dualist paradigm is inadequate in treating the
organic relations between people and nature. Many societies that
have been studied by anthropologists and geographers, have lacked
this kind of dualistic thinking, and provide an empirical foundation
for challenging this kind of thinking. The Achuar of the Upper
Amazon, for example, consider most plants and animals as persons,
living in societies of their own, entering into relations with humans
according to strict rules of social behavior. Game animals are treated
as affines by men, while cultivated plants are treated as kin by
women (Descola 1994). The nature–culture dichotomy is inadequate
in making sense out of non-Western realities, and even of Western
ones. In short, to understand both humanity and the rest of the
natural world, we need new ways to think about the interactions
taking place. A monistic or biocultural approach to these interactions would take us part of the way there. People are part of the
environment and, likewise, the environment is part of the person
(Descola and Palsson 1996:18). But since the dichotomy is deeply
ingrained in Western philosophy and practice, we face a constant
linguistic challenge to formulate the place of people in nature free
of this in-grained mental dichotomy.

This Western philosophical fault line between nature and humanity
at present stands in the way of resolving our environmental crises.
Tim Ingold, in his book *The Perception of the Environment* (2000)
offered a synthesis derived from developmental biology, ecological
psychology, and relational approaches in anthropology. His approach
begins by thinking about people as organisms-in-their-environment,
rather than apart from it. Crucial to this way of thinking is the
consideration of exactly how people-as-organisms act towards the
nature within which they find themselves. Materialist-thinking analysts tend to oversimplify this process by suggesting that individual
organisms or agents respond largely to the material conditions of
life, while more cultural or non-materialist analysts tend to suggest

that agents act according to memory, symbolism, social relations, and other factors (e.g., Rival 1998). It is in this domain, in particular, that one needs to move away from these dichotomies and push towards a synthesis wherein the agent, or organism, acts in a holistic fashion that does justice to the nuanced way in which we all make decisions in whatever context we find ourselves.

Thinking less dichotomously will allow us to think more like other societies. The Cartesian dichotomy between humans and nature is a peculiar notion in Western society that is not widely shared cross-culturally. Most peoples in the world do not externalize nature in this manner. Rather, they see humans as very much a part of nature. In its more extreme forms it takes the form of ideologies where we are reincarnated in forms other than human (i.e., plant, animal), and vice versa. Mythologies across the globe have always pointed to the close connection in both origin, and continuity, between animals in nature and us; between the plants in the landscape and our spiritual and material lives (Pretty 2002:13). Australian Aborigines' Dreamtime embodies these beliefs, for example, in how the land came to be, how closely they are still connected to these ancestors, and why the land must be respected – that it belongs to no one, but that it belongs to everyone.

One of the challenges before us is how to re-conceptualize the interactions between people and nature. One step forward is to think organically, as organisms-in-nature, bringing our own versions of meaning to it in accordance with our histories. Dichotomous thinking led us to think of people as apart from nature, and charged with controlling nature for human purposes – and crucially, as distinct from the inherent dynamics of the Earth system itself. It is from this error that a lot of our post World War II spiral towards destruction comes. Treating the whole of nature as we treat industrial products, as if it was inanimate, as if what we did to it did not matter to us. It does matter, and profoundly so. What happens to the air we breathe, the water we drink, and the land upon which we depend for our food matters. If we take care of it, it will nurture us – and if we damage its capacity to provide us with sustainable goods and services, and the comfort of aesthetic beauty, we will put ourselves at risk. We cannot do this alone, but it must be a partnership of trust in human communities bound by covenants that favor life over material accumulation, that favor dignity for members of the community and the pleasures of taking care of each other, and nature, as the highest good. We need to re-conceptualize our relations with each other, and with nature – and to think of human agents as organic parts of nature.

Can one Conceive of Ecosystems Without Human Agents?

It is a lovely fantasy to think of ecological systems in the absence of human agents – a fantasy used frequently in the past in ecology when speaking of natural systems in the absence of humans (e.g., Ricklefs 2001:1), and indeed there was a time many millions of years ago when that was a reality. Yet, it is also true that for several hundred thousands of years, human agents have been having a steady impact on the structure, function, areal extent, and species composition of the Earth's ecosystems (Ricklefs 2001; Cronon 1996). This has two important consequences to how we begin to develop solutions and strategies for a sustainable planet: one, there was a time when we were not running the Earth down; and two, the crisis is relatively recent and reversible if we act with consistency and alacrity.

Ecologists in the past had a tendency to blame human agents for our current crisis, and indeed there is some merit in this view as we will see throughout this book (Ricklefs 2001). However, doing so does not begin to move us towards solutions. Ricklefs notes that Cronon (1996) in his book, *Uncommon Ground*, challenges the ecologists' view of pristine nature, of nature as tending towards a self-restoring equilibrium when left alone, and that in the absence of human interference nature exists in a pristine state. Ricklefs (2001) agrees that recent ecological studies show major variations in nature and with and without human "interference" nature experiences cyclical disturbance. Human presence adds a further element of change into the processes of nature. Fortunately, we know one thing: human agents are eminently self-interested, and capable of amazing self-organization when properly motivated and led. So, if we are so capable of looking after ourselves, and to organize to achieve our goals, why are we in the current crisis? I think the answer lies in our evolutionary tendency to think primarily in terms

Figure 1.2   San hunter–gatherers with harvest. Traditional diet in the Dobe area relied heavily on nuts, roots and grass seeds gathered by women.
© Anthropology Photo File

of our local territories or immediate environment, even though our contemporary capacity to use resources from distant places has grown enormously (Bates 2001; Bodley 1996). We still have not been able to internalize the consequences of our contemporary consumption of environmental resources from throughout the world, and have not developed effective, believable ways, to have the information and feedback on what the impact of our consumption has been in those distant places. In other words, economic globalization since World War II has been very effective at using global resources, but not in giving consumers the information they need to make a decision on whether they want to have that kind of impact. That has not always been the case in how we use resources.

In the past, human agents went out from their communities to gather needed resources to sustain their population at a very local level. We must recall that for most of our experience as a species, we were hunter-gatherers (Lee and DeVore 1968, 1976; Bicchieri 1972). The range of a given hunter-gatherer band was fairly limited, and when they overused resources they were forced to move considerable distances until they could find another, familiar, territory not occupied by others, to sustain them. As hunter-gatherer populations increased, they found themselves running into other bands, and experiencing conflict with them. In short, it was preferable in many cases to limit the group's consumption to sustainable levels, rather than face a very uncertain access to distant, and possibly dangerous, territories.

Even with the advances in control made possible by domestication of plants and animals, human agents could easily understand how the local land and water were affected by their agricultural management. What was happening in China's fertile valleys, was of no interest to those living in Europe, or those living in Africa. It mattered only to parts of China. Products came from relatively close distances and anyone could assess whether they were putting themselves at risk through given practices or levels of consumption. There were, without any doubt, many cases of poor judgment in human history, but in those cases populations paid a dear price and had to move or take some other radical path to survive – and these processes took centuries rather than decades (Redman 1999; Diamond 2005).

Those familiar ways to adjust our behavior to existing resources are completely changed now for much of the human populations of the Earth. Today, whether in China, Germany, Argentina, or the United States, human agents can obtain coffee from Brazil, Sumatra, or Kenya, bananas from Honduras, Philippines, or Gabon, fish from oceans on the other side of the world, and powdered milk from places unspecified on the label of the cans. The human consumer has no way to know how much forest was cut to grow that coffee, how many people were displaced to make room for those banana plantations, what fish stock was depleted, or how much methane was emitted by that hog farm. In short, we have a complete disconnect today between what goods we use on the Earth, and the consequences of that use on People and nature. In short, we lack information on the consequences of our consumption.

If we are to begin to move towards a sustainable Earth system, we must begin to have awareness of what we do – no matter where it might occur – and to reflect on whether that is an impact we want to have. Just as consumer movements have, after much effort, succeeded in having many products labeled by corporations as to their nutritional and caloric content, we need to consider requiring that products indicate where they come from, and to post in public sites on the internet, environmental impact statements that give consumers an idea of what the cost to ecological systems is of that form of resource use in that place. Is this naïve? Some colleagues have suggested that it is. It certainly would be difficult, and companies promoting use of their products would oppose this form of exposure to consumer evaluation, and consumers driven only by lower prices would certainly not take the trouble to read an "impact label." But let's consider the options. The most common one has been to think of prices as the best regulator of consumer choice. In this case, however, prices are insidious in their consequence – as the products with the least concern for environmental impacts are likely to be cheaper and more attractive to the consumer resulting in an ever increasing spiral of products with high environmental impact. As we will see later in this book, it is the human agents individually and through their institutions, which must demand that consumer products be responsibly produced, and consumed, using their ability to choose to consume a given item or not as a tool in changing business-as-usual. In chapter eight, I go into considerable detail on strategies to begin to change business-as-usual and to regain control over how we can interact with nature in ways that are more biocentric.

The question at present is whether consumers have choices given to them between items with different environmental impact. The greatest difficulty comes from the propensity of policymakers in many places to respond more to the lobby of powerful companies, than to the demands of citizens. Companies currently make efforts to show the public, and shareholders that they are responsible corporate citizens towards the environment. To that end they produce visually attractive brochures showing their contributions to environmental conservation. At the same time, they engage in lobbying activities that prevent enactment of legislation that regulates their emissions into the environment. It is difficult for the average citizen to be cognizant of these two faces of a given company and to be able to decide whether to consume products from a given company on the grounds of their environmental position or products.

Human Agency: Individuals Making a Difference

There is a very fine line between endowing individuals with agency, or the ability to take decisions and actions, and ignoring them altogether. In ecology, we have tended to do the latter. Reading almost any major text or popular book (e.g., E. Odum, Ricklefs, Miller, to name just a few of the most popular ones), we read about how people disturb natural ecosystems, degrade a landscape, or pollute rivers. Just as the socialist literature treated the workers as a *lumpenproletariat*, (i.e., as an aggregate proletarian mass), so does ecological analysis sometimes treat people as homogenously the cause of environmental problems without recognizing the diverse ways that people in fact act towards their physical environment. Not all people in developed society behave destructively towards the environment, nor are all people in developing countries noble in how they treat nature. But in giving individuals the attention they deserve, and in trying to understand their actions, we can also fail to see the complex and diverse patterns in their actions. After all, human agency takes place within an environmental and social matrix, and individuals are members of social groups with distinct shared economic, social, cultural, and political interests. Thus, in ensuring that we give individual human agents their due, we must balance this attention with a concern for how agents share similar values and make similar decisions that have cumulative impacts.

It is all too appropriate to consider how human agency can make a difference, and how social movements can make an even greater difference. Individuals, as members of given societies, do not represent the entire society but some segment of it characterized by a given social and economic origin, acquired education and wealth, and political linkages to segments of society. As such, when individuals act they commonly represent the interests of those parts of the social fabric within which they are embedded – although on occasion they rise above those origins and represent the interests of those less fortunate than they socially, economically or politically. Time and again we see evidence of how an individual through his or her actions can change how we think about the world, and what we might do. Think of Rachel Carson and her book, *Silent Spring* (1962), and how it launched the modern environmental movement. She, herself, may not have had the right characteristics to lead the environmental movement, but she laid the foundations for public concern and outrage over what was happening to our streams and water. Others, more capable at public mobilization followed and took action that over the next several decades provided protection of species, of air and water, and of landscapes under threat.

In short, human agency does make a difference whether expressed as ideas in books and articles, in speeches, or in action. Until 1985, there were hardly any stories in any major magazine or newspaper about Amazonian deforestation – even though there had been a growing discussion of it in scientific journals, and research attesting to the rapid rates of forest destruction. The appearance of an interview with Tom Lovejoy in the *New York Times*, Science Times section, in 1985 overnight mobilized the considerable resources of the press and other media and over the next decade there was an exponential growth in the number of stories in major newspapers and magazines that resulted not only in stories but in considerable international pressure on Brazil to stop the subsidies to cattle ranchers which were fueling the high rates of deforestation – and resulted in a temporary but notable decline in both subsidies and rates of deforestation. It also resulted in funding being provided for research to monitor and understand the impact of deforestation on biodiversity, biogeochemistry, hydrology, land use and land cover, and socioeconomic impacts (e.g., Moran and Ostrom 2005; Gutman et al. 2004; Steffen et al. 2003 for recent syntheses of work carried out as a result of funding for global change).

Lay people's views of climate change, just as an example, can differ from scientific evidence. Ethnographic research by anthropologist Willett Kempton (1991) showed that most informants had heard of the greenhouse effect but that they conceptualized climate change very differently from scientists because they interpreted it in terms of stratospheric ozone depletion; plant photosynthesis; tropospheric pollution; and personal experience with temperature variation. Concern with species extinction was high but unspecific. Few informants in the study recognized the connection between energy consumption and global warming, and they did not view their fuel consumption as subject to much change. These views are further explored in Kempton et al. (1995).

So, one characteristic of human agency seems to be that we need to have the accumulation of information over an extended time, gradually shaping into a picture of a process that results in concern in some quarters, and in some individuals taking action. When that action is associated with some notable event or overwhelming evidence, it appears that public response to this news can result in remarkably rapid mobilization and effective action – as took place with ozone and the quick adoption of the Montreal Protocol to reduce use of chlorofluorocarbons (CFCs) responsible for destroying ozone. Agrawal and commentators of his article in *Current Anthropology* (2005) take note on how citizens who may not be environmentalists can gradually evolve into having a strong commitment to environmentalism sometimes through getting involved in enforcement and regulation mandated by government. From this engagement came the rise of an environmental conscience that went far beyond what the government foresaw, and that saw in some of the government regulations deep flaws in resource management. But none of this would happen if individual agents did not take the considerable risks involved in trying to change business–as–usual and to advocate a significant shift in how we do things. Change is resisted by all complex systems, largely in self-defense, and because it can be very costly if the change was unnecessary or wrong-headed. Thus, human political and economic systems, like ecological systems, resist changing their patterns until there is overwhelming evidence that something fundamental has changed which requires a shift in the structure and function of the system, if it is to survive. Are we there yet? Do we have overwhelming evidence?

Overwhelming Evidence for Concern with the Condition of the Earth System

> The Earth is currently operating in a no-analogue state. In terms of key environmental parameters, the Earth system has recently moved well outside the range of natural variability exhibited over at least the last half million years. The nature of changes now occurring simultaneously in the Earth system, their magnitudes and rates of change are unprecedented.
>
> (Steffen et al. 2003)

The above quote, from scientists associated with the International Geosphere and Biosphere Program, in a synthesis of over a decade of research, and involving thousands of scientists, and Figure 1.3, illustrate what is happening in the realm of People variables – and it raises a number of concerns. Population has been increasing rapidly since 1750 but it is really since 1950 that the exponential nature of this growth is manifest, and shows very little sign of subsiding in the next 30 to 40 years. In the past 50 years we went from 2.5 billion to 6 billion. In less than 40 years the human population will be in excess of 10 billion. Total Gross Domestic Product, foreign direct investment, damming of rivers, water use, fertilizer consumption, urban population, paper consumption, and the number of motor vehicles, have all jumped exponentially since 1950, with no evidence of a turn around in this upwards increase. This increase would be enough cause for concern, if it were happening in one or two of these measurable areas, but they are all happening simultaneously.

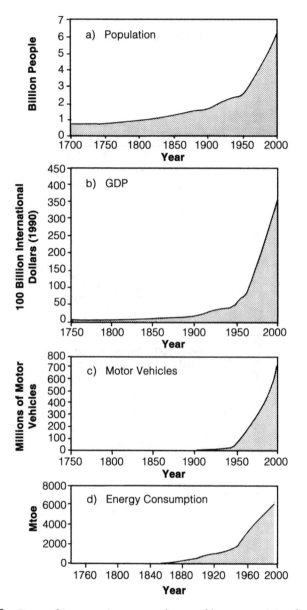

Figure 1.3 Rate of increase in many spheres of human activity for the last 300 years: a) population (U.S. Bureau of the Census 2000); b) world economy (Nordhaus 1997); c) motor vehicles (UNEP 2000); and d) energy consumption (Klein Goldwijk and Battjes 1997). *Source:* Steffen et al. 2003, p. 5

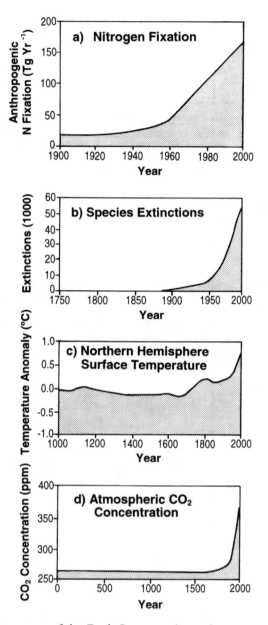

Figure 1.4 Responses of the Earth System to increasing pressure from human activities: a) nitrogen fixation (Vitousek 1994); b) species extinctions (Smith 2002); c) northern hemisphere surface temperature (Mann et al. 1999); and d) atmosphere CO_2 concentration (adapted from Keeling and Whorf 2000). *Source:* Steffen et al. 2003, p. 6

As if this were not enough reason for concern, similar synchronous events are happening on the nature side (see Figure 1.4): CO_2 concentrations, N_2O concentrations, CH_4 concentrations (all three earth-warming gases); ozone depletion, Northern Hemisphere average surface temperatures, the number of natural disasters, the rate of loss of fisheries, the increase in nitrogen fluxes in coastal zones, the rapid loss of tropical rain forests and woodlands, and the number of species gone extinct have all jumped exponentially since 1950. While some might argue, for example, that there is evidence that CO_2 concentrations are actually beneficial to many plants and that there is increased productivity in some places, experimental studies have shown that increases in productivity when CO_2 concentrations are up to 56 Pa, are lost when concentrations reach 70 Pa, at which time there is a steady decline in productivity (Granados and Korner 2002). There are also notable differences in how different species and types of forest vegetation respond to CO_2 enrichment. At Duke Forest, one species of pine, *Pinus taeda*, increased 20–25 percent in both net primary production and in woody biomass, whereas in nearby Oak Ridge, Tennessee another tree species, *Liquidamber styraciflua*, increased only 7 percent in woody biomass (Norby et al. 2002).

One of the most troubling changes in the planet has been the human alteration of the global nitrogen cycle. We know with a high degree of certainty based on available scientific evidence that we have (1) doubled the rate of nitrogen input into the terrestrial nitrogen cycle and that these rates are still increasing; (2) that increased concentrations of the greenhouse gas N_2O globally, and other oxides of nitrogen drive the formation of photochemical smog; (3) that this nitrogen increase has caused losses of calcium and potassium from soils, essential for soil fertility; contributed to the acidification of soils, streams, and lakes; increased the quantity of organic carbon stored in terrestrial ecosystems; and accelerated losses of biodiversity particularly plants adapted to efficient use of nitrogen (Vitousek et al. 1997a).

Surface temperatures over the Northern Hemisphere at present are warmer than at any other time over the past millennium, and the rate of warming has been especially high in the past 40 years (Hurrell et al. 2001:603). Agricultural yields, water management, and fish inventories are affected by this warming – having as it does its origin in an upward trend in the North Atlantic Oscillation, dictating climate variability from the eastern seaboard of the United States to Siberia and from the Arctic to the subtropical Atlantic. Changes in the North Atlantic Oscillation, in turn, affect the strength and character of the Atlantic Thermohaline Circulation. Climate changes can have profound effects on society as suggested by recent research suggesting that the lowland Maya collapse was associated with an increase in droughts in Yucatan resulting from bicentennial oscillations in precipitation (Hodell et al. 2001). The Maya were dependent on rainfall and small water reservoirs for the sustainability of their agriculture, and these multidecadal and multicentury oscillations in precipitation probably exacerbated other challenges faced by the Classic Maya (Demarest 2004). One of the conclusions of recent climate change studies is not that it will be warmer everywhere but, rather, that we will see more extreme events more frequently, such as the occurrence of El Niño events – with drought in some places and flood in others (Caviedes 2001). In Brazilian Amazonia there is already serious concern with increased frequency of devastating fires entering into Amazonian forests as a result of El Niño. In 1997, climate scientists and ecologists were in agreement that the droughts associated with that El Niño were responsible for a fire that consumed 13,000 square kilometers of forest in just one location (http://www.diariodecuiaba.com.br for January 25, 2002). We know of similar vast fires during the 1982–83 El Niño over Borneo (Prance 1986:75–102) and of devastating fires in the Amazon 250–400 years ago (Sanford et al. 1985).

Climate change will increase the severity of population and species declines, especially for generalist pathogens infecting multiple host species. The most detectable effects relate to geographic expansion of pathogens such as Rift Valley Fever, dengue fever, and Eastern oyster disease. While other factors are surely implicated, such as land use change, there is very little doubt in the end that warming trends will affect crop and human diseases [e.g., potato late blight; rice blast; cholera, and Rift Valley fever] (Harvell et al. 2002). Climate warming is also expected to alter seasonal biological phenomena such as plant growth, flowering and animal migration (Penuela and Filella 2001). Some Canadian tree species (e.g., *Populus tremuloides*) show a 26 day shift to earlier blooming over the last century, and biological spring in Europe is about 8 days earlier from data for the period 1969–98 (ibid.). In the Mediterranean, leaves of deciduous plant species now unfold 16 days earlier and fall on average 13 days later than they did 50 years ago (ibid.).

In short, the simultaneous and interconnected nature of these changes in human and in environmental conditions since 1950 suggest that human activities could inadvertently trigger abrupt changes in the Earth system with consequences that we can only faintly imagine. The most troubling of all is, of course, triggering a disruption in the "oceanic conveyor belt," as it is called, which regulates world climate (see Figure 1.5 and Broecker 1991). The increases in greenhouse gases can trigger changes in the North Atlantic circulation and computer simulation results have most of the scenarios resulting in rather dramatic collapses. We know already that the Atlantic Thermohaline Circulation (THC) can have multiple equilibria and multiple thresholds, that THC reorganization can be triggered by changes in surface heat and in freshwater fluxes, and that crossing thresholds can result in irreversible changes of ocean circulation (Rahmstorf and Stocker 2003). Our current situation with regards to CO_2 alone, not to mention all the other earth-warming gases being emitted exponentially, is well above the experience of the past 500 million years as recorded in the Vostock Ice Core (see Figure 1.6).

The evidence for the seriousness of climate change has been affirmed at a meeting of members of 63 national academies of science from all parts of the world, affirming support for the work of the Intergovernmental Panel on Climate Change (IPCC) which says that it is at least 90 percent certain that temperatures will continue to rise by at least 5.8 degrees Celsius above 1990 levels by 2100, and urging prompt action to reduce emission of greenhouse gases (IPCC 2000). In their joint statement, the representatives of the 63 national academies of science concluded that "the balance of the scientific evidence demands effective steps now to avert damaging changes to Earth's climate" (Interacademies 2000 and also see http://interacademies.net/intracad/tokyo2000.nsf).

Once we begin to operate well above any recorded levels not just for one but for many measurable parameters, the question has to be asked if we have begun to play a reckless game with the survival of

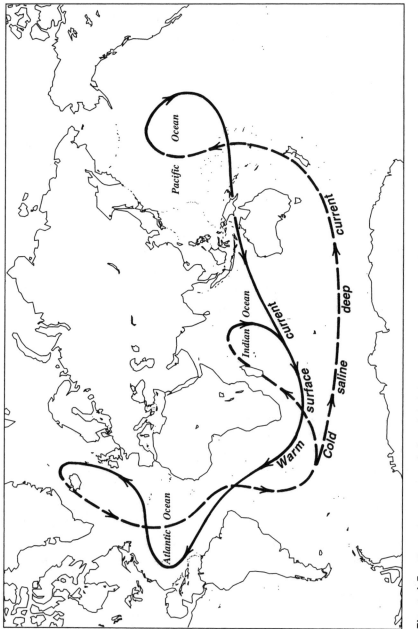

Figure 1.5 Oceanic conveyor belt. Global warming is expected to disrupt the conveyor belt that regulates climate. *Source:* Broecker 1991, p. 79

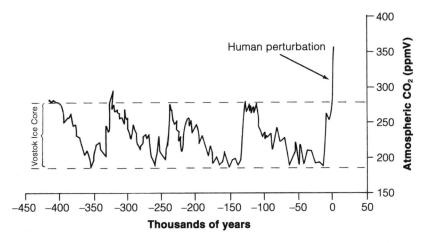

Figure 1.6   Vostock ice core provides the best current record of CO_2 for the past 450,000 years. *Source:* Petit et al. 1999, p. 399

our species on planet Earth. Do we recognize that business-as-usual threatens the end of life as we know it? Do we recognize our own contribution to it in choices made each day? Are we willing to use the considerable mental capacity, and exercise our political will, to ensure our survival and that of our children? Or are we so self-satisfied in our own material success that we cannot recognize overwhelming evidence when we see it? Is the evidence above sufficient? What else might one need to know? In the answer lies our likelihood of having a future in a world worth living in.

Looking Back and Looking Forward

In the chapters that follow, we look back at our evolution as a species and how we have managed our relations with nature, and we look at what we might have to do in the near future to reverse current destructive trends. This story is characterized by changes in how we have made use of our social and cultural tools to learn about and use natural resources. In chapter 2, we examine the history of human–environment interactions with a focus on Western cultural traditions in the study of human–environment interactions.

The dichotomy between people and the physical environment is deeply embedded in Western thought and in Western religions – a dichotomy that to this day influences our choices and actions – and that seems to facilitate a view that treats the environment as external to our being, and subject to control and domination. This is in stark contrast to some of the Eastern religions and cultures which view human existence as profoundly embedded in nature through cycles of incarnation and re-incarnation. An examination of the archeological record further elucidates this problem in the frequency with which it seems that societies which built complex systems of control over key resources, such as water, collapsed in time due to a series of miscalculations and both internal and external forces (discussed in chapter 3, and in Diamond 2005). In other words, chapters 2 and 3 review approaches from the social sciences to the study of environmental issues. In chapter 4, we discuss the web of life and how closely tied we are in it, and what are fundamental principles of ecosystem productivity that lay the foundations for our capacity to use the Earth's biotic resources. This examination of human impacts focus in this chapter on land use changes with particular attention given to the dynamics of contemporary deforestation in the Amazon Basin (an area where I, and colleagues, have worked for over 30 years). In chapter 5, we look at one important aspect of adaptation, i.e., how we use information and make decisions that affect our environment, the role of population dynamics in shaping our decisions and how our modes of production have been shaped by population growth and by our decisions to either mitigate or adapt to changes in our environment. Information and learning are discussed in the context of demographic patterns, choices about reproduction, and the various ways different populations think how to manage population-and-environment. It is important to recall that our current environmental crisis is tied at some level to the breakdown of local institutions' capacity to manage the local environment because of the larger forces unleashed by population growth, globalization and other political economic forces. In chapter 6, we examine the role of institutions and self-organization, how we can avoid tragedies of the commons, and how we might address the restoration of trust and community as part of a strategy to find once again balance with nature. Chapter 7 examines patterns of consumption in developing and developed countries, and provides a critique of our current patterns of consumption that value accumulation of material goods over other things such as human dignity, trust, and reciprocity. In the eighth and final chapter, I provide a personal examination of our environmental crisis and of viable solutions that can be tried to restore our balance on the planet by valuing community, trust and reciprocity, and to find happiness in each other and in a biocentric world, rather than in a self-centered materialist world that is leading our planet towards a collapse as has never been seen before. Do we value life more than we value things? Our own self-interest should help us make the choice.

2
A Reminder:
How Things Were. . . .

The Study of Human Ecological Relations

A decade ago, an international effort began to understand how the Earth functioned as a system. This involved taking apart the earth's components (e.g., oceans, terrestrial ecosystems, atmosphere, hydrological systems) and studying each one separately and how they connected to, and influenced, the other parts of the Earth system. This was a very successful effort that elucidated how the Earth system worked and that permitted major advances such as improved climate prediction (see synthesis volume, Steffen et al. 2004). Over this same ten year period, Earth system scientists began to appreciate how much human activities impact the various components of the Earth system (Crutzen 2002). Burning of fossil fuels results in emissions of vast amounts of carbon dioxide and other earth-warming gases that are changing the atmosphere, the productivity of terrestrial vegetation, and are at the highest levels known over the past 400 millennia. More nitrogen fertilizer is applied in agriculture than is fixed naturally in all terrestrial ecosystems (Crutzen 2002). Fishing fleets have depleted the stock of many species (removing more than 25 percent of the primary production in upwelling ocean regions, Crutzen 2002), and the catches are collapsing. Irrigation and other alterations of surface and underground water are increasing the vulnerability of hydrologic systems and the people that depend on these precious water sources, with more than half of all accessible water being used already by mankind (Crutzen 2002). Agricultural activities have resulted in massive deforestation and alteration of land cover at huge scales – with the amount of land devoted to agriculture increasing five-fold over the past three centuries. In short, human activities are so pervasive that they are capable of altering the Earth system in ways that could change the viability of the very processes upon which human and non-human species depend. Interest in understanding this reciprocal relationship between people and the environment goes a long way back. The following section provides a compressed history of Western ideas about human–environment interactions.

The history of studying human ecological relations goes back to the very beginnings of Western thought, and can also be found in non-western societies (e.g., discussions in Moran 2000; Glacken 1967; Alavi 1965; among others). Contemporary theories about the nature of human ecological relations are only understandable in the light of the historical roots of such theories. Modern notions of homeostasis reflect ancient assumptions about order in nature, that persist to this day (Cronon 1996). This same yearning for order keeps making its way into ecological explanations through the attribution of purposive motives to biological populations.

Every society has philosophical or mythological explanations about the natural world and human beings' place in it. It is through such explanations that members of society articulate both their behavior as individuals and understand the requirements of survival. Neither the behavior nor the requirements of survival are at all obvious to human agents. Each agent must be socialized as a member of a given culture and society to understand what, at this time and in this place, is acceptable behavior, what is the accumulated knowledge that members of that society can pass on that could serve each person well (and this is differentially shared among households due to differences in experience, income, and expertise). Cosmologies and mythologies were widely used in the past to embody the sacred and the profane knowledge of people in the place where they found themselves. Today we learn in schools, at home, and in church what society expects from us, and what knowledge we must seek to be functioning members of society.

Ancient Greece's theories arose from observations of nature and society. At the heart of their argument was that their political power was based on their strategic location in the Mediterranean. Writers explained that their geographical location was most conducive to favorable cultural developments because there people were subject to an ideal proportion of the basic four elements (fire, water, earth, air). A hot and humid tropical climate was believed to foster idleness and resignation (Thomas 1925:227), while the climate of Greece was more conducive to progress. These ideas, which were endorsed by Hippocrates, Aristotle, and other major figures of ancient Greece, set a trend that was followed by the Romans.

Roman writers gave environmental reasons for the Roman conquest of the rest of the civilized world. Cicero attributed this success to the strategic location of Rome itself; Vitrivius attributed it to the all round superiority of peoples located in the middle latitudes. He pointed to Rome's dominance as proof of the correctness of his judgment. Pliny, another Roman author, added to this assertion by describing Rome's location as so salutary to human development that "the manner of the people are gentle, the intellect clear, the genius fertile and capable of comprehending every part of nature. They have formed empires which has never been done by the remote nations" (Pliny quoted in Thomas 1925:38).

Human–environment theories of classical times survived the turmoil that followed the breakdown of Roman rule (Castaglioni 1958). Theoretical contributions of the Arab world elaborated on classical theories. The Arab conception of the human–environment relationship consisted of an astrological explanation that considered humans to be part of the cosmos, and their character determined by the ruling stars of their environment, and of a purely geographical explanation based on climatic considerations (Alavi 1965:68). Elaborating upon the geographical explanation, Arab scholar Al-Mas'udi discussed the importance of the availability of water, natural vegetation, and topography in determining the sites of human settlements (ibid.).

As Europeans began their colonial expansion into the Americas, Africa, and Asia, information on new environments spread, and writers of the Renaissance began to question Greco–Roman theories on the relationship between environment and human character, including whether climate had the same influence on all living things. The role of human culture in buffering the impact of environment upon society began to be appreciated, and the scope of possible explanations for similarities and differences in human populations grew. In the eighteenth century, however, climatic influences once again became the focus of deterministic explanations with Bodin and Montesquieu, among others, affirming the superiority of middle latitudes. The eighteenth century was also a period when natural historians, concerned with notions of human progress, formulated evolutionary sequences that attempted to explain human society in terms of increased human control over nature. Turgot (1727–81) in his *Universal History* foreshadowed the cultural ecological approach of Julian Steward. Turgot interpreted the band-organization of hunters as a response to the necessity of pursuing game over vast areas. Such pursuit resulted, in turn, in the dispersal and diffusion of peoples and ideas (Moran 2000).

In the late nineteenth century, attempts were made to illuminate the processes by which human–environment interactions occur. This resulted in the cultural area approach, one of the most popular theories that dominated the late nineteenth and early twentieth century explanations and was an early version of what one might call biogeography. In his 1939 book, *Cultural and Natural Areas of Native North America*, Kroeber organized his material into regional categories developed from data on subsistence systems, habitat characteristics, and population densities. Kroeber gave extensive examples of how environmental factors limit cultural practices such as maize farming, population concentration, and tribal and linguistic boundaries. Kroeber's approach can be likened to that of British geographer/anthropologist C.D. Forde (1934). Both of them emphasized the need for collecting ecological data and viewed such data as potentially valuable in explaining cultural similarities. Despite his inability to deal with irregularities in human–environment interaction, Kroeber's book is of major importance in that it forms the backdrop to the formulation of the cultural ecological approach (Steward 1955; Netting 1977).

On the biological side, the nineteenth century was a creative period for natural historians. Their careful recording of the similarities and differences in living organisms stimulated the development of theories that influence all of us still today. The contributions of Charles Darwin to ecological theory stand out. Darwin found inspiration for his theory of evolution in the works of Charles Lyell and Thomas Malthus. Darwin took a copy of Lyell's *Principles of Geology*

(1830) with him on his Beagle voyage and confided in his diary that it "altered the whole tone of [his] mind." Through Lyell's account of the geological record, Darwin saw an alternative to the narrow Biblical timescale and was impressed by the relationship between environmental change and modifications in biological forms. Malthus's *An Essay on the Principle of Population* (1798) influenced Darwin with its idea that the natural trend of the human population was to increase unless stopped by disease, war, or famine. Darwin extended this notion to plant and animal populations.

Darwin's synthesis, *On the Origin of Species by Means of Natural Selection*, appeared in 1859. In this work, Darwin did not really explain the origin, but rather the mechanisms by which species develop and diversify. Darwin began by assuming that all living things are related and that the diversity of species results from a continual branching out. Such branching is a product of the process known as natural selection. According to the principle of natural selection, those organisms most fit to survive and reproduce in a given environment will out-reproduce less well-adapted organisms; species not adapted to current environmental conditions will be reduced to insignificant numbers.

Modern evolutionary theory and genetics have elaborated on the Darwinian synthesis. The basic elements of evolutionary theory are, briefly: (1) all populations have genetic variation through the mechanisms of mutation and recombination, (2) all populations seek to increase their numbers exponentially until restricted by environmental constraints, (3) under a given set of environmental circumstances, the best-adapted phenotypes in a population will be selected for, and (4) the effect of the environment on the genotype is indirect. Adaptive changes in all organisms, including human beings, are mediated by the genetic hereditary material passed on from generation to generation. Since more fit individuals who possess the best-adapted traits must replace a population, evolutionary change is slow. A population thus often reflects earlier conditions and is always in process of change – just as the environment is always changing (Levins 1968:11).

Biological adaptation is seldom perfect and is opposed by numerous factors. Among these are mutations and gene flow, evolutionary opportunity, physical limits, problems of allocation, and changing environments (Ricklefs 1973:71–73). No matter how well adapted a population may be, new random mutations are introduced into a population, leading to change. The past history of an organism limits future changes, so that major changes in anatomy are rare and may take millennia. The range of adaptation is also limited by the properties of the natural world, and these cannot be easily altered either. Adaptation is essentially a compromise. The results are seldom the "best." Adaptation is never perfect because environments are always changing, and populations must constantly readjust to the new environmental conditions.

The period since the 1950s has seen fast growth in ecological approaches, not surprising given the gradual deterioration of the global environment. Julian Steward began to formulate his themes in the 1930s, but his research strategy was not implemented until the 1950s. Unlike Kroeber who sought general theory in his research efforts, Steward delimited a range of phenomena and sought to explain the cause-and-effect relations between such phenomena. Steward's approach, which has come to be known as cultural ecology, led young scholars into the field and remains influential, particularly in archeology and geography. A more biological approach to cultural ecology followed in the 1960s (Rappaport 1968; Baker and Little 1976). This approach, which relied heavily on evolutionary and ecological theory, has come to be known as ecological anthropology to indicate the importance assigned to the ecological system. The ecosystem concept provided a conceptual framework more satisfactory to some scientists (Geertz 1963; Rappaport 1968) than the behavior/ social structure equation stressed by Steward (but see critiques of the ecosystem approach in E.A. Smith 1984; Winterhalder 1984). By studying human populations as parts of ecosystems, attention is paid to human adaptability, physiological, cultural, and behavioral. The research strategy of ecological anthropology is to study a wide range of human responses to environmental problems, to social constraints, and to environmental problems. On the other hand, the focus tends to give less attention to individual variation and the behavior of agents (Moran 1990).

Studies with an ecological anthropological approach focused in the 1960s and 1970s on isolated populations such as Alaskan Eskimos and Aleuts, South American Yanomamo Indians, New

Guinea tribesmen, and Miskito Indians of Central America. The choice of such small isolated groups was made because it permitted easier monitoring of the interaction between the human population and their environment. Monitoring the complex relationships between such environmental stresses as disease, low energy and food availability, heat, cold, and altitude in technologically complex societies is more feasible in small populations. Although one might have expected to see ecological anthropologists study human response to environmental degradation, urban pollution, and other contemporary stresses following these two decades – and we can find some cases of such studies – on the whole specialists have continued to prefer to work on largely rural populations in less developed settings.

The Contemporary Study of Environmental Issues: The Rise of Cross-Disciplinary Team-Based Approaches

A number of other approaches emerged in the 1980s and 1990s and which were nicely reviewed in a volume organized by the Anthropology and Environment section of the American Anthropological Association, and edited by Carole Crumley (2001), among the approaches covered were: biocultural anthropology, cognitive anthropology, the archeology of global change, environmental justice, and concern with grassroots environmental non-governmental organizations. Biocultural anthropology emerged from the growing interaction of biological anthropologists with cultural anthropologists and archeologists. It was characterized by an effort to develop joint research activities and to examine carefully the way social and cultural features affected the biology of human populations. It took its most extreme form in the charges that hunting-gathering populations were nothing more than populations that had been marginalized economically at certain times in their history (Wilmsen 1989). More commonly, however, it reflected a growing incorporation of political economy into biological analysis (Goodman and Leatherman 1998; Coimbra et al. 2002). It is still a growing area, resulting from the growth of team-based research addressing complex biological and political economic interactions. Not all biocultural approaches make a connection to political economy.

Other approaches emphasize the coevolution of biology and culture (e.g., Boyd and Richerson 2005; Durham 1991; Winterhalder 1994).

Cognitive anthropology grew out of the work of ethnoecology earlier (e.g., Conklin 1957) and has always had an interest in cognition of the environment. It has focused heavily in the past on how indigenous societies understand human–environment relations, and with folk classification of biological species (Posey and Balée 1989). During this period it also extended to the study of contemporary urban Americans (Kempton et al. 1995) and shed light on the diversity of environmental views of contemporary Americans. This new approach asks "what mental models does a culture use to understand and predict the ways in which species interact with each other and with human perturbations?" (Kempton 2001:59). Atran and Medin (1997) have shown how a Maya cultural model operates to ensure sustainability of the forest through emphasis on inter-dependence of parts and of the unity of forest and the people. This shows that there can be vastly different cultural models of the environment across cultures. A more detailed discussion is found later in this chapter.

Environmental justice has been a topic of interest for a few years and one that has attracted several disciplines concerned with the disproportionate burden of exposure to pollution borne by ethnic minorities (Johnston 2001). This connection between environmental quality and social justice is important but one that requires great attention to methodology since it is not always easy to document the precise exposure in time and space that may cause a series of ailments to a given group. There is a small but growing presence at the Environmental Protection Agency (EPA) of social scientists that promises to provide in the future valuable input in the area of environmental justice and environmental regulation. Much of the work on environmental justice is invisible to academics, since many of its practitioners work in NGOs and are too engaged with the political mobilization to become visible in academic journals but some of this activity may be visited in the web at http://www.igc.org/envjustice/training.

Anthropology and geography in particular have paid attention to the interactions among traditional populations, such as those practic-ing shifting cultivation, pastoralism, and other forms of traditional cultivation (including paddy rice production). Findings have elucidated little known facts at the time, such as the high efficiency of traditional cultivators using input/output analysis of caloric costs (Rappaport 1968; Pimentel and Pimentel 1996), and the energetic inefficiency of our allegedly efficient systems of mechanized grain production. This wave of research was the first to scientifically question the mantra that modern methods of agriculture were more efficient than traditional ones. Modern methods do indeed have greater output per unit of land, but only if one leaves out the high cost of fossil fuel inputs. As a result, there has been a softening of the rhetoric of promoters of intensive mechanized approaches, and an acceptance even by members of the National Research Council that "alternative agriculture" is an option worth examining that offers many advantages to people and the environment (NRC, 1989; see also Pretty 2002, 1998; Netting 1993). By alternative agriculture is meant a return to more organic, lower input, and greater emphasis given to selection of varieties for their efficiency in the use of nutrients and in resistance to pests, rather than going always for highest output and applying chemicals to crops to fight off the inevitable pests and pathogens. This trend has reversed in recent years as advocates of genetically modified crops (GM) have taken a strong position that seems to once again downplay the value of low input approaches. A battle between industry, which wishes to generalize the use of GM foods, and many farmers and some nations that see in GM foods a further exacerbation of the negative trends in environmental conditions looms in the decades ahead.

In the late 1980s, interest in the human dimensions of global environmental change and growing awareness that the environmental crisis had only deepened during the 1980s grew. Interest during this period arose from concern with potential climate warming, but it soon became clear that that was just one of many potentially threatening issues that needed attention. Unlike the earlier wave of research, which maintained the traditional disciplinary tendencies to work alone, in small areas, using traditional research methods, the new wave of research emphasized early on that these problems were just too complex to be addressed by single disciplines or single scholars, but required large teams representing multiple disciplines (NRC 1992). Geography, anthropology, sociology, political science, psychology, and economics became participants early on and began to work together in unprecedented ways as they cobbled research recommendations (NRC 1992, 1994, 1999a, 1999b) and began to work on topics such as land use and land cover change; decision-making; consumption; regional climate change; and sustainability/vulnerability.

Land use and land cover research has been of long standing interest under rubrics such as agrarian studies, rural sociology, and cultural ecology (Thomas et al. 1956). From the outset it was one of the prime topics for research on global change, since land use and land cover change account for most of the changes in the terrestrial biosphere. Research since 1995 has focused on the drivers of land cover change (Geist and Lambin 2002; Lambin et al. 2001) and the complex and highly variable causes from place to place. Research in this area has led to advances in techniques and methods, particularly in the application of remote sensing and geographic information systems (Guyer and Lambin 1993; Skole and Tucker 1993; Moran et al. 1994; Liverman et al. 1998; Walsh and Crews-Meyer, 2002; Goodchild and Janelle 2004; Gutman et al. 2004; Moran and Ostrom 2005).

Decision-making research tends to be dominated by no single discipline but economics and psychology bring some of the stronger theories to bear upon it. The issue of individual choice is at the core of what needs to be understood in the study of how we make decisions. Psychologists ask questions as to whether the individual makes the decisions, or whether context and other pressures of the organizations within which individuals act most often explain the choice (Stern 2000). Values and attitudes are very important in shaping individual choice. It appears that favorable environmental behavior lies at the end of a long, causal chain involving both individual and contextual factors (Stern et al. 1999). Personal and contextual factors condition the effect of values and attitudes on specific behaviors. Taking a pro-environmental behavioral position is affected by environmental concern, attitudes, information, beliefs, abilities, and external conditions that either impede or facilitate taking a particular course of action. While this seems to downplay the role of values and attitudes, it does confirm the complexity of how people make decisions and the need to better understand how these choices are made. The current context within which people live clearly favors more consumption and less concern with conservation. It has been suggested that one way to bring about more favorable conservation is to focus on goods that have a disproportionate impact. Among the upper and middle classes in America the purchase of a home, motor vehicles, home heating and cooling systems, and major appliances can have a huge environmental impact. Purchasing high-efficiency homes and equipment which have decadal impacts is particularly important. Yet, there is evidence that these social classes are buying larger homes and larger motor vehicles just when their household size is smaller. What could reverse this trend? What is behind this counterintuitive preference for larger autos and homes? Is it the construction of demand by advertising? Status competition? How different are the patterns of consumption of poor and lower middle households? Are they driven by the same or different external incentives? Attention to these topics needs to move front and center of researchers wishing to contribute to solutions to the environmental crisis.

Another approach from the social sciences to environment comes from cognitive anthropology and ethnobiology. This approach focuses on cognition as mediated through language (naming and classification of things), through cognitive models that organize environmental sensory inputs, and through issues of identity and socially distributed cognition (Kempton 2001). Early work focused on ethnobotany and ethnozoology, or how people organized their cultural knowledge of plants and animals, with the former being far more extensive (Conklin 1954; Berlin et al. 1973; Berlin 1976). Remarkable correspondence was found between indigenous systems of ethnobotanical classification and the Linnean system. In some cases indigenous systems surpassed it for domains of particular importance to them or because of inherent biological richness unexpected by the Linnean system. For a comprehensive view of research and findings in ethnobiology see Berlin (1992). The second trend, focusing on cognitive models, can be found as early as Rappaport (1968) who developed an elaborate cognitive model of how ritual cycles operated to regulate the timing of swiddens and pig slaughters and thus the use of land. It is found in many other cases, including Chernela (1987) where she found that the Tukano Indians of the

Northwest Amazon applied their model of clans and ancestors to the regulation of their fishing activities, thereby avoiding degradation and resource overuse. The third trend emphasized identity and group formation. It is based on the notion that a growing number of people associate, for example, being an environmentalist with whom they are. Three-quarters of adult Americans have identified themselves in Gallup polls as environmentalists (see Kempton et al. 1995: 4–5). Cultural models affect behavior and cognitive approaches deserve an important place in how we think about human–environment interactions (Atran and Medin 1997). While cognitive models alone cannot be used to predict behavior, decision-making on the environment is strongly influenced by these cognitive models.

Consumption research is relatively recent but growing quickly in interest among social scientists, particularly those who wish to understand the environmental impact of those consumption choices (see a longer discussion in chapter 7). The National Research Council (1997) convened a panel of experts to set an agenda for this topic and they came up with an exciting set of issues that require immediate attention. For some scholars the issue of decision making and of consumption can be boiled down to "lets get the prices right". There is a voluminous literature in economics that discusses the difficulties of determining the right prices for things like clean air that are not traded in markets and the imperfect functioning of markets for "public goods" (e.g., Cropper and Oates 1992; Stern 1999; Stern et al. 1986).

Regional climate change studies emphasized the significance of climate variability and extremes in how people perceive and respond to climate change (Giorgi et al. 1998; Justice and Desanker 2001; Liverman et al. 2001). Parry (1990) showed how climate variability and change might affect agriculture and food production across the world. Some of the most exciting work focused on El Niño events. Climate variability associated with El Niño and La Niña events (based on an alteration in the surface temperature of the Pacific current) which results in drought, floods, and severe storms across the world (Caviedes 2001, Stern and Easterling 1999).

A number of recent approaches further strengthen the contributions of the social sciences to the study of environmental issues. One of them is a historically informed approach under a variety of rubrics:

historical ecology (Crumley 1994; Balée 1989), environmental history (Worster 1984), and demographic anthropology (Childs 1998, 2004; Fricke 1986). These approaches are characterized by efforts to provide a long-term perspective to human–environment studies. Each of these approaches offers distinct points of view. Environmental history, which began as an intellectual history of the environmental movement, has developed to emphasize social and political theory of human–environment interactions taking both macro-historical approaches (e.g., Diamond, 1995, 1997, 2005), and more micro-historical approaches (e.g., Worster, 1998, 1984). Historical ecology, on the other hand, tends to explore the in-space and over-time changes that characterize those ecological relations (e.g., Crumley 1994, Balée, 1998), often within the context of landscape change (Crumley 1994:6). Demographic anthropology focuses more on within group dynamics of fertility, mortality and migration (Childs 2004; Kertzer and Fricke 1997; Fricke 1994). There is also a growing number of syntheses which pay close attention to long-term historical processes that affect forest ecology and landscape change, such as the study of New England, and Harvard Forest in particular (Foster and Aber 2004); the study of land change in southern Yucatan (Turner et al. 2004); and the study of forest ecosystems across the Americas (Moran and Ostrom 2005).

Related to this are approaches that are regional but set within a local context. Early efforts in this regard, such as Geertz (1963) and Bennett (1969) were largely historical studies set in a regional rather than local context. Bennett defined the Northern Plains in terms of its historical unit and not solely on the basis of its biogeography (1969:26). Other well-known efforts are those of the !Kung San Project (Yellen 1977; Lee and DeVore 1976), the Chiapas Project (Berlin 1992), and our own studies of Amazonia (Moran et al. 1994, Moran and Brondizio 1998; Moran et al. 2002). Research in the past decade on the human dimensions of global change has further intensified the contributions of the social sciences to environmental research (NRC 1999a).

The study of sustainability and vulnerability is relatively recent and addresses concerns in contemporary society over the design of sustainable systems, and the growing vulnerability of people to chang-ing environmental conditions (e.g., sea level rise, extreme weather events). Kasperson and Kasperson (2001) provide a synthesis of what we know about vulnerability and make efforts to design rigorous study of such processes. Vulnerability studies also extend to non-human species (Abbitt et al. 2000). The goal of the latter is to identify species and areas of vulnerability before they become endangered.

The Evolution of Human–Environment Interactions

Many introductory ecology and environmental science books begin with a picture of a natural world without humans – one in which the forces of nature and natural selection operate without the intervention of people. It is a convenient image: it allows researchers to look for patches of ecosystems in which the human presence is not evident, and to study them "as if" no people have ever altered the ecological relations between species, populations and communities. Indeed, without such an assumption, research would be more difficult and results less clear. This assumption has served well the cause of science and helped advance our understanding of ecological systems. Yet, if our goal is to also be able to bring about changes in how people relate to nature in order to address our current environmental crisis, it is an assumption that distracts us from the reality that practically every ecosystem on Earth has been shaped by human action not just over the past 10,000 years, since the beginning of agriculture, but ever since hominids walked the earth millions of years ago (Redman et al. 2004). Our ancestors may not have brought about the sorts of conditions that we see in the dawn of the 21st century, but they did steadily and throughout the world impact ecosystems by their hunting, their gathering, their use of fire, and by changing predator-prey balance, and even herbivore pressure on plant species.

Evidence keeps accumulating that our human ancestors spread out of Africa a very long time ago, and that they spread quickly worldwide, and that they made considerable advances in their use of resources. They followed game wherever it might flee, and carried seeds with them and broadcasted them wherever they went. The evidence is growing that our ancestors did not passively adapt to their environment but modified it to facilitate their quest for food – familiar food at that. This should not surprise us. Study after study of migrant populations show that they carry few material possessions, but they often carry seeds and plants and animals which will allow them to produce food that they are familiar with, and to have animals that they understand, or can help them in the quest for food security. In short, we know that the first imperative of survival is aided by the tendency of all people to reproduce the patterns of production that they know, and that have sustained them in the past. While people learn about new environments over time, it is a process that takes years, if not generations. Initial "adaptation" is a result of reproducing the familiar mode of production and reproduction in new environments – and gradually modifying it as the success, or failure, of the transferred mode of production proves their worth, or failure to meet their needs (Moran 2000; 1981).

It is this dynamic that probably explains why most migrations, in the distant past, and even today, are short distance migrations. In this way, people are less likely to encounter totally different ecosystems, and resources, that are totally unfamiliar to them and their adaptation to the new area can be more successful since it implies minor changes towards resources encountered. Migrations to totally different ecosystems is fraught with risk, and with a high probability of failure. An adaptive strategy to the use of resources, to the climate patterns, and to the behavior of plants and animals in a different environment takes decades to be acquired, and few people could survive it without subsidy or external support. Until the nineteenth century, cases of such subsidization were rare. For most of human prehistory, human groups which splintered off to seek new territories, and resources, were totally on their own – with only their wits, the strength of their arms, and their acquired patterns of resource use to guide them into the unknown.

Another important component of migrations in the past to keep in mind is that until relatively recent times human populations moved with only what they could carry on their backs (see Figure 2.1). The use of carted wagons and the use of the wheel are relatively recent in human history. This had as a direct consequence that human groups did not accumulate possessions that they could not carry themselves, or that they could not reproduce quickly at their new location. Thus, light baskets served a multitude of purposes

Figure 2.1   San hunter–gatherers carrying all their possessions.
/Du/da People moving south along the fenced border road, 1969.
© Anthropology Photo File

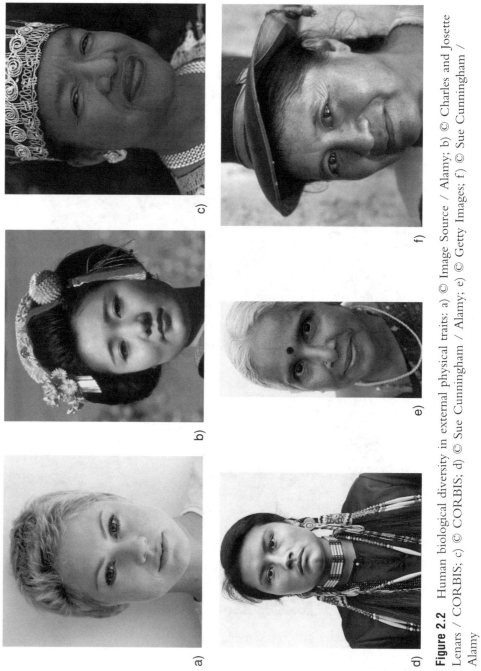

Figure 2.2 Human biological diversity in external physical traits: a) © Image Source / Alamy; b) © Charles and Josette Lenars / CORBIS; c) © CORBIS; d) © Sue Cunningham / Alamy; e) © Getty Images; f) © Sue Cunningham / Alamy

and were light to carry. Tools were often multipurpose or man-ufacturable with ease. A lot of the cultural knowledge of human groups was invested in teaching each member, and each generation, the skills of making the full set of tools required to make a living and survive effectively in their habitat. This knowledge has been shown time and again to have been profoundly sophisticated and effective (Schick and Toth 1993; Demarest 2004).

The exemplary populations who are responsible for our occupation of Planet Earth, and for our success in learning to use its plant and animal resources have come to be known as hunter-gatherers (see Figure 2.1). They not only moved, of course, but they were also changed biologically by the experience of migration. Human migration injects DNA from one gene pool to another (Lasker and Mascie-Taylor 1988). In small populations, such as hunter-gatherer bands, the effects of migration might be similar to those of random genetic drift (ibid: 2). Yet, while the human race is one genotypically (i.e., there is one human genome) it is characterized by great phenotypic variability and that we differ largely in the proportions of given traits that have resulted from both past and current mixing between human groups (see Figure 2.2). Studies long ago, by Boas (1910, 1912) and others (e.g., Goldstein 1943), showed that the children of migrants varied in stature, in the shape of their head, and in other anthropometric measures as a result of changes in diet, in swaddling practices, and in exposure to environ-mental stresses or opportunities. Thus, as human groups have migrated they have changed the human-environmental interactions with consequences to their own biology, as well as their cultural repertoire. Environment plays an important role in bringing about biological consequences in human populations: temperature, humid-ity, altitude, wealth or scarcity of resources, disease vectors, quality of foodstuffs, hours of sunshine, inches of rainfall, all vary with location. Temperature, humidity, precipitation and hours of sunshine are likely to impact the development of coloration, and the scheduling of activities by human groups and their housing preferences. The quality of foods consumed and the pressure from disease vectors will result in different height and weight tendencies at the popula-tion level. Altitude has been associated with differences in chest capacity, and in capillary development to reduce the effects of hypoxia for high altitude dwellers such as in the Andes (Baker and Little 1976).

Hunter-Gatherers: Setting our Preferences

Much of what we do, and don't do, has its roots in the preferences and habits that our hunter-gatherer ancestors found to be of adaptive value. Sometimes, these may even go back to our primate ancestors, as growing evidence suggests. This is as it should be. Insofar as we have gradually evolved as a species, we have kept and honed skills that have proven to be useful: our capacity for self-organization, to use language to transmit information, and to flee when the odds don't look particularly good. Other traits also vary in response to the great variability of environments and situations that groups encounter reflected in differences in patterns of marriage, kinship and descent; clothing and housing forms; food preferences; and world views.

For a long time, studies in anthropology and geography suggested that the hunter-gatherer (HG) mode of subsistence was relatively homogeneous − a result of the harshness of making a living with simple tools in sometimes difficult environments. A not insignificant component of this perspective of HG as homogenous came from the impact of a few studies that were very influential because of the detail and quality that they brought to understanding this mode of production (e.g., the San Studies led by Lee and DeVore 1968, 1976). These important empirical studies began to construct a picture of hunter-gatherers (Damas 1969a; Netting 1971; Helm 1962) that showed the exquisite linkage between HG and the biogeography of their habitats. The view was one known in anthropology as "environmental possibilism" in which characteristics of people resulted from constraints posed by the environment. Like the rest of anthropology and geography at the time, the emphasis was not on internal variability but on accounting for the broad shared patterns of each group as a whole. Functionalist approaches went further and began to account for the adaptive value of particular forms of social organization in the achievement of adaptation to environmental resources. Julian Steward, in particular, is responsible for leading the field of anthropology, along with Carl Sauer in geography, towards a view known as cultural ecology. This view gave us considerable insights not just about hunter-gatherer populations but across the entire array of pre-industrial modes of production (see Netting 1977 and subsequent editions).

The picture emerging from these studies was that hunter-gatherers were not at the mercy of unpredictable resources, facing the danger of starvation at every turn. Instead, the studies began to point out the great variety of adaptive strategies, and the often leisurely way in which HG groups lived. Most influential in this regard were the papers published in *Man the Hunter* (Lee and DeVore 1968), *Hunter and Gatherers Today* (Bicchieri 1972), and the many publications from the studies of San peoples of the Kalahari (Yellen 1977, among others). These studies showed, first, that the view of the marginality of HG resulted from their relatively recent occupation of unfavorable areas. In the past, before agricultural peoples and states pushed them into these marginal environments, they had occupied more productive areas and had enjoyed a better life. Secondly, they showed that even in unfavorable environments they had managed to adjust their population size and their mode of production to achieve their needs with a modicum of ease and short hours dedicated to subsistence (see Table 2.1).

Perhaps the most important characteristic of HG in these writings is that they have lived in small bands or groups. This has the advantage of reducing their immediate impact on the landscape and also allows them to have a very immediate read of the landscape and

Table 2.1 Work Hours per Week: Men and Women

	Subsistence Work	Tool Making and Fixing	Subtotal	Housework	Total Work Week
Men	21.6	7.5	29.1	15.4	44.5
Women	12.6	5.1	17.7	22.4	40.1
Average, both sexes	17.1	6.3	23.4	18.9	42.3

Source: Lee 1979, p. 278

their impact upon it. The other, and closely related, characteristic is reliance on frequent movement to further reduce their impact on the area immediately around their habitation sites, thereby also gaining access to a greater variety of resources seasonally and inter-annually. The disincentives to frequent movement were apparently addressed by frequent visiting of neighboring, and often interrelated, bands with whom they socialized, exchanged information, and often exchanged partners and members.

Male hunters and female gatherers fanned out from base camps and brought back resources that were shared with the entire community. Clearly this would not work well with large groups, but given the small size of bands this system of sharing and reciprocity has been shown to spread the risk of any given day's harvest of resources being low for part of the band. This emphasis on sharing and reciprocity also militated against accumulation of material goods. Even if a group was particularly successful, this success was likely to attract neighboring bands or those out to harvest resources, to whom there were comparable expectations of sharing. This had huge advantages in ensuring the survival of individuals, and cementing their bonds over long time periods. This was important since mating often took place across bands (band exogamy) and assessment of which men were good hunters and which women were good gatherers must have surely played into mate choice, and acquisition of respect for those abilities.

Bands were not always the same size, but had enough inherent flexibility to grow in size, at least seasonally, in response to resource availability. Research by optimal foraging theorists (e.g., Winterhalder 1981; E. A. Smith 1983) have shown the importance in HG adaptations of risk minimization. Much of the strategic food sharing which is so important to HG is rooted in their efforts to reduce risk (Winterhalder 1986; Kaplan and Hill 1985). Without food sharing strategies, HG populations, and contemporary populations in rural and urban areas with scarce resources, are highly vulnerable to fluctuations in access to food necessary for survival (Winterhalder 1986). In those cases when HG were able to locate near a very abundant food source, and retain control of this location, studies have shown that they can and will abandon their migratory ways and small band size. The classic example of this are the indigenous peoples of the Pacific NW in North America that began as nomadic bands but developed large settlements with large populations, and accumulated significant property, because of the abundance of salmon and other resources (Suttles 1968). Interestingly, they also developed annual rituals wherein they destroyed significant amounts of those same material goods, as well as shared them with groups less fortunate than they (see Figure 2.2).

In short, our HG ancestors laid a very important behavioral foundation for our species: they excelled at survival and populated the planet by maintaining flexibility in the size of their groups, by frequent movement to reduce their impact and to gain access to a wider set of resources, they reduced their risk from the unpredictabilities of climate and the environment by emphasizing the value of food sharing and reciprocity not only within the band but with other bands in their territory. They ensured vitality by putting in place exogamous patterns of marriage that ensured that individuals from other bands came into each band and that genetic and cultural information flowed across them. These values that resulted from choices made millions of times across our evolution on the planet are still at the core of what we must keep in mind to survive in difficult times. Potts (1996) has suggested that these patterns of adaptability and flexibility were characteristics even earlier, among the hominids and allowed their spread over a variety of the planet's landscapes. This flexibility in the past was treated as a lack of variation in these groups but is now viewed as much more based on kin relatedness and autonomy, or a toleration of diversity (Bird–David 1996:303). This would seem to further strengthen the notion that the success of this form of subsistence is its range of diversity alongside a foundation of shared kinship. In other words, cultural diversity laid an important foundation for dealing with changing environmental circumstances, and the shift in thinking adds a further layer of complexity to how HG adapted over millennia to their changing planet.

Views of HG have changed considerably in the past 20 years. Ellen notes that the use of the term HG deceptively suggests uniformity (2002:201). Some groups rely more on harvesting vegetable matter, while others rely more heavily on hunting. Some do not hunt at all but fish instead. Today, the number of extant HG or food collecting populations is very small and their distribution restricted to marginal areas for cultivation. There is evidence that so-called HG have participated to various degrees in cultivation, when the opportunity arose, and that they have engaged in trade and economic relations with non-HG for centuries. It has been suggested that the prevalence of hunting as compared to gathering goes back only to the time in the Upper Paleolithic when mostly plant collectors moved into temperate and arctic zones where the prevalence of plant foods was much reduced, and where sources of animal protein were by contrast richer (Ellen 2002:204). Whether this view is correct or not what we can be sure of is that HG adapted to available resources by shifting their strategies of food obtention with climate and biome changes. Populations with rich fishing resources probably did not move very much, nor did HG with rich nearby plant resources. However, where resources were widely distributed or highly seasonal we can presume that movement became a key strategy for subsistence.

How Did We Decide To Become Farmers?

The move from a HG way of life to a farming one must have been difficult, and evidence shows that this transformation was a long and complex process (B. Smith 1989:1566). Anyone who has ever farmed, or lived for any length of time among farmers, knows how hard that work can be. Gone are the pleasures of going on trips to hunt and gather honey. Gone are the long walks on spectacular landscapes, the pleasures of the chase, and the freedom to follow the game or of finding new groves of trees with desired fruit. Instead of this freedom of movement, farmers have to get up each day, at the same place, and go out to the same place to carry one more step in the careful nurturing of plants that have become so dependent on our care that they cannot survive without us. If animals have been domesticated as well, the tedium is even greater. Each day animals must be milked (sometimes several times in the day), taken to pasture or feed brought to them from far away places, and the farmer lives with the constant worry that if he is too successful, his grain and his animals might become targets of raiders who have been less successful or less fortunate but are better armed.

Studies over the past several years have shown that this transition from HG to settled agriculture was not rapid, and that the two modes of production coexisted for very long periods of time (B. Smith 1989). In fact, as one might have suspected, HG learned the arts of domestication of plants and animals early, but they were reluctant to let go of the freedom and advantages of HG (Butzer 1976; Ellen 2002). This also meant that in most places, the evidence for domestication as seen in distinctive morphological changes was sometimes slow because the human population was itself between exploiting wild sources and beginning to change the plants and animals in permanent ways.

Cultivation and domestication of animals permitted a degree of control and predictability over harvests that was not part of the HG worldview. In the early centuries of the transition from foraging to agriculture, the difference in productivity between the cultivated varieties and the wild varieties was less dramatic than it is at present. It is now believed that the shift began in settings that required nothing other than inadvertent soil disturbance and enrichment, providing a habitat for colonizing weed species with desirable grain heads. This provided a predictable supplement of food to the natural floodplain stands that were the basis for foraging (B. Smith 1989: 1568). Thus, a gradual coevolutionary process starting with tolerance, then inadvertent disturbance, and ending in intentional encouragement and manipulation took place that was slow but steady (occurring in North America over a period of two to three millennia). As HG grew in number and filled the earth, the very lifestyle of HG began to be threatened by this population growth. Boserup (1965) and others (Netting 1968, 1981, 1993) have shown that the most important driver of the intensification implied by the shift from HG to agriculture has been population growth leading to greater applications of technology to production in order to stave off famine and meet the basic needs of growing populations. It is associated with greater competition over resources and the growing need to store supplies for times of scarce resources. The need to store provisions, rather than move to get them, resulted in a shift in how labor was invested, and in the settlement pattern of peoples worldwide.

At first, and still in some places where population density is low and land abundant (e.g., much of the Amazon Basin), the preferred form of subsistence was a combination of HG with extensive cultivation of crops that did not require constant management. This allowed people to spend part of their time in the satisfying activities of getting fresh and varied meat or fish, the gathering of a varied diet, and to have the security of harvests in settled areas. In some places, like central Brazil, the populations still go on trek for months at a time, leaving the cultivated crops to fend for themselves, or watched over only by some older community members and those unable to keep up while on trek (Gross et al. 1978; Coimbra et al. 2002). This allowed a maximum of flexibility, and resulted in diets that were balanced and healthy. Except where their life has been disrupted by contact, efforts to find nutritional deficiencies among indigenous Amazonians have largely failed. Under conditions of low population density and abundant land, extensive cultivation with HG constitutes the best of both worlds: freedom, flexibility, and growing capacity to self-organize into larger groups. When these groups grew too large for the resource base, it was common for them to fragment into smaller groups and re-settle elsewhere to ensure the efficient use of the natural resources (Chagnon 1968).

However, over time these populations grew more numerous and they began to compete with each other for natural resources. Chronic warfare ensued as groups competed for the prime lands, the prime spots along the river or mountain, and sought ways to recruit more members to their communities. In a world of hand-to-hand combat, having strong, and numerous men to field was the top determinant of success in holding on to territory. Over time, some groups developed from single village communities into networks of communities and chiefdoms emerged that provided some capacity to mobilize larger social units when any of its member communities was threatened. The evidence is quite substantial that as human communities grew more successful in production, the temptation was great for other communities to take away their accumulated wealth (often in the form of grain or animals). As in the shift from HG to extensive cultivation, the shift from extensive cultivation to intensive cultivation appears to have been driven by population growth putting too much pressure on resources (Boserup 1965; Netting 1993). One study showed that a given area of irrigated land could support 14 times as many families as it could under shifting cultivation (Palerm 1968; Spooner 1972). However, another explanation offered by scholars has been that this intensification was forced upon people either by external domination and colonialism (cf. Geertz 1963) or by internal domination brought about by elites wishing to control land resources for their own political and military objectives (Demarest 2004).

Herding and Farming: An Uneasy Relationship

In some parts of the world, farmers and pastoral peoples coexist. From a resource point of view it is a coexistence that offers many advantages to both: each group can specialize; animals can be kept well away from crops thereby reducing the chances that the animals will destroy the cultivated fields; animals can roam over wide areas and take advantage of marginal areas, while the prime land can be devoted to cultivation (Barth 1956, 1961). At various times and places, this symbiotic or complementary relationship works out just like this. However, at other times the relationship is an uneasy one: if harvests are not bountiful, cultivators raise the cost of grain and pastoralists find the exchange rate too onerous to pay; there are suspicions on both sides that the other is gaining the upper hand in their trading relations (Lees and Bates 1977); and the greater mobility and aggressiveness of pastoralists (necessary to defend their herds from other groups as they transmigrate) makes them feared by cultivators who tend to be far less ready to deal with attacks than their pastoralist neighbors (Edgerton 1971). Psychological studies in E. Africa of both cultivators and pastoralists showed that pastoralists manifested considerable psychological similarities, as did the cultivators among themselves, despite membership in different cultural or ethnic groups (Edgerton 1971).

However, over long periods of time there is evidence that pastoralists become cultivators and vice versa. It is still unclear under what conditions this might occur. In the contemporary period, this appears to be forced upon pastoralists by the state which sees their armed presence and freedom to move about as a political and military threat to their sovereignty. Thus, campaigns to sedentarize pastoralists have been common since World War II. Whether similar politically motivated forced settlement explains past shifts or not is uncertain. Pastoralists need access to large areas of territory to graze their animals and political boundaries are hardly ever coincident with environmental needs or boundaries, yet they seem to be among the most flexible populations anywhere in terms of their adaptability. It is likely, therefore, that in the past as in the present the boundaries between chiefdoms or between states altered the viability of pastoralist subsistence and its trade relations with cultivators.

One thing is emerging clearly from excellent studies of pastoralist adaptation: mobility is even greater than was ever imagined. Studies on the Turkana in the past decade show an exquisitely complex pattern of movement that uses information in complex ways to achieve a very effective use of resources (McCabe 2004; Little and Leslie 1999; Coughenour et al. 1985). Pastoralists far from bringing about desertification ensure the biodiversity of savannas and prevent them from evolving into less desirable mixed scrubland. They do so by a combination of how they graze their animals and their occasional use of fire to improve pastures. The use of fire has the benefit of preventing the invasion of savannas by woody species. The result is not only better fodder for the domesticated animals but also for the many wild species that inhabit the savanna ensuring that their biomass is also increased by higher quality grasses.

Pastoralist social organization shows much greater flexibility than other forms of subsistence because of the flexible nature of managing animals. Sometimes it is possible to gather people and animals in areas when rain is abundant and pasture is rich, but for at least half of the year or more, the drying of the savannas results in scattering of people and animals. This scattering would put these populations at risk if it were not for mechanisms such as segmentary lineages that allow segments of large lineages to call upon others to come to their assistance in times of trouble. Thus, pastoral societies have developed impressive capacity to field armed men to defend their animals and people – and then to return to a very scattered and apparently disorganized pattern of moving to find the best forage (McCabe 2004). It is a remarkable example of social self-organization that results in politically sophisticated outcomes.

More Food for The Masses

The success of pastoralist and extensive farmers provided the means to support more and more people. The result of this success was greater pressure on resources, the need to continually increase productivity to meet the needs of a rapidly growing population, and growing specialization with more and more people dedicated to tasks other than farming, and who required food to be provided to them. This was particularly the case as chiefdoms and states undertook wars to protect and/or defend themselves. These armies required food supplies, often sent at great distances. The more people stored food in case of production shortfalls, the more they became a target for other groups wishing to take over their supplies. As this insecurity grew, more people had to be taken out of food production to defend those supplies thereby increasing the pressure to intensify effort and technology for food production. Intensification of agricultural production took many forms: water management, commonly through irrigation and terracing; changing the crop mix towards higher yielding combinations; the use of chemicals and other external inputs; the use of technology; and more intensive use of land and labor (Netting 1972; Boserup 1965).

Water management has been one of the first ways that farmers increased the output from agriculture, particularly in areas where either reliable moisture during the growing season was not assured, or where nutrients were in short supply on the land but not in abundant water. Water management requires considerable human densities because of the high labor costs of building canals and of maintaining the terraces or the slope of the land in a way consistent with effective draining of the water after it has been supplied to crops. Considerable research has been done over this topic, and it is associated with complex systems of social organization to manage the water and ensure its provisioning. In some areas, the institutional rules for managing water go back centuries, and in some places remain operative to the present (Butzer 1976; Guillet 1987, 1992).

Irrigation and terracing takes many forms, from canals to carry water to field, to terracing in mountainous terrain and fed by gravity irrigation, and sunken fields wherein deserts could be made to bloom.

These sunken fields can cover vast areas as in the desert coastal plain of Chilca, Peru where seven square kilometers have been documented (Knapp 1982). The sunken fields constitute the excavation of areas so that cultigens can more easily uptake moisture from the water table. At some point they were thought to be flooded, but more recent research suggests a more sophisticated approach based on moisture wicking. By contrast, irrigation in the humid regions of the tropics, as in Bali, is associated with very intensive rice production, complex systems of temples that manage the supply of water, and the provisioning of water and nutrients (Lansing, 1991; Geertz 1963).

Changing the crop mixture has been a common way to increase the production of the land by adding crops or varieties that add to the nutritional value of the output from the land. This allows one to take advantage of shifts in nutrient uptake by existing plants so as to improve efficiency in nutrient use and water availability, and to spread labor over the calendar year more effectively (Netting et al. 1995). With modernization and development this has been particularly the case, with shifts from staple crops to commercial crops, by the use of interplanting and intercropping, or by producing previously staple crops for the market (McConnell and Keys 2005).

Use of chemicals and other inputs has been a common way to intensify land use and increase productivity. For a very long time the most common form was through the application of animal manures and plant mulches (Winterhalder et al. 1974), or through the application of irrigation water which carries nutrients in suspension (Geertz 1963). With the industrial revolution one sees a growing number of chemical inputs used that permit the same area of land to be continuously cultivated, rather than periodically fallowed. This led to many advances in production, and reached its zenith (as was thought at the time) with the Green Revolution which combined plant breeding for high yielding varieties with a sophisticated package of inputs. Currently, debate is on-going on the practical development of transgenics or genetically modified crops in the field. A growing concern exists in Europe, Japan and other countries on the dangers of using these GM crops because of the probability of those features affecting the entire ecosystem with consequences which are unknown. Already concern has been expressed over the fate of the Monarch Butterflies as a result of GM corn in North America. There is some evidence of high mortality from the butterflies coming in contact with the pollen from this type of corn (Losey et al. 1999).

Genetic modification is just one of a very large range of technologies which are brought to bear on food production (Marvier 2001). More commonly one thinks of tractors, combines, and other mechanical devices which reduce the amount of human labor required by substituting manual with mechanical power and the use of fossil fuels. This advance permits much larger areas to be cultivated and harvested. Debate over the efficiency of manual vis-à-vis mechanized agriculture is rarely settled because of the differences of what is included in the input/output equation by advocates of each type of approach. Some crops are more amenable to mechanization than others, and thus technological applications need to be adjusted to the characteristics of the crop and to the quality that consumers expect from the product. Strawberries, for example, in the past were produced on very large farms, but the quality expected by consumers led to returning production to smaller owners who were better able to ensure a high quality product, resulting in strawberry sharecropping in California (Wells 1990).

In short, over a period of 400 generations, or 10,000 years, the human population has grown from a few million to more than 6 billion. This change has taken place quickly in recent decades; and has changed the nature of how we deal with each other (Raven 2002). The biggest shift has been since World War II and is connected to rising living standards and rising consumption levels for materials and energy. This compounding of population and consumption is recent and without precedent. An important question to ask ourselves is how well prepared we are to think in new ways about our relationship to the environment. Human populations do not respond in homogeneous ways to the environment, or anything else. Human society and culture is characterized by high diversity, and in the past this has gone along with biological diversity. The number of people who live by hunting-gathering today is shrinking, and most of them are connected to the global economy to some degree, and they have been for some time. Horticultural populations still constitute significant populations in rural areas of developing countries – and among those in developed countries who seek to return our food production system to more organic methods. As we will see later in this book, this is a fast and expanding movement that questions the industrial mode of food production and seeks to return to more organic ways to take care of the land and produce the food we need. Pastoral peoples have been under pressure for decades to abandon their migratory ways, but they still constitute an important component of how grasslands are managed, despite efforts to block the routes of their movements. Intensive farming is growing ever more intensive, now including genetic modification to a degree that has not been seen before. Despite the efforts to homogenize our systems of production, there is still considerable diversity to serve us in the future to restore what we have destroyed unwisely. As single-minded ways of thinking about materials and energy have arisen – i.e., trying to think of these things in largely monetary terms – the question is whether this simple way of thinking about complex human–environment interactions may not be appropriate and may, in fact, be destructive. In the next chapter we discuss the consequences of intensification, in the past and in the present.

3
The Great Forgetting

Earth Transformations in Prehistory

Ask people in the street what they think an ideal environment is and one discovers they have very different ideas (Kempton et al. 1995). For some, it is nature untouched by humans, for others it is a "pretty landscape" mixing forests, grasslands, and human habitations. The latter show a preference for a human constructed environment, while the former prefer an environmental Eden before Adam and Eve and the rest of us spoiled it. Yet, pristine nature is very hard to find anywhere (Cronon 1996). Time and again when we think we have found untouched nature, we discover that the area had been occupied by prehistoric humans, sometimes at great density.

When Europeans first came across the Maya regions of Mexico and Central America they found ruins of past civilization, and unbroken forest. It took decades of research to begin to understand that that primeval-looking forest was really old growth moist forest following intensive use of that landscape for agriculture (see Figure 3.1). Estimates now are that up to 75 percent of that landscape was cultivated (Redman 1999), and that only with collapse of these civilizations and the subsequent depopulation did tropical forests regain the space they had lost to these great Maya civilizations (Demarest 2004; Turner et al. 2004). In other cases, humans shaped the composition of the "pristine" forests we admire not just in the Maya region, but in many other areas as well (e.g., New England, cf. Foster and Aber 2004). Another example is the grand old growth forest of ponderosa pines found in Yosemite Valley. Until relatively

Figure 3.1   Maya ruins in forest of Belize. Photo by Emily V. Moran

recent times, the area was covered with widely spaced oaks amongst an expansive grassland occupied by the Ahwahnechee Indians who collected acorns, hunted, and farmed at a very small scale. They used fire to keep the area open – but an unintended consequence of the regular use of fire led to the gradual replacement of oaks with ponderosa pines, which are more fire-resistant. Today, hardly an oak remains of the native forests of the region, and they have been replaced by nature, and human use of fire, with the magnificent ponderosa pines we all admire today (Redman 1999:201). The most admirable and pristine environments today, as in the past, bear the imprint of human manipulation and/or the restoration by nature of disturbed habitats.

In other words, people transform landscapes to ensure a productive environment familiar to them, and one that meets their image of what an aesthetically pleasing landscape should look like. How else can we explain the preference of wealthy Californians to build very expensive homes in the fire-prone forests in the hillsides, despite repeated cases of devastating fires. How else can we explain the tendency of people moving into the arid Southwest of the United States to plant lawns and trees from more humid regions in an area lacking in water resources? And, if they plant environmentally appropriate desert or xeric vegetation proceed to water them excessively to keep them flowering (instead of accepting the rare flowering events of desert plants kicked off by those rare rains) thereby using even more water than those who plant mesic vegetation (Central Arizona Project)?

Just as migrant populations try to reproduce the production system, and the social relations, that they are familiar with in a new location, so do populations in a given place try to construct their lives in familiar ways. Thus, a culturally defined "appropriate" environment is a powerful force that struggles constantly with the logic of environmental appropriateness and adaptation to changing environmental conditions. If we are able, we tend to change nature to fit an image we have of it. In other words, there is no absolute nature because natural forces and human forces are always shaping and re-shaping nature so that over time it is reconstituted with different assemblages of plants and animals – and given enough time, even its geology and climate can be shaped, since these are systems characterized by biological complexity. It deserves to be noted that not just people but even plants do something similar. Plants through the action of their roots (and the chemicals that many of them can release) are capable of changing the soil conditions in which they grow to some degree. Posey and Hecht (1989) suggested that the Kayapó Indians also modified their soils to facilitate the creation of forest islands in the savanna.

The notion of conserving nature is relatively recent. For most of human history, nature has been seen as wilderness – by some viewed as forbidden and by others as wilderness to be tamed when they have the means to do so. Nature, and wilderness, have been seen as powerful – and dangerous. Our current tendency to value wilderness comes from its rapid disappearance, and the importance of having those areas available to us along with those areas we have tamed all too well. It is not surprising, for example, to find vigorous NGOs and environmental activists in mega-cities like São Paulo,

Brazil – but an absence of them, or very weak presence, in important wilderness areas like the Amazon. For non-native people in the Amazon, the impression is that there is a lot of forest that they need to convert to economic uses quickly in order to achieve a modicum of well-being, and the discourse of environmentalism sounds to them naïve. They seem to want to transform that forest into a landscape that is more amenable to their goals. Yet, we can expect that with every year that passes, and another percent of the Amazon forest gone to see a gradual emergence of vigorous local environmental movements. We already begin to see it in areas where 50 percent of the forest cover has disappeared, and local farmers begin to worry about their water supplies, the stability of precipitation for their rain-fed crops, and rising temperatures (Moran, field notes, 2002). One local NGO, for example, wants to protect a large area of forest, known as the "Terra do Meio," not to protect its species diversity and structure, but because they see forest as producing moisture and precipitation needed for the agriculture of local people (Moran, field notes, 2004).

What ideas, and experiences, from the distant past can we recover to understand our impact on nature? Archeology offers many insights into human–environment interactions (Redman 1999:4) because of its focus on long-term change. Archeologists have documented the massive extinctions of birds brought about by Polynesian colonizers; the deforestation of the Maya lowlands; the salinization of lands in southern Mesopotamia; and soil erosion in Ancient Greece (Redman 1999:6). One of the most interesting, and tragic, cases is that of the settlers of Easter Island. The colonizers who came there from Polynesia seem to have found a tropical island with lush vegetation, dominated by a palm, *Jubaea*, which may have been as tall as 25 meters, and by a woody tree, *Sophora*. They thrived for a thousand years, but in that time they deforested vast areas and by 1400 AD the palm appears to have gone extinct and the other woody species declined to insignificant levels recorded in the pollen record. Zoo-archeological studies have shown that Easter Island may have had the richest seabird populations in Polynesia – yet during their occupation the settlers virtually eliminated all bird fauna, aided by the rats they brought with them unintentionally (Steadman 1995; Diamond 1995). With the end of the large trees, they probably found it difficult to build their large canoes to go after sea mammals. The archeological records suggests that soil fertility was depleted, local shellfish stocks declined, and chickens became their only source of animal protein, and that they abandoned their large settlements. Increasingly they raided each other's villages, and in time began to topple the exquisite statues for which Easter Island is well-known. The question must be asked, though, why did the inhabitants of Easter Island not foresee this collapse? Did they not see the environmental signals that the productive system was threatened by their actions? Clearly, small islands are more likely to experience this sort of collapse than large continental areas because of the limited area they encompass, the lack of opportunity to easily move elsewhere, and the suddenness with which they can be impacted by storms, hurricanes, or economic disasters. But are we that much different today? Are we reading the evidence for our current environmental crisis and doing anything to prevent it from reaching dangerous levels?

Looking at a few more archeological cases may help us see why we so often seem to misread the environment. The first great impact seems to have been the impact of hunters on the megafauna. While the issue is still contested among scholars, over whether it was climate change or hunters who were responsible for the extinction of the megafauna, there is little doubt that human activities accelerated whatever climate events may have started. At the end of the last Ice Age, upper Paleolithic hunters of Siberia moved across the Bering Straits and brought about a rapid end to the megafauna of the Americas – most notably American mammoths, mastodons, ground sloths, horses and camels (Martin 1972, 1984; Mead and Steadman 1995; Redman 1999:77; Martin and Szuter 2004).

More clear misreading, and better documented, are cases surrounding intensive agriculture. It is much harder to see cases of extensive agriculture leading to environmental crises because the populations tend to be low and their imprint on the landscape hard to detect by archeological methods. In arid lands, and lands with a Mediterranean climate, we can find much clearer evidence of the impact of people over time on the physical environment. In the Levant, fire has always been an important natural force shaping the landscape, as it is true in other parts of the world, where people use fire to open up the canopy and favor the growth of plants for grazing animals. The risks of natural, and human-induced, fire increase the longer the dry season is – thus, the Levant has a high vulnerability to fire. Fire, if too frequent (say, more often than every ten years) can lead to a shift in vegetation from forest to shrubs, herbs and grasses. Fires also increase patchiness, and thus create a landscape at various stages of succession with greater diversity of land covers. Over the past 10,000 years, the landscapes of the Levant have been transformed under the impact of people (van der Leeuw 1998). Natural oak woodlands have yielded to scrub ecosystems, and sometimes to still shorter heath or open turf. As the soils became more exposed, soils eroded, and agriculture became increasingly restricted to areas that could be reached by irrigation.

In the Levant we see a clear sequence of occupation. Beginning with *Homo erectus* about a million years ago, the area began to be occupied by hominids (van der Leeuw 1998). About 50,000 years ago one begins to see evidence for fully modern humans in the area and the use of stalking techniques in hunting. About 15,000 years ago there is clear evidence for sedentary permanent structures built by the Natufians – talented peoples who lived by gathering plants and hunting animals. Over the next several thousand years to 7,000 years ago, one begins to see evidence that some of the plants they previously gathered were domesticated, and possibly that some of the animals were also being herded rather than hunted. Through this period, we see the coexistence of wild and domesticated plants and animals playing a role in the diet of these early Neolithic peoples. We also see evidence over the next 4,000 years of contractions followed by expansion in Levant villages, a result of population ebbs and flows. Several possible explanations for these population changes have been offered. One that seems particularly notable is the widespread use in Ain Ghazal, in Southern Jordan, of lime plaster. Lime plaster making requires enormous quantities of timber as a fuel, and this probably led to massive deforestation near villages. It seems that houses were plastered frequently and this preference may have resulted in rapid changes in forest and soil cover. Their use of goats, rather than sheep, probably is also implicated in a rapid loss of plant cover given the devastating impact of large goat populations on any vegetation, resulting in further erosion. Without vegetation, the steeply sloping terrain of the region would have resulted in loss of soils needed for cultivation, and to loss of water from the area through rapid run-off (Redman 1999).

These impacts are not restricted to arid and semiarid regions. McGovern and others (1988) have documented how the Scandinavian settlers in the Medieval North Atlantic overstocked the islands of that region, including Greenland, and depleted the stands of willow, alder, and birch that were there before. As in so many other places, fire appears to have been used in initial land clearing, then pressure came from the need to make charcoal for making iron, and forest resources were used for fuel in their hearths. Not all forms of land use were destructive. There is evidence that the Norse redistributed water to increase productivity of pastures, and that they used dung and organic garbage to enrich soils. By 1100 BP, even the most marginal grazing resources in the western islands were in full use and they were beginning to have a negative impact upon the environment that sustained them. So then, why did environmental feedbacks fail to trigger appropriate management responses? It seems, at least for this case, that the experience of the settlers from central Norway, the British Isles and the eastern islands provided disastrously false analogies. In the western islands, such as Iceland and Greenland, the environment is far more exposed to the effects of small-scale and short-term climatic fluctuations, and thereby is more vulnerable to even small scale shifts in climate (Ogilvie 1981; McGovern et al. 1988).

The initial Viking expansion took place during a warming period known as the Little Climatic Optimum. Even a one degree shift in temperature, in an area already marginal for cereal cultivation, would have been disastrous. But there were social and political changes as well that contributed to the collapse. Local farmers grew increasingly subordinated to regional and national powers. As the population put greater pressure on resources, the local middle and lower classes grew impoverished and lost their autonomy to wealthier land owners, who viewed the distress of the small holders as someone else's problem, not theirs. By the end of the seventeenth century, 94 percent of farmers of Iceland were tenants, rather than owners and the pasture area of the country had been reduced by 40 percent (McGovern et al. 1988:264).

These degradational forces did not mean the abandonment of the area by humans. Rather, it meant that they moved and probably fragmented into more flexible social units with a lighter impact upon the environment for a time. These ups and downs in population and environmental impact continue to this day. Each year thousands of hectares in southern Europe, even today, are transformed into near-deserts as a result of human activities. We can see evidence for these millennial changes in southern Spain, Greece, Italy, and France (Redman 1999:116). What is clear is that following a period of intense human occupation, there was an environmental crisis which required a change in exploitation techniques – commonly from more intense to a lighter use of the environment to allow restoration of the landscape. Famine, migration, and loss of territory have been the usual consequence for people.

Another clear example of human impacts is the case of the American Southwest. Even more so than in Mediterranean landscapes, the Southwest United States is an *arid* region, with trees occurring only at higher altitudes and with considerable sensitivity to climate change. Here we see frequent cases of occupation, growth, followed by abandonment of villages. Why? According to archeologist Tim Kohler (1992), growing populations in favorable areas intensified food production to meet the needs of the increasing population, resulting in greater deforestation of the region, depletion of local soils, and ultimately to abandonment of the region – speaking at least for the Anasazi living in the Dolores River Basin. This process took only about two centuries to play itself out, rather than the millennia it seems to have taken in the Levant. The Anasazi seem to have emphasized concentration in larger villages to improve their competitive advantage vis-à-vis other smaller groups. In doing so they also became more vulnerable to shifts in climate, to declining soil fertility, and to the loss of woody species needed to build houses. A key element is understanding the balance between resource use and resource depletion, and the possible rate of recovery of the ecosystem. When any human population undertakes more intense use of an environment, it is often rewarded with improved returns if the environment has had low rates of exploitation. However, as resource use intensifies, and if this rate is higher than the natural rate of restoration of the nutrients and resources taken out, there is gradual resource depletion and eventually degradation. Humans have the capacity to invest in helping with the restoration of some of the resources removed (e.g., through reforestation, application of nutrients), but they seem to do so rarely – or perhaps, the evidence for such restoration may be hidden from archeological evidence. In the present, at least, evidence is that restoration efforts are postponed, until there is hardly anything left of the initial habitat.

It was just a matter of time, and opportunity, for people to have their growing villages develop into something larger and more complex that we have come to call cities. Urban areas provided a site for trade, for the exchange of information, for specialists in a large number of skills to meet the needs of a more technologic-ally intensive society, and for redefining the nature of human–environment interactions. The rise of urban centers is most commonly associated with irrigation and the rise of complex water control. As these systems grew in size and complexity, breakdown became more common and more costly. In time, when they had grown to pharaonic proportions, the systems could collapse when either information or climate or both, were beyond the capacity of managers (Butzer 1976).

The Archaeology of Environmental Change

Some archeologists trace the interest of archeology in human–environment interactions to the work of Julian Steward (1955, 1938), particularly his defining of an approach that he named "cultural ecology" (see chapter 2; and Fowler and Hardesty 2001). Prior to 1940, archeologists treated ecology as the physical environment. After Steward, it became clear that once humans became a presence in any environment, there was no such thing as a natural world, but one that had to be examined as human–environment actions. For several decades cultural ecology guided archeology. This approach tended to ask how people in a particular landscape made a living from the natural resources present (Butzer 1971, 1976; J.D. Clark 1960). It emphasized understanding how people organized socially to exploit resources, and how such behavior related to the behavior of other groups who lived in environments with similar challenges.

In other words, Steward laid the basis for comparison across human–environment interaction situations or places by focusing the research on characterizing the resources culturally recognized or cognized, and on how people organized themselves to effectively exploit those resources (Netting 1976; Moran 2000, 1979a).

This approach produced excellent characterization of archeological populations and is still used to some degree by a very large number of practicing archeologists. However, other approaches have emerged as well with strong environmental dimensions. In the 1960s and 1970s systems approaches were formulated (Hardesty 1977; Flannery 1968). Flannery, for example, focused on ecological processes such as the gradual changes in ancestral maize that led to its higher productivity, and to greater dependence on it for food, and the pressure to develop farming. In this approach, as in the earlier ones derived from cultural ecology, a central concern was with how people adapted to environment.

However, some archeologists found that these adaptational approaches seemed to pay little attention to "agency" or the individual. The result was a set of theoretical emphases that led archeology away from focusing on adaptive systems and towards a consideration of how agents pursue their goals under both ecological and social constraints (Brumfiel 1992; cf. also Fowler 1993). A major element of this shift in the thinking of some archeologists has to do with a greater focus on landscape history. Crumley (1994) and others began to emphasize that archeology is first and foremost a historical discipline whose task is to write landscape histories or ecohistories at a variety of scales. This means trying to find historical evidence for how they were created and changed by both human activity and natural processes and their interactions. The implication, of course, is that archeologists cannot forget to try to find the meaning that underlay the decisions made by agents and the consequences of those decisions.

Excellent ecohistories have been produced for all the major ancient civilizations, i.e., Egypt, Mesopotamia, the Indus valley, China, Mesoamerica, and the Andes (found for example in Redman et al. 2004; Bahn and Flenley 1992; Fish and Fish 1992; Kohler 1992; McGovern et al. 1988). These ecohistories provide detailed examination of the complex interactions between climate change and the landscape changes resulting from human activities. The record is clear, for example, that the Sumerian, Akkadian and subsequent civilizations of the Tigris–Euphrates, and the Harappan civilization of the Indus river basin were all hurt by deforestation, overgrazing and salinity built up from the use of irrigation over long periods of time (Fowler and Hardesty 2001). While human action alone was not responsible, as noted earlier in this chapter, it was human actions pushing a system too far, and then climate change pushing it beyond the capacity of the system to restore itself and provide for the growing human population that had begun to make too many demands from these ecosystems-on-the-brink. Ecohistories comparing archeological studies of farming populations in the Mediterranean with those in Mesoamerica find that climatic instability coupled with human-induced ecological damage affected population distributions and the success of farming (Butzer 1996).

As one gets closer to the present, i.e., the last 300–600 years, it is possible to get even more detailed archeological records and a greater understanding of agency and processes. Kirch's study of environmental change in the Anahulu valley in the island of O'ahu (Hawaii) describes the impact of settler introduced taro irrigation and husbandry of pigs and dogs on the islands's ecology, changing the forests into patches of secondary vegetation and gardens. The arrival of European plants, animals and diseases after Captain Cook in 1778 dealt a second major blow to the native species of the island (Crosby 1986:89–90). Deagan's study of St. Augustine, Florida (1996) showed that change often involves cross-fertilization across ethnic groups as each seeks to adapt themselves to the local environment, given their social position – but that many of the indigenous people were able to sustain their food habits long after they had intermarried Spaniards.

The contributions of archeology to understanding our contemporary environmental crisis are evident in the current work of the group at Arizona State University. Using an archeologically inspired sampling approach, a grid overlaid over the city of Phoenix, a sample of grid cells is sampled every five years for evidence of change in measurable parameters such as soils, arthropods, bird species, and land cover. These grid cells are also sampled over historical time using aerial photos and satellite data, archival data, and archeological research. The result is a historically deep, spatially explicit, and social and environmentally informed understanding of the dynamics of human–environment interactions. A similar study of urban environment, using other methods than a gridded approach, is the study of Baltimore, Maryland, U.S.A as an urban ecosystem (e.g., Grove and Burch 1997). They use a social ecology approach that links urban revitalization with environmental restoration and that combines methods from ecosystem ecology with social ecological theory and community forestry perspectives drawn from international research on forest ecosystems.

An important theoretical approach that contributes to the understanding of these complex processes is resilience theory (Redman and Kinzig 2003; Holling 2001; Gunderson and Holling 2002). This approach is built on four key features: change is episodic; patterns and processes are patchy and discontinuous; ecosystems have multiple equilibria; and ecosystem management must be flexible because ecosystems are always changing. Archeological research offers a great deal to the advancement of this theory because archeological case studies provide evidence for multiple, completed cycles of adaptive behavior and thus to study how systems change as systems organize and re-organize under changing conditions. Major innovations such as the beginnings of agriculture, the rise of urbanization, and the development of industry which caused major changes in human–environment interactions can be studied over the long-term using archeological evidence and the theoretical insights of resilience theory (Redman and Kinzig 2003).

The Urban–Industrial Revolution and the Unleashing of Prometheus

If the rise of cities and a growing network of linked villages into states proved to be a considerable source of disturbance in human–environment interactions, imagine what happened with the rise of that technological wonder that is the industrial revolution. Cities are symptomatic of human impacts on nature: they are creative centers where some of the best and brightest of every society are concentrated to develop the arts, technology, education, science, and commerce. Yet, they are also often chaotic, with erosion of social controls, and distant enough from day-to-day realities of environment to ignore environmental feedbacks with remarkable frequency. That is because urban areas have too many layers of information between the environment and the decisions managers take – who are motivated by many other incentives than just ensuring good environmental management: political pressures, mis-valuation of the resources, self-interest, and corruption.

We can trace the beginning of our current environmental crisis, particularly the changes that have resulted in significant global warming and climate change, to the Industrial Revolution (Landes 1969). The burning of fossil fuels to power industry have emitted the bulk of the carbon dioxide that has made global warming a serious threat, the intensification through technology of agriculture led to a rural exodus into the cities clamoring for cheap labor for the emerging industries. The result was both a short-term public health crisis due to the unsanitary conditions of those early industrial cities, and the smog from burning coal that made cities like London, and then Pittsburgh, famous for their smog-filled air. Despite their unsanitary conditions, however, cities grew ever larger (as they continue to do today throughout the developed and developing countries) and in time conditions become sufficiently disastrous that society began to provide enough public health services to reduce child mortality from those experienced by those living more isolated lives in rural areas (see Figure 3.2). This transition to high fertility and low child mortality resulted in very rapid increases in human populations that led to the kinds of exponential increases in environmental impacts discussed in chapter one.

The industrial mode of production is accompanied by major technical innovations that also result in a reorganization of the division of labor. The industrial revolution's larger environmental impact is the product of discovering the use of fossil fuels. First, and for a very long time, this involved only the use of coal. Oil and natural gas came much later. In using fossil fuels humans did not have to compete with any other animal species to use the resource, as we had often had to do with the use of plants (hervibores) and animals (carnivores). This would seem to be a win–win situation, and it certainly allowed a quantum increase in the amount of energy that humans could harness for productive purposes. Unfortunately, the

Figure 3.2   Pollution obscures the Hong Kong skyline. Air pollution causing acid rain is costing China in excess of 100 billion yuan (US$12 billion), according to China's State Environmental Protection Administration (SEPA). Photo Mike Clarke/AFP, *The Epoch Times*, May 14, 2004

exploitation of the huge amounts of fossil fuel materials stowed away for geologic periods of time in subterrestrial sinks and the launching of the byproducts from their use into the biosphere kicked off biogeochemical changes in the atmosphere that took a couple of centuries to be felt and which now threaten our planet. But these changes were not entirely surprising. Local and regional consequences of the use of fossil fuels were felt quickly: the fogs of industrial cities like London, with serious health consequences for people living in these locations being the most recognized. While the rich could escape to their rural estates to breathe fresh air, the poor in the cities grew sick from the constant exposure to foul air.

One of the ways in which industrial society addresses this problem today is by exporting the problem (and not just the finished products). It has become a common strategy to move industries from those locations in the heart of industrial societies to the less developed world. In great part this is driven by the rising wages of workers in the industrially more developed regions who over time develop the self-assurance to strike and demand higher wages than industrialists are willing to pay. As these wages rise, there is greater pressure on profits for the industrial companies, and greater pressure to move operations to regions where wages are lower and labor is not yet unionized. At first, this is a move from large urban centers to more rural areas or emerging urban areas where labor is more malleable (as in the move some decades back out of the industrial North to the rural and growing cities of the Southern United States). But eventually, these within-country moves also became too costly to companies. The move overseas results in loss of high paying jobs in the industrial world (note the importance of the debate over "outsourcing" in the 2004 presidential campaign), and the availability of low paying jobs (but jobs nevertheless) in the developing countries – but like in an earlier era in industrial heartlands – with associated pollution and foul emissions into the environment. The result is a "cleaner" environment in the industrial countries (but greater unemployment), but a more polluted environment in the less-developed countries, with the same associated indices of poor health, respiratory distress, water poisonings, and fouling of the water and air due to poor regulations to control emissions. As in the North Atlantic Islands archeological cases discussed earlier in the chapter, as control over the resources becomes distanced from the local environment, there is a tendency for those distant corporate and national agents to show little concern for what local people experience, and to ignore the feedback from the environment as environmental conditions worsen. Even efforts by citizens in developed countries to improve working conditions and environmental practices in developing countries seems to fall largely on deaf ears, as long as consumers continue to buy the products from these corporations. In chapters 7 and 8 we address this challenging problem.

The Contemporary Situation: Human-dominated ecosystems

The past 50 years have been devastating to the Earth system's functions (see discussion in chapter 1, and Steffen 2004). Many experts agree that these changes have been of sufficient magnitude to rival climate change in both environmental and social terms (Vitousek et al. 1997a; NRC 1999b). During the first 50 years of the twenty-first century, demand for food and other commodities by a wealthier and larger global population will be a major driver of global environmental change. While some of this change may come from more intensive and efficient agricultural production, much of it will come from converting further land areas and natural ecosystems into agricultural fields. This will result, at least, in a 2.5 fold increase in the amount of nitrogen and phosphorus making its way into terrestrial freshwater and near-shore marine ecosystems resulting in unprecedented eutrophication and habitat destruction (Tilman 2001). People already release as much nitrogen and phosphorus to terrestrial ecosystems as all natural sources combined (Vitousek et al. 1997b). Much of the nitrogen and phosphorus from fertilizers and animal wastes enters surface and groundwater untreated and unimpeded to any significant extent (Tilman et al. 2001). The result is eutrophication of estuaries and coastal seas, loss of biodiversity, changes in species composition, groundwater pollution, and tropospheric smog and ozone. The conversion of up to 1,000,000,000 hectares of natural habitat to meet our expected demand for food is viewed as conservative. This is expected to occur largely in Latin America and Sub-Saharan Africa. Can the Earth system withstand this kind of additional burden without approaching at global scale the conditions of regional systems that collapsed in the past?

At the start of the twenty-first century, we have some critical choices to make. For most of the 400 generations that we have been farming, production and consumption of food has been intimately linked to social and cultural systems, to systems of beliefs, and respect for the environment. Foods were given special meaning, and were surrounded with ritual. First crops harvested were treated with deference and gratefulness. We still see some of these practices in some ethnic rural populations, and even in an industrial superpower such as Japan. Rivers and mountains embodied the divine and the forces of creative and destructive nature that were respected. Over the past two or three generations we have changed all that in too many places. Industrial agriculture has steadily replaced family farms worldwide, and while they seem to produce a lot more food in absolute terms, they do so at a huge cost in terms of loss of soils, damage to biodiversity, pollution of the air and water, and negative impacts on human health through heavy use of chemicals (Pretty 2002:xii). The need to restore sustainable systems of food production that nurture the spirit of those who grow the food, and those who consume it – and not just fills their belly – has to become a global priority. We will need to redesign whole systems of food production, more directly linking those who grow food to those who consume it, using methods that have a lighter impact on the environment, and in which the land takes on, once again, the nurturing value that it had for most of our history. Community-supported agriculture, farmers' groups, farmers' markets and slow food systems are just the front-line today of what needs to be a priority to put total human well-being and the well-being of the land-air-water system front and center (Pretty 2002:125).

In the past 35 years, we were able to double food production but we did so with a six-fold increase in nitrogen fertilization, a three-fold increase in phosphorus fertilization, and a substantial increase in the area under cultivation (Tilman 1999). Another doubling of food production would result in a three-fold increase in nitrogen and phosphorus fertilization and an increase of 18 percent in cropland cultivated. These increases will further eutrophy fresh and marine ecosystems, leading to biodiversity losses, shifts in the structure of the food chains, and impairment of fisheries (Tilman 1999). Is this what we need to do? Or can we improve the distribution of food so that these huge costs are not imposed upon the environment. Global agriculture has passed a threshold. It has gone from being a minor source of environmental degradation to becoming the major source of nitrogen and phosphorus loading to terrestrial, freshwater, and marine ecosystems. A business-as-usual continuation of agricultural practices will bring about growing and increasingly severe environmental costs. In the next chapter, we ask a few more questions about our current food production orientation, the impact it is having on the web of life and on ecosystem interactions, and how demographic processes play a role in food production and landscape change.

4

The Web of Life:
Are We In It?

The Web of Life and Trophic Relations: Thinking Ecologically

One of the clearest ways to think about the interactions of people and nature is in terms of the web of life (see Figure 4.1). The web of life teaches several important and fundamental lessons: (1) we are all interrelated; (2) we eat and are eaten (at least through decomposition); (3) we depend on the other parts of the web to be able to eat and exist; and (4) we have a role to play in the existence and sustainability of this intricate web of life. Let's think about each of these lessons.

1. *We are all interrelated.* A web is a superb image of a system that depends on the closely-knit connection between the parts, very much like a spider web depends for its success on the symmetrical weaving of the web and the constant repair of it to maintain its effectiveness in providing a steady food supply. In the web of life, we are all interrelated, as recent DNA research suggests. We share a remarkable portion of our DNA not only with our closest primate relatives, but also with distant organisms whether they be insects, amphibians, and even plants. We are only recently beginning to appreciate how we might be able to repair genetic damage in our DNA by tapping into the DNA of other organisms to solve many of our health problems. At a more fundamental level, we share our evolution with that of other coevolving species from which we may have branched but to which we are still connected as living organisms and sharing any number of genetic markers, and probably even behavioral and cognitive characteristics.

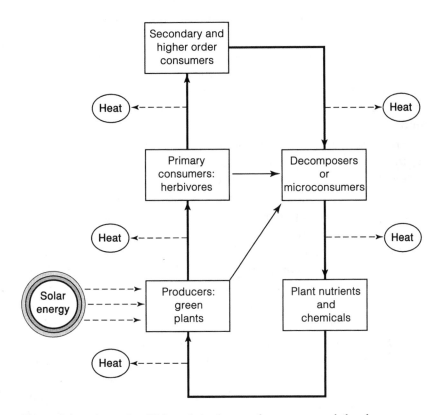

Figure 4.1 The web of life and the losses of energy at each level.
Source: Moran 1979a, p. 15

2. *We eat and are eaten.* Life is not possible without eating and in the web of life we depend on a lot of other life forms to sustain us, yet we too die and decay and are consumed by detritivores who are fundamental to maintaining the cycle of life. This gets at that most crucial element we have already talked about: our pattern of consumption can maintain us in the web of life, or it can be responsible for undermining the integrity of the web. For much of human evolution, people used what they needed to survive and reproduce. Because life was difficult and strenuous in our hunting-gathering experience, and dangers from predators and disease lurked everywhere, populations grew slowly. This combination of modest consumption to meet needs and slow rates of population growth resulted in a balanced

relationship between people and nature. As our numbers grew, and we began to consume far more than we needed, and began to accumulate possessions, this balance began to destabilize the web of life and now threatens the sustainability of our life on the planet.

3. *We depend on others.* The balance achieved by hunting-gathering and other populations in the past was a result of some important mechanisms: reciprocity, trust, and community. These mechanisms played a crucial role in our evolution as social animals, and account for a lot of our success as a species on Earth. During that early and long-lived experience as hunter-gatherers, we achieved great success in spreading over the face of the Earth by relying on small groups of agents closely tied together by bonds of trust and reciprocity, often strengthened by bonds of kinship and biological relatedness; and by the emergence of a sense of community sharing in values and in a common purpose. Thus, individual decisions were balanced by a sense of mutual obligation based on trust and the need to maintain the group's unity vis-à-vis the many dangers, and enemies they might confront. We still see evidence for these behavioral traits within families, who treat each other differently than they treat "outsiders" to the family; sometimes within members of religious congregations, who treat each other as family members sharing the same faith vis-à-vis those who do not share those same beliefs; and within some closely-knit voluntary associations which share common values or represent somewhat common economic status. Within these "insider" groups, we can still see the practices that made us strong through trust, reciprocity and community.

4. *We have a role to play in sustaining the Earth.* One consequence of our alienation from nature, through our vast numbers, our technology, and our industrial forms of deriving our food has been a loss of a sense of what we can do to change the world. In a world made of billions of people, what can one person do? It is precisely by recalling the first three characteristics of the web of life that we can begin to regain a sense of our ability to contribute to a sustainable planet. If indeed our actions have cumulative impact, and if we are interrelated and have the capacity for self-organization, there is really nothing that can stop any person from playing an important role, as a single person, or as a member of a group, in protecting the web of life.

People, plants, and animals interact with the physical world. These interactions result in food chains wherein the accumulated energy harnessed by plants are consumed by herbivores, who in turn are eaten by carnivores, who in turn are recycled by detritivores. Food chains do not exist in isolation but are interconnected in what we call food webs. People occupy a position near the end of a chain of food items and we are commonly thought of as the "top carnivore." That does not mean that we eat only meat, but rather that meat is part of our diet. In fact, people can choose, as they have done throughout human history, to be vegetarians. This is a choice which, for whatever reason is undertaken, has huge implications for the cycling of nutrients, and for how many people can be supported by the environment. The growing number of young people who have chosen to be vegetarian in developed countries reflects a growing awareness in the younger generations for the conditions of our planet.

The longer the food chain, the more energy is lost as entropy and the less is accomplished in net terms. Thus, the greater the consumption high up in the food chain, the fewer the number of individuals that can be supported, sustainably, on the same food base. Thus, when a human population moves from a mostly vegetarian diet, to one where meat is a higher proportion of the diet, there is much greater pressure on the environment, and the potential increases for environmental problems such as environmental degradation. The current crisis is associated with the multiple pressures brought upon the environment. Even hunter-gatherers ate a diet that was mostly vegetarian on a day-to-day basis since it took so much more effort to harvest meat than it took to harvest vegetable products from the environment's net primary productivity.

Even a partial food web is very complex (see Figure 4.1). Even the most simple ones often have the producer trophic level or green plants that convert solar energy into biomass, this is followed then by a primary consumer trophic level, then a secondary consumer trophic level. Complex food webs specify trophic exchanges between plants and herbivores and then primary and secondary carnivores. Some organisms occupy intermediate positions between trophic levels where they consume from both the level above and below it. Human beings have been particularly effective at exploiting all food sources available, restraining themselves culturally for a variety of reasons, among them to reduce their effort at subsistence (as with hunter gatherers) or to make statements about ethnicity (e.g., avoidance of ethnically defined "unclean" foods such as pork and shellfish), or to express solidarity with animals' rights to live (as with some vegetarian and animal rights activists).

Another important implication of food chains and food webs is that they can concentrate harmful chemicals as one moves up the food chain, as has been the case with mercury in top predator fishes (such as swordfish and tuna), and DDT in the American eagle, cormorants, and other top predator birds. Activities such as gold mining in the Amazon have resulted in very high concentrations of mercury in fish and human populations (Boischio and Henshel 2000). Mercury is used to separate gold from soil in the extraction of this precious metal and is transformed from its solid state to its gaseous form which then precipitates in the ecosystem. An implication of food chains is that we need to care a great deal about our emissions of harmful substances into the atmosphere, water, and land because these elements will enter and move along food chains and result in harmful consequences for many plants and animals, particularly higher up in the food chain – particularly for that top predator known as the human species!

As a concept, the food chain and the food web remind us that we are all connected in chains of who eats whom, and that we are all connected in this chain with consequences for all for what happens to elements of the food chain. The top predator, in particular has to exercise restraint in the demands placed on the lower elements of the food chain to avoid what has been noted time and again in insects and smaller mammals in which population crashes result from over expansion of population when food is abundant, and crashes when food supplies decline. The collapse of Maya and Egyptian civilizations has been associated with the collapse of productive capacity in agriculture due to a combination of climate events and human mismanagement of agriculture or irrigation (Butzer 1976; Hodell et al. 2001; Demarest 2004). In fact, observing the human population's growth in the past couple of centuries, and especially after 1950, looks ominously like that of classic insect models (see Figure 4.2a and Figure 4.2b), with exponential increases followed

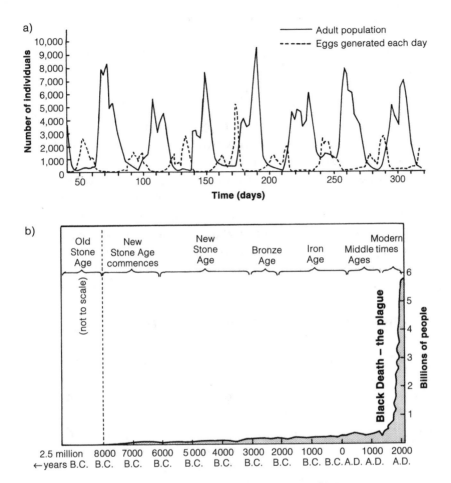

Figure 4.2   a) Insect population exponential increases; b) Human
population exponential increases. *Source:* Kormondy and Brown 1998,
pp. 82 and 87

by major crashes. How long can we expect to continue along our
exponential growth rate without a crash?

The concept of the food web also raises the importance of paying
attention to both gross and net productivity as a factor in ecological
systems. The more complex the system, the more chains there are,
and the more likely that net yield from such a system may be low
due to the costs of maintenance and respiration. Such is the case

with tropical moist forests, one of the most productive systems on the planet, but one also characterized by relatively low animal populations due to the costs of maintaining the complexity of the trophic levels operative.

One of the classic ways that ecology has visualized food chains has been through ecological pyramids, particularly of energy or biomass. Biomass pyramids tend to overemphasize the importance of large organisms, whereas energy pyramids underrates them. Thus, it is important to use multiple measures of trophic levels so that a more balanced view of food chains can be obtained from overrelying on a single pyramid that may under- or overestimate. A pyramid provides a quick overview of the structure of the food chains and trophic levels but it does not provide a guide on how such a food chain might be restructured. To do so one needs a different kind of analysis, which we discuss in the following section.

Ecosystem Productivity and Net Primary Production

Ecosystem productivity ultimately derives from the conversion of solar energy into biomass, interacting within a biogeochemical and climate context. Gross primary productivity refers to the total rate of photosynthesis, whereas net primary productivity refers to the rate of storage of biomass in excess of the costs of respiration by plants. Biological productivity differs from the agricultural concept of yield. The latter assumes a single time point at which the yield is harvested, whereas in biological communities the production is continuous and it is essential to designate a rate of production per unit of time to define what that amount is, as there is no harvest point.

Ecosystems vary a great deal in ecosystem productivity in light of these differences in climate, biogeochemistry, and the photosynthetic efficiency of the plants present. Deserts and arctic regions have some of the lower rates of net primary production whereas tropical rain and moist forests, and wetlands are among the highest (see Table 4.1 illustrating ecosystem productivity for major biomes). In thinking how to manage the various ecosystems of the planet it is important to take into account these differences, or to consider the costs of providing energy, water, biogeochemical and other forms of

Table 4.1 Net Primary Production and Plant Biomass of Major World Ecosytems

	Net Primary Productivity Unit area in dry g/m²/hr		Net Primary Production (10⁹ dry tons)	Biomass/Unit Area (dry kg/m²)		World Biomass (10⁹ dry tons)
	range	mean		range	mean	
Tropical rain forest	1,000–5,000	2,000	40.00	6.0–80	45	900
Tropical Savannas	200–2,000	700	10.50	0.2–15	4	60
Temperate Grasslands	150–1,500	500	4.50	0.2–5	1.5	14
Tundra/Alpine	10–400	140	1.10	0.1–3	0.6	5
Semiarid	10–250	70	1.30	0.1–4	0.7	13
True Desert	0–10	3	0.07	0.0–0.2	0.02	0.5

Source: Moran 1979a, p. 73. Based on Whittaker 1970

subsidy to overcome the factors that limit the current net primary productivity of plants in these systems. In many cases the costs may be too high to justify, but throughout history certain locations have been heavily subsidized for long periods of time if they represented important locations for human settlement, regardless of the environmental constraints that they may represent (e.g., the Negev desert during the Nabatean era when it served as an important stopping point and service center for the caravans connecting the spices from the East to the markets in the West – Evenari et al. 1971).

For obvious reasons, people manipulate ecosystems to increase the amount of net primary production that they can obtain from nature, whereas natural systems such as mature forests tend to maximize gross primary production. The latter puts more energy into developing complex and overlapping food chains that increase system resilience, whereas the former in increasing the harvestable portion exposes the system to external shocks and diminishes resilience from climate, pests, and other disturbances. Eugene Odum noted long ago (1971:50) that people should not harvest more than one-third of gross primary production or one-half of net primary production, unless we were prepared to pay dearly for subsidies to ensure system sustainability. Not being willing to pay results in environmental degradation and declining capacity to sustain structure and function.

An important line of thinking in recent years has been trying to put a "price tag" on the productivity of nature. Conservation-minded ecologists and economists have been struggling with this question by trying to put a price tag on "ecosystem services." One such effort (Constanza et al. 1997) put the price tag of replacing nature's services (such as fresh water, soil, climate regulation, crop pollination, etc) at US$33 trillion per year, nearly twice the combined gross domestic product of the Earth's 194 nations. While this exact figure may not be right, it does point to the enormous scale of nature's bounty to all of us, and the need to tax those who reduce or destroy wetlands, eliminate forest cover, and engage in activities that reduce the ability of nature to produce these services.

For example, a 1981 study estimated that for each hectare of U.S. wetlands destroyed by development, the annual flood damages caused by the lost ability to soak up floodwaters increased up to US$11,000.

Table 4.2 Putting a Price on Nature's Bounty

Ecosystem	Area in millions ha.	Value/ha/yr	global value In trillions/yr
Open ocean	33,200	252	8.4
Coastal	3,102	4,052	12.6
Tropical forests	1,900	2,007	3.8
Other forests	2,955	302	0.9
Grasslands	3,898	232	0.9
Wetlands	330	14,785	4.9
Lakes and rivers	200	8,498	1.7
Croplands	1,400	92	0.1
Total worth of the biosphere =			33.3 trillion

Source: Roush 1997

Table 4.2 provides a summary of the estimates from the Constanza study (based on Roush 1997).

Land Use and Long Term Disturbance

There is growing evidence that people have brought about modifications in the world's ecosystems from the outset. First, through the use of fire to drive animals into areas where they could more easily be hunted, to clear fields of vegetation, and to favor particular assemblages of wild life. Then, through their management of plant and animal densities, through cultivation, and through particular regimes of land use that exerted a variety of selection pressures upon native flora and fauna (see earlier chapters, this book). Regional vegetation, for example, tends to correspond to climate gradients (see Figure 4.3). This is the case for example for the dominance of hemlock and northern hardwoods (maple, beech, and birch) in the cooler Central Uplands of the United States, and oak and hickory at lower elevations in the Connecticut Valley and Eastern Lowlands. This stands in strong contrast with the modern vegetation of these areas which shows little relationship to broad climatic gradients. The

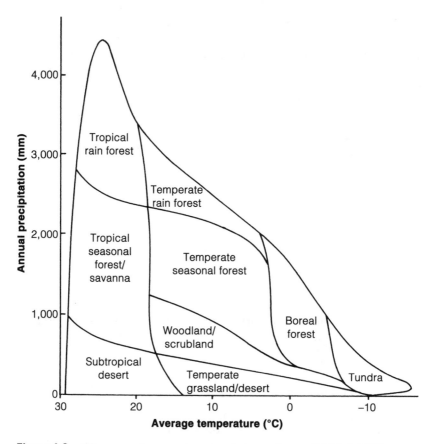

Figure 4.3   Climate and vegetation associations. *Source:* Ricklefs 2001, p. 105

process of forest regrowth for the past 100 years, the on-going low-intensity disturbances, and some permanent changes in certain aspects of the biotic and abiotic environment have maintained the regional abundance of shade intolerant and moderately tolerant taxa (e.g., birch, red maple, oak and pine) and restricted the spread and increase of shade tolerant long lived taxa such as hemlock and beech (Foster et al. 1998a and b).

For an area like Central New England, the pattern is one of increased population and settlement through the early nineteenth century, a period of stability in the mid nineteenth century, and with growing industrialization in the cities begins a rapid process of rural depopulation, land abandonment and reforestation. At the peak period of intensive agriculture and settlement in the mid nineteenth century, forests were restricted to narrow lowlands, steep slopes and wetlands (Foster et al. 1998b:105; Foster and Aber 2004). In other words, those lands that could be productively tilled and were well-drained were cultivated, and those which were excessively well-drained and sandy or poorly drained wetlands were forested. The regrowth, even after 150 years, is surprisingly dissimilar to the Colonial forests in terms of composition, inferred structure, and relationship to environmental gradients. Thus, forest vegetation itself has proven highly resilient to human impacts, but individual taxa have responded in highly variable ways to produce landscape patterns that contrast with those found in the Colonial period (Foster and Aber 2004; Pacala et al. 1996). Oak has increased in the north-central region and declined at lower elevations; birch and maple have increased substantially especially at lower elevation; and hemlock has declined in the north and increased in the west and south. The initial clearing, cutting, burning and cultivation favored species resilient to frequent disturbance such as beech and sugar maple in uplands. Beech remains at low abundance due to the large extent of its initial decline, very poor dispersal, and disease (e.g., beech bark disease) (Pacala et al. 1996).

Soil losses through erosion continue unabated in the modern world at ten times the estimated sustainable rate of soil losses. More than 10 million hectares per year are lost to erosion. Erosion results from the action of wind and rain upon the soil. Erosion is intensified further on sloping land where as much as half of the soil contained in the splash may be carried downhill. In dry places, soil particles can be transported thousands of miles, e.g., soil particles from Africa have been blown as far as Brazil, where they have had a sustaining effect upon the Amazon forest by providing nutrient inputs in otherwise nutrient-poor soils (Pimentel et al. 1995).

The Amazon provides a classic example of an environment being placed at risk on behalf of "development" even though there is little evidence that these development activities to date have achieved the goals of benefiting local people through better income. Instead, the result of 30 years of deforestation has been the loss of at least 17 per-cent of the forest cover, and the generation of some significant wealth to a small number of persons benefiting from government subsidies and wood extraction. The region continues to produce insignificant amounts of food and nearly half of the area deforested is in various stages of secondary forest and degraded pastures (Moran et al. 2002; Moran 1993; see also Collins 1986 for Peru). For the tropics as a whole, Lambin et al. (2003) find a number of dominant pathways for observed patterns of land use change. Achard et al. (2002) found that between 1990 and 1997 close to 6 million hectares of humid tropical forests were lost each year or 42 million hectares and that an area nearly half that large was degraded through logging and the impact of nearby development. Lambin et al. (2003) identify five major causes of land use changes at global scale: resource scarcity; changing opportunities created by markets; outside policy interventions; loss of adaptive capacity and growing vulnerability; and changes in social organization and attitudes towards nature.

It is important, too, to dismiss myths that are frequently held about land use and land cover change. It is not the case that deforestation is driven largely by population increases and poverty. Rather, it is government policies that target forested areas for agricultural development that explain most large-scale conversion of forest to agriculture (Lambin et al. 2001) – although differences have been noted between continents, with logging concessions preceding agricultural development in Asia and Africa but less so in the Americas. It is also not the case that rangelands are natural climax vegetations. Rather, they are a product of long-term interaction between pastoral peoples and the animals that graze and browse in those ecosystems. Land use intensification is not just a product of population increase but has been promoted in recent years by government policies that promote development through commercial crops and market-driven priorities, sometimes without adequate provisioning for conservation practices to protect the more heavily used habitats. Finally, urbanization needs to be seen as a form of land use whose impact is not so much in the place where cities are located, but on all the habitats upon which its inhabitants draw their goods and services from. Whereas cities occupy less than 2 percent of the terrestrial surface area of the planet, their impact is several orders of magnitude larger than that because of their consumption levels drawing from all over the planet (Lambin et al. 2001). As noted in chapter 1, globalization disconnects the sources of demand from the location of production and results in greater impacts through an insufficiency in feedback to inform resource users (Folke et al. 1997).

The Amazon region had experienced deforestation prior to 1975, but on a small scale. The population collapse of indigenous communities by war and disease following European discovery resulted in a pattern of small communities practicing shifting cultivation and moving their settlements frequently (Beckerman 1994; Roosevelt 1989; Meggers 1971). Assessments using satellites (Landsat MSS) found less than 1 percent of the Amazon Basin evidenced deforestation in 1975 (though the resolution of MSS probably hid some areas that were in secondary succession, and of course these satellites could not look back historically to pre-Columbian chiefdoms' land use in the region). Initiated in 1970, Brazil's Program of National Integration, associated with a major initiative to build roads across the Amazon and to settle land along these roads with colonists, began to change the rates of deforestation. The east–west Transamazon Highway, constructed in less than four years, cut a path from the northeast of Brazil to the frontier with Peru. The north–south Cuiabá-Santarém highway and the Belém-Brasília highway linked, respectively, the central and eastern parts of the Amazon to the central part of Brazil (Moran 1981, 1993).

These roads were catalysts of land cover and land use change in the Amazon. Human settlements were promoted by a series of settlement schemes providing incentives and virtually free land, attracted people who quickly began cutting forest in order to ensure their claims to land (Moran 1976, 1981; N. Smith 1982; Fearnside 1986). For the period up to 1988, Skole and Tucker (1993) were able to document that up to 15 percent of the Brazilian Amazon had been deforested and seriously fragmented – a rate close to 0.5 percent per year (see Figure 4.4). This rate actually hides the real local rates of deforestation. In settlement areas the rates of deforestation were commonly in excess of 1 percent per year, while vast areas remained out of reach of human occupation by Brazilian society. Percentages, too, tend to hide the scope and magnitude of deforestation in the Amazon: 1 percent of the Brazilian Amazon is equivalent to 50,000 km^2 or an area the size of Belgium. Thus, while the percentage of deforestation is higher in Ecuador and Mexico's tropical

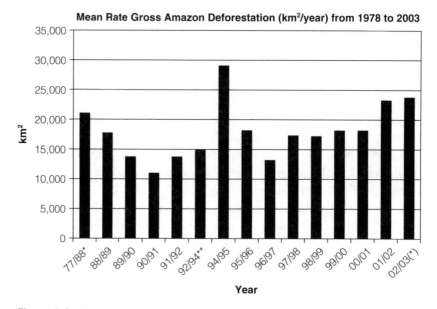

Figure 4.4   Deforestation in the Amazon, 1978–2003. Modified from INPE data (www.inpe.br)

forests, the absolute area being deforested in Brazil per year is several orders of magnitude larger.

Rates of deforestation in the Brazilian Amazon reached a initial peak in 1987, followed by a notable decline, then an increase that topped that peak in 1995 and in 2004 (see Figure 4.4). The drop in the late 1980s was not a result, as some thought, of more effective conservation or of a more effective set of policies, and turned out to be temporary. It was, rather, the result of hyperinflation and a serious credit deficit in Brazil. After the introduction of the new currency in 1994, and effective control over inflation, the rate of deforestation surpassed the first peak of 1987, generating serious concern. This second spike in the rate of deforestation can probably be explained by the suppressed rates of deforestation from 1988 to 1993, and the opportunities that economic stabilization offered. Within two years, deforestation rates settled down to the more common rates of about 0.5 percent for the Basin, and in settlement areas the rates remained considerably higher, i.e., above 1 percent annually (Wood and Skole 1998; Moran et al. 2002; Brondizio et al.

2002; Lu et al. 2003). The recent expansion of soybean cultivation into the Amazon, from the adjacent savanna regions, is expected will lead to new increases in deforestation.

Land change begins with the clearing of forest through slash-and-burn techniques, commonly followed by the planting of annual crops or the creation of pastures. In some cases, fields are kept in cultivation continuously, but this is rare. Only in areas with alfisols of relatively high fertility with favorable texture are there examples of continuous cultivation for over 25 years with some crop rotations in place (Moran et al. 2002, 2000a). In most places the low nutrient conditions of oxisols and ultisols, dominant in over 75 percent of the Amazon Basin, present constraints to continuous cultivation without major fertilizer inputs – which remain prohibitively expensive throughout most of the Amazon basin. Without fertilizers, farmers have tended to plant pastures and graze cattle at very low densities as a preferred strategy. Cattle ranching has a long tradition in Latin America and receives favorable treatment by policy makers as a repository of value and a hedge against inflation and uncertain economic cycles. It is the traditional tool for occupying large areas of the vast frontiers of Latin America with few people and labor scarcity (Walker et al. 2000). Thus, Rondonia (predicted in the 1970s to become a center for cocoa production) and the Altamira region of Brazil, both of which have patches of high quality soils, are dominated by pasture land despite the presence of fertile soils (Moran 1988). Less than 10 percent of the land area is in crops, with less than 4 percent in annual or staple crops (e.g., rice, corn, beans, manioc), and the rest in some form of plantation or tree crop (e.g., cocoa, rubber, sugar cane, coffee) (Brondizio et al. 2002). Nevertheless, the typical nature of change is one from undisturbed forest to a landscape cleared for management for cultivation or ranching, with a significant component of secondary regrowth on abandoned land (see Figure 4.5).

Farmers experiment with a variety of strategies. They tend to clear more land than they can manage at the outset, and rates of 6 percent per year are not unusual when first arriving (McCracken et al. 2002). This rate quickly drops as farmers realize the high cost of managing regrowth (Mesquita et al. 2001; Laurence et al. 2001; Zarin et al. 2001, 2002; Moran et al. 1994, 1996, 2000a; Tucker

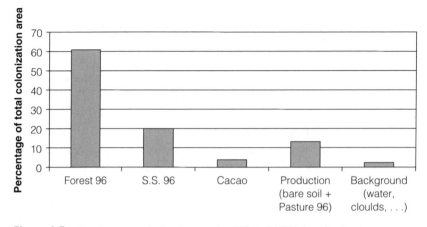

Figure 4.5   Landscape scale landcover in 1996. INCRA colonization area of Altamira, Brasil Novo and Medicilandia. Study Area = 355,295 ha. *Source:* Brondizio et al. 2002, p. 147

et al. 1998; Steininger 1996). Those with more favorable biophysical initial conditions and some capital move towards plantations and pasture formation; those with less favorable conditions continue to combine annual crops with modest increments in pastures on lands with exhausted fertility. Over time, those with favorable conditions tend to evolve a balance of crops and pasture, while those with unfavorable soil conditions and poor labor and capital resources tend to concentrate most of their land in pastures (see Figure 4.6).

While legislation in Brazil has sought to protect up to 50 percent of the areas occupied by settlers, raising this figure to 80 percent more recently, there is little enforcement of this legislation even if it were wise to do so. Given poor enforcement and the likely fragmentation of these "back of the property" conservation areas, this legislation seems less than effective as a means of conserving flora and fauna biodiversity. Recent evidence from a study in Rondonia suggests that extractive reserves, provide the only effective mechanism for conservation in areas of settlement (Batistella 2001), largely through the protective actions taken by the inhabitants of the extractive reserves who care and look after the forest which provides them with the resources to live on.

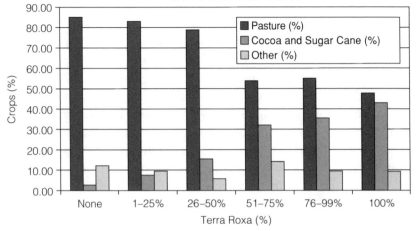

Figure 4.6 Crops and Terra Roxa soils. With an increase in the proportion of good soils like Terra Roxa, farmers diversify their crop portfolio. *Source:* Moran et al. 2003, p. 78

Research on causes and driving forces of tropical deforestation reveals that neither single factor causation (e.g., poverty, population growth) nor irreducible complexity adequately explain the dynamics of tropical deforestation (Geist and Lambin 2001). Deforestation is driven by regional causes, of which the most prominent are economic, institutional, and policy factors which seem to drive agricultural expansion, logging, and infrastructure development (Kaimowitz and Angelsen 1998; Lambin et al. 2001). Logging appears to be a more important driver at the outset of forest clearing in Africa and Asia than in Amazonia, where farming and ranching seem to precede logging activities. In Middle America, selective logging (not clear cutting) has provided road networks ultimately followed by farmers (e.g., Turner et al. 2001). The vastness of the Amazon, and the precariousness of infrastructure has probably mitigated the impact of logging in the Amazon as a primary driver of land change. Recent work by Cochrane and Schulze (1998), Cochrane et al. (1999), and Nepstad et al. (1999, 2002) suggests that loggers are beginning to lead the way in places where some primary road infrastructure has been created. Predictions are that the migration of major multinational logging interests from Asia to the Amazon may destroy what remains of the last great rain forest, for the benefit of a few international interests, leaving local people with an impoverished landscape.

In short, land use and land cover change in the Amazon, as elsewhere is having notable consequences on people and nature. While we commonly think of these changes largely in terms of conversion (i.e., from forest to farmland), it is important to note that often the change is modification (i.e., from low density to high density of a given species of economic interest) rather than conversion. Conversion of land cover to more intensive and economically valuable uses is one way to reduce environmental impact and to increase the sustainability of systems (Brondizio 1996). In the Amazon estuary, Brondizio found that farmers could achieve a five-fold increase in income while only having less than 1 percent impact on land cover by changing the density of a desirable palm species from which a fruit could be extracted and marketed (Brondizio, in press). While such impressive results may not be possible in non-estuary areas, where water acts as a constraint on productivity, it is conceivable that two- to four-fold increases could be achieved with other agroforestry activities.

Such increases may be possible not only in terms of income and biodiversity but also possible in terms of carbon stocks (Lugo and Brown 1992). Increasing density of some species can actually increase carbon accumulated in a system with only a marginal impact on total diversity. However, economic activities such as growing opium poppies for the production of drugs has been noted to have had a negative impact on species diversity in Colombia and other montane tropical forests (Goodman 1993). Since 1970 it is estimated that more than 700,000 hectares of montane forests have been cut down in Peru alone to make room for coca growing and production. Over 50,000 hectares of poppies have replaced forests in Colombia. The use of herbicides to combat the drugs in Peru and Colombia have had devastating downstream effects on fish and bird populations compounding the damage to nature. The focus on fighting drugs seems to blind policy-makers to the effects of some of the strategies being used which cause grave damage to the environment and the entire food web in ecosystems affected. In the next chapter we explore what makes people use, and misuse, information in making decisions.

5
What Makes People Do That?

Learning, Adaptation, and Information

An important aspect of our current dilemma is grasping under what conditions human populations learn and adapt to their environment. The reverse may be even more important: under what conditions do we seem to want to change the environment to our purposes and without regard for cost or consequences?

In the interest of formulating theories that adequately deal with the interrelations between people and nature, several authors have advocated a range of approaches that deal with meaning, ritual, and cognition combined with ecological research (e.g., Alland 1975; Adams 1974; Rappaport 1971, 1979; Brosius 1999). Adams, in his book *Energy and Structure*, detailed how the concentration of decision making and social power at higher levels of a social system leads to the concentration of control over energetic flows (Adams 1974). Interestingly, he found distinctive ways in which colonial powers organized themselves to exploit and use energy – and that countries they colonialized, had distinctly similar bureaucratic organization to exploit resources, long after the colonial power had left. In other words, how nations are politically structured to use resources has deep roots that often remain unexamined for decades, and even centuries. This suggests that the way nations use resources embodies histories, and myths, which remain hidden from public scrutiny because they have become culturally embedded.

Similarly, Rappaport discussed how ritual can act to adjust the relationship between a population and its resources in a New Guinea society (1968). According to Rappaport, ritual reduces ambiguity by putting complex analogic information into simple signals (i.e., like an on–off switch). In general, he noted that religious ritual affirms group values and asks individuals to abandon their selfishness and take on the social good. It does not rely on cost-benefit analysis, but on faith in the community through the act of participation in ritual. It runs counter to the immediately pragmatic. Ritual is an "expensive" cultural investment, but it pays off by providing unequivocal information of value for adaptation to changing conditions (1971). In his collection of essays, *Ecology, Meaning, and Religion* (1979), Rappaport explored these themes a great deal more. In it he argued that higher-order meanings, those that are most important to grasp complex processes such as how nature is constituted, and what our place in nature might be, are not based on discursive reasoning and logic but on more philosophical and mystical forms of reason (1979:157). These higher order meanings have a place in the adaptive structure of humanity because they incorporate more profound options than are readily apparent by the simple calculus of short term cost/ benefit to the individual. Moreover, he argued, maladaptations leading to things like "environmental problems" become increasingly dangerous with growing complexity of the system, because information must pass through many nodes and many scales, at each of which information can be distorted, resulting in inappropriate responses or errors in the scale of the response (e.g., "too little, too late" responses – Rappaport 1979:161). In short, our increasingly global system is subject to frequent errors in response to perturbations because it overaggregates information, and fails to define the appropriate scale of response due to informational anomalies as one goes from local to national to global scales. The result is loss of adaptiveness, and the erosion of evolutionary flexibility. Following Bateson (1972), Rappaport suggests that purposefulness is a characteristic of the human mind, and that this way of thinking about the world inclines human beings towards self-interest, and even selfishness. This had evolutionary value when we were hunter-gatherers as they decided what game to chase, where to locate their camps, and how to self-organize (Rappaport 1979:169). However, both Bateson and Rappaport suggest that when applied to complex systems, this way of thinking becomes increasingly prone to systemic disruptions. "To argue that more than reason may be required to maintain adaptive structure in human social systems. . . . is not to argue for the banishment of reason nor for its replacement by blind commitment or mystic insight" (ibid.). Rather, it is simply to recognize that linear reasoning alone is insufficient, because socionatural systems are so complex that we do not, and probably never will, fully understand all the interactions that must be considered in managing them. Therefore, we need to develop ways to make decisions based upon incomplete knowledge (and not pretend we have "perfect information" as neoclassical economics would have us do), and to take into account the need to preserve local systems by restoring the ability of local communities to rely on adaptive and cognitive flexibility in managing their resources (Kempton 2001; Potts 1996).

In a provocative discussion many years ago, Howard T. Odum (1971) argued that we would only begin to address our environmental crisis when priests and ministers of our major religions made saving the Earth an important component of the religious obligations to which they held believers to. One of the figures who defined "liberation theology," Leonardo Boff, suggested a few years ago in an interview that hugging a tree was like hugging God! While tree hugging is generally criticized in our society, here is one of the most profound theologians of the late twentieth century suggesting that this simple action could lead people to recognize the sacredness of the environment and the importance of giving it centrality in our actions. Boff felt that saving the world God created was no less important than loving one's neighbor as a testament of faith (Boff and Berryman 1997). He has continued to write about Ecosophy, a combination of philosophy and ecology, despite criticism by the Vatican. Major churches have not been forthcoming with this level of commitment to environmental stewardship, and until such a time as they do, many citizens may continue to prioritize linear thinking, rather than community thinking or biocentric thinking in making choices that affect the sustainability of the planet. Sponsel (2000) has written a compelling discussion of an emerging field, that he calls spiritual ecology, which combines spirituality with solid attention to ecology and which seeks to mobilize some of these same forces that H.T. Odum, Boff, and deep ecologists argue are necessary to tear many in our societies from the forces of materialism which distort our values.

Religion survives the challenges of science and secularism because it offers a needed complement to these alternatives. In times of vulnerability and stress, which are pervasive in human communities or for individuals, self-interest and deception can run rampant as people seek their self-preservation. As a result, commitment to ideals may be abandoned and the social fabric can be threatened. Religion, and faith, insist that one break out of this viciously rational cycle of self-interest and that one adopt group interests, exercise charity, and concern for others. In so doing, it holds greedy self-interest in check and encourages what has been called "organic solidarity" that makes social life more than a contract among self-interested individuals. It creates the basis for altruism, devotion to the group, promotes the value of sacrifice, and enhances the capacity to endure difficulties as a community (Atran 2002:278–279). This capacity to endure in the face of difficulties through trust in the supernatural, through sacrifice for the community, and to see a way to overcome difficulties that appear rationally to be beyond explanation has served humanity well. Our current addiction to material things and to making decisions with a calculus that privileges maximizing one's utility, results in a loss of faith, trust, and community that leads to both greater unhappiness and a destructive way of dealing with the world that sustains us.

While faith and meaning as embodied in ritual are ways to knowledge, there are many other modalities. Mackay (1968a:204) suggested that an organism required a repertoire of acts from which to make decisions. Work must be done to update the adaptiveness of these acts through the informational system. If one defines information as that which does logical work in orienting the organism toward better coping behaviors, then information is the establishment of logical relations (that is, the creation of logical structures). Human systems, like biological systems, are self-organizing – that is, able to receive inputs of new information and to develop characteristic organizing sequences by combining new and old information. Since the environment manifests consistent and recurrent features, an individual can use probability in deciding which routine is most likely to be successful (Mackay 1968b:363–364).

A number of authors have questioned the assumption that humans act according to the principles of probability. Some argue that human choices respond to empirical experience – that is, if it worked in the past, try it again; if it did not, try something else. Others suggest that the choices are made from a limited set of options or past routines, usually those that have occurred in the most recent past and that have the least uncertainty associated with the outcomes (Slovic et al. 1974). This continues to be a topic of lively research in the cognitive sciences. Figure 5.1 represents a schematic representation of how information flows in human–environment interactions. It begins with sensory reception of signals and symbols, some of which are ignored and others perceived, depending upon the sensory quality of the information and its fit with current logical structures that result from linguistic and cultural categorization, and from the portfolio of past routines that can be drawn on. This then allows for several possible new re-orderings in the process of evaluation. When a perceived stimulus does not fit neatly into categories, the cognitive domain may develop structured analyses of the stimulus so that it can create hypotheses and assign meaning to the information acquired. After this occurs, the information is processed and put into the realm of "information-for-decision." Information continues to be used throughout this process with past behavior being used as a ruler against which new options are judged, and with feedback a crucial element of decision making. Individual decisions are influenced by external constraints such as level of income available, vulnerability of the individual, and available information provided. The entire process depends on the quality of the information available to the decision maker and the individual's past set of routines. Each decision is then fed back to the past routines portfolio to be used or not in the future depending on the outcome of the current routine vis-a-vis other routines. This is part of the reason why we seem to persist in some behavior routines even when we have information provided that could lead to change. It is easier to keep doing past routines than start a new routine, unless the benefits from developing a new routine are substantial.

The human informational system probably works at various levels, depending on the level of difficulty in making choices. Decisions

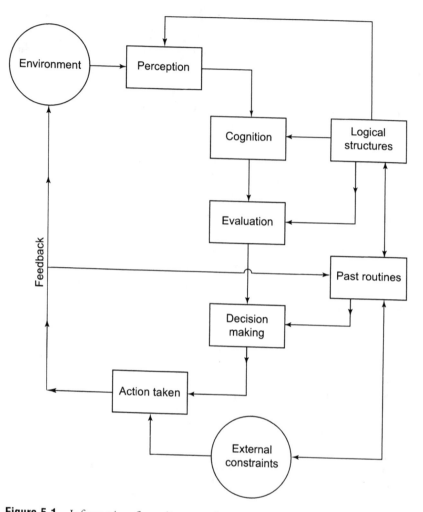

Figure 5.1 Information flow diagram. *Source:* Moran 1979a, p. 19

can be made in a climate of certainty, uncertainty, or risk. Certainty exists when one can predict what will happen in the period relevant to the decision. Uncertainty describes a situation wherein one cannot specify the probability of outcomes. Risk refers to situations where one can specify the probability distribution of several possible outcomes (Levin and Kirkpatrick 1975:106).

Under conditions of certainty about a situation (e.g., at breakfast I have a choice between cereal and eggs, with coffee in either case), a set of simple rules or pathways may be followed in arriving at a decision between cereal and eggs (e.g., which one we had yesterday, whether one will have lunch today, one's cholesterol level). As certainty decreases and there is a greater possibility of inappropriate or maladaptive choices, increasingly complex logic and structure must be used to help sift the information and allow for decision making under conditions of risk and uncertainty. Solutions may be elicited from the use of simulation, probability, and "judgment heuristics" (that is, non-probabilistic methods that make use of consensus between knowledgeable people). Effective research tools for dealing with conditions of risk have not achieved the sophistication of those dealing with uncertainty (but progress is taking place in the study of risk, e.g., NRC 1996, 1994). Both areas offer fertile ground for new contributions given the paucity of analytical tools available and the importance of this aspect of human systems (Levin and Kirkpatrick 1975:529–530). A decade of research on natural hazards yielded important results on why people seem to prefer risk to uncertainty (White 1974). Whereas risk involves an assessment of probabilities, uncertainty tends to immobilize people, as they have no idea of how to assess what might be the consequences of a given course of action.

Methods developed in microeconomics and in the field of management and decision theory can be usefully applied to the problem of choosing among courses of action. If one has too many choices, one may be immobilized by indecision. Thus, one of the typical responses of information flow systems is to develop rules to simplify the number of options considered. Over time, social scientists have presented a variety of theories that seek to give primacy to one factor or another. Perhaps dominant for many years has been the assumption behind the behavior of Economic Man (that is, maximization of expected utility). Behavior has been simplified so that economists can focus on those aspects of behavior that are aimed at advancing the interests of business, households, and so forth. However, some scholars have attacked those assumptions. The key assumption that the decision maker's objective is maximization of expected utility is useful for analysis, but does not represent the actual behavior of actors.

Critics have shown that economic men sometimes seek to maximize "non-economic" things, such as prestige (Cancian 1972; Schneider 1974), or that they simply try to minimize risk and uncertainty (Johnson 1971). Leibenstein in his book *Beyond Economic Man* (1976) has called for an overhaul of economic theory that takes into account "selective rationality" – that is, choice making that reflects a compromise between what one might do in the absence of constraints and what one does when they are present. One's preferences reflect social, cultural, and psychological standards of behavior that may be in direct conflict with the calculus of maximization. Similar theories have been proposed by business psychologists (March and Simon 1958; Lindblom 1964; Cyert and March 1963) and geographers (Heijnen and Kates 1974; Slovic, Kunreuther, and White 1974). The emphasis of these studies is on how decision makers do not necessarily maximize utility, but aim instead at satisfactory solutions to problems – often invoking simplified "programs" that lack the complete knowledge often assumed in economic analysis, or values such as family unity over economic gain – as in refusing a transfer on the job to ensure that the kids stay close to friends, and that community engagement in voluntary organizations is maintained over time. It has been suggested by some authors that one reason why we are in the midst of an environmental crisis is that so many people in our society lack roots to "place" because of the high frequency with which households move. The average American moves every five years and this surely is one element that militates against households committing to ensuring that the environment is conserved where they live.

Economic textbooks have tended to presume that individuals seek to maximize their benefits and that they are driven to particular production and location decisions by factors in their environment. Further, that unless they had secure private tenure they would not consider long-term consequences in their decisions – with the result that they would take decisions that would negatively impact the environment (Dales 1968; Dasgupta and Heal 1979). The work cited above by Simon (1985, 1997) and others (Camerer 1998, 2003) more recently shows that people make decisions taking into account a much broader set of values and that they recognize the imperfections of the available information. Theories of collective action have entered into this arena to further highlight the role of contingent human decisions (Olson 1965; Ostrom 1990). Davis first pointed out that individuals facing decisions independently without an external enforcement agency to make them keep agreements would have trouble making decisions. Hardin (1968) in his classic article on the tragedy of the commons further predicted that individuals using a common pool resource would degrade it as they each sought to maximize their utility, unless government imposed regulation. These views have been challenged more recently by noting that the above assumes that individuals do not communicate with each other, and that government performs effectively. Researchers have been able to identify key attributes of a resource, of users, and of government within which one might predict that individuals will, or will, not self-organize to protect resources (Libecap 1995; Ostrom 1999; Dietz et al. 2003).

An important component of achieving a sustainable society is a growing participation of citizens in environmental decision making. This means that environmental governance needs to involve those most affected, not just those who profit from the exploitation of resources. Who gets to decide often determines what we decide. Therefore, better environmental governance where those affected actively express their views and have those views translated into policy is one of most direct ways to reverse the world's environmental decline. It is not at all obvious to most of us how decisions are made about using ecosystem resources. Environmental governance is associated with institutions and how societies organize themselves to achieve goals. In the next chapter we delve more deeply into the role of institutions in mediating our relations with nature.

Governments are major players in how ecosystems are managed and conserved. Laws and regulatory frameworks set the formal rules by recognizing discrete property, mineral and water rights. They establish mandates for regulatory agencies charged with environmental protection and resource management. Governments also act internationally to set rules that apply across national boundaries – e.g., the Convention on Biological Diversity, the Kyoto Protocol on greenhouse gases; the Montreal Protocol to protect the ozone layer. Also involved are non-governmental organizations (NGOs), industry groups, and shareholders in expressing their views sometimes through lobbying efforts. Finally, and perhaps most importantly, governance involves individuals in society making choices on what resources to use, whom to vote for when elections are held, and each and every one of our consumer choices (see chapter 8 on the importance of recognizing the power of the consumer in a democratic and capitalist society). The choice to buy environmentally friendly products, organic produce, certified lumber, and a fuel-efficient car influences the behavior of businesses through the market – just as buying products just because they are slightly cheaper sends a different signal to them.

There is evidence of the effectiveness of action by citizens and their governments: in the UK a law requiring industrial facilities to provide information to the public about toxic releases led to a 40 percent reduction in the release of cancer-causing substances to the air in three years. Laws in 1998 in South Africa, mandated that a water reserve be maintained to ensure the sustainability of freshwater systems, thereby reducing overuse of water resources. The Montreal Protocol, a treaty passed in 1987, successfully eliminated the manufacture and use of chemicals harming the ozone layer and turned around an environmental and health disaster-in-the-making. A key element in successful governance is making information available to citizens and creating mechanisms for them to provide a degree of vigilance and oversight over the resources that matter to them.

Mitigation and the Cautionary Principle

Two chief responses dominate the literature on global change and human–environment interactions: adaptation and mitigation. Adaptation refers to the effort of the human population to adjust to changes as they occur. These can take the form of behavioral changes, such as changing clothing in response to heat or cold, or physiological adjustments such as increasing red blood cells when exposed to low oxygen pressure at high altitude. We rely on such social and behavioral adaptations to deal with most environmental changes – as in moving to a different neighborhood to avoid exposure to poor air quality – if we can afford to do so. In many cases, government policymakers prefer that their citizens adapt to environmental changes, as this requires lesser effort on their part, and less conflict. Thus, when faced with the demands of European countries for the United States to lower its carbon dioxide emissions, the response has been to prefer to argue that we will develop better technology to address the problem, or to argue that the evidence is incomplete, rather than to mitigate the levels of carbon dioxide through reduction of current levels.

Mitigation speaks to the efforts of people to change the current conditions so that exposure to poor air quality, for example, is eliminated through regulation, by reducing carbon emissions from fossil fuels through a change in consumption patterns. The Kyoto Protocol is an example of an international effort to mitigate the effects of global warming by setting goals to reduce current levels to those of 1992, thereby reversing a trend that seemed unstoppable. Mitigation and adaptation are not only strategies that individuals pursue but they are also political choices around which major debates are taking place. Some countries, like the United States prefer a wait-and-see attitude, trusting that technology will offer solutions in the future (NRC 1992, 1999a, 1999b). Other countries, such as the advanced industrial nations of northern Europe, take a mitigation strategy based on the cautionary principle that if we are uncertain about the future of the planet in light of current trends, we must act now to mitigate the impacts just-in-case the predictions prove to be true that current trends will do permanent damage to the Earth system. We must ask ourselves which strategy seems more reasonable to the sustainability of the planet we call our home.

Transforming the Face of the Earth: Making Better Decisions

In order to make better decisions one needs to begin by ensuring that decisions are made at the appropriate level. Often decisions are made far from the resource and the people most affected by the use of those resources (see earlier discussion of the work of Rappaport (1979)). In other words, decisions are made by government agencies, or companies, without input from citizens and communities affected. In some cases, it would be better to let communities decide what is best for them. But this may not be practical in many cases, and there is an important role that government agencies and higher level actors play – for example, to ensure that higher standards are applied than a given local community may be ready to accept without a fight. Generally speaking, the appropriate level for decision making should be determined by the scale of the resource system to be managed. The more localized the resources, the more the decision should be up to the local population, but the larger the area, and the more likely it is to have effects on other watersheds, the more the decision must involve a larger number of decision makers. Problems such as acid rain which involve movement of air pollutants across watersheds and even national boundaries must necessarily involve cross-national decision-making, international treaties, and other extra-local decision makers.

An important element of good environmental governance is to provide citizens with access to information and opportunities to participate in the decision-making process armed with that information. The Rio Declaration, from the 1992 global conference on the environment and development, and adopted by 178 nations, defined that access has three components: access to information, access to decision making, and the opportunity to seek legal remedies. Without all three of these elements there is a lack of public participation, and probably a lack of effective governance of resources. The information needed involves access to important data such as air and water quality in the local community (as this affects whether they drink the water or not); information about environmental trends through time (to see if things are degrading or improving); information on pollution from industrial facilities (to empower citizens and NGOs to pressure companies to behave responsibly); and information on how to deal with emergencies and risks present in their environment (e.g., if a large water impoundment is present, what are the risks that it may give way and flood the area). These should be minimum standards of information that citizens need to act responsibly in a democratic society. Access to decision making requires that citizens and other groups be able to influence national policies and plans, provincial and local policies and plans, and to take part in environmentally significant projects, such as licensing a power plant or a chemical plant. Access to legal remedies implies that it is possible for citizens and citizen organizations to seek legal remedies for irresponsible corporate behavior, ineffectiveness in the enforcement of pollution standards, and other failures in the decision-making process that endanger the public's health.

An important and growing element of citizen participation is through the proliferation of non-governmental organizations (NGOs), such as environmental NGOs, which have more than doubled since 1985 with more than 40,000 officially recorded. These organizations have helped pressure government and corporations into opening up to public scrutiny and to allow greater citizen participation in decisions. On the other hand, NGOs themselves are caught in the larger political economy which does not question the foundations of uneven development, poverty, and inequality (for a critical analysis of these issues, see Bebbington 2004). Further, economic globalization has been effective in growing also very fast, as a growing number of companies (more than 60,000 operate in the global marketplace) operate in a global market with few environmental strictures and little transparency. Some of these corporations, such as logging companies operating in Asia, remove trees illegally and work with corrupt officials who permit the continued removal of trees that violate existing laws.

One of the proposed solutions to better environmental governance has been decentralization, or devolving decision making to local governments. This solution is not a panacea to the problems noted above. More than 60 developing countries claim to be devolving power to local units – but few cases of true decentralization have been recorded, and rarely are adequate funds devolved to local agencies to permit them to operate effectively in monitoring the environment and in giving them power to prosecute those who violate local rules. In most cases, local agencies are charged with implementing decision made elsewhere without local accountability. When done fully, decentralization can work (Andersson 2003, 2004). In the next chapter we examine the role of institutions in mediating human interaction with environment, and the key role that trust and shared values have in the robustness of human institutions.

Decisions that people make apply to many things related to the environment. The choice of which crop to plant, what soil to use for a given crop, how many children to have, and how much to produce all involve complex decisions. One of the most crucial ones are decisions regarding the size of the family, and at larger scales, what one might do to direct the size of the human population at national and global level. At present, for example, European scholars, and policymakers are trying to figure out what to do with the fact of an aging population, and how to deal with anti-immigration movements in some of these countries (Lutz et al. 2001). Earlier, China's one-child policy became a classic of draconian intervention to reduce population pressure on national resources that worked in turning around the rate of increase of the world's most populous country. India, which did not put into place any radical population policy, is expected to surpass China's population in 50 years. More commonly, countries create incentives either to have, or not to have, more children, through their social welfare policies, the tax deductions provided for children, and other interventions that are more indirect (e.g., ease or difficulty of getting affordable daycare).

Population and the Environment

It has been all too common to make a direct association between population numbers and things like CO_2 emissions, environmental degradation, global warming, and other manifestations of climate change. Indeed, human activities now contribute a substantial percentage of the accumulating greenhouse gases. But more people does not mean more emissions. Per capita emissions of CO_2 are two times higher in North America than in Europe, and two times higher in China and Latin America than in the rest of the developing world (O'Neill et al. 2004). Moreover, the role of population in energy use, and thus in emissions, changes whether the population is an aging one, or a younger population with high dependency ratios. One of the future major drivers of increased energy use will not be population size itself but the growing number of households resulting from high rates of divorce worldwide, and the creation of two households where before there was just one (Rindfuss et al. 2003; Liu 2001; Liu et al. 2003). This growth rate of households is greater at present than the growth rate of population in both developed and developing countries (O'Neill et al. 2004).

Theories of population-and-environment go back at least to the time of Malthus, who writing in 1803 noted that human populations have a tendency to increase exponentially, unless limited by starvation, disease or fertility limitation policies – but that agriculture only increased its productivity in linear fashion, resulting in famines. Malthus failed to predict for the possibility that agricultural yields, and area under cultivation, could also expand exponentially and technological breakthroughs like the Green Revolution have proven that it is possible, at least episodically, to catch up in the race between agricultural yields and population demand for food. Neo-Malthusians have been at work ever since refining these views, while remaining basically consistent with the prediction that there is a race between population and food supply.

In contrast to the neo-Malthusians, who posit population as the driver of negative environmental changes, those who follow the views of Boserup (1965) find that population growth is the force that stimulates technological change and intensification. Boserup suggested that increases in population density, resulted in land scarcity, and that this triggered agricultural intensification through application of improved technology (such as better tools, irrigation, terracing, and shortening of fallows). Indeed, a number of studies show that some populations have come up with dramatically more efficient technologies which are also less harmful on the environment than more extensive technologies (Netting 1986, 1993; Turner et al. 1993a).

A theory which borrows from the above theories and some others was formulated first by Davis (1963) and revived more recently by Bilsborrow (1987) and is known as the theory of multiphasic response. While it was originally applied to refer to country level dynamics only, its applications have been more on communities. In this formulation, populations respond to population pressure first by increasing food production to keep pace with population growth through putting more land under cultivation or intensification. If insufficient, temporary labor migration removes some of the rural labor and generates income in urban areas; households then entertain more permanent migration to take pressure off the rural residences; and only then does fertility reduction occur (Bilsborrow and Carr 2001), its impact only being felt in the next generation.

Another influential theory was generated by Thünen (1966 [1826]), in which he introduced the importance of how land values and rents relate to distance from a central place, thereby adding transportation costs to production costs as central to the maximization decisions of farmers. There is now strong empirical support for the impact of transportation costs on what crops are planted, and how other decisions are affected by this consideration (Webber 1973; Visser 1982; Moran 1981; Chomitz and Gray 1996).

The impact of population growth on land cover changes over time. Students of population describe the changes in rates of birth, death, and migration in terms of a demographic transition (see Kirk 1996 for a history of this concept). Human populations for much of their history experienced high death and high birth rates. These rates balanced each other off and growth was minimal (see Figures 4.2 and 5.2). In the nineteenth century, improvements in public health began to reduce death rates and population increase began to take place at ever growing rates. In the next stage, death rates stabilize at low levels and birth rates begin to fall. Once birth rates have fallen to the same low level as death rates, population growth is once again very low as it had been when birth and death rates were high (but because of the high growth period, the total

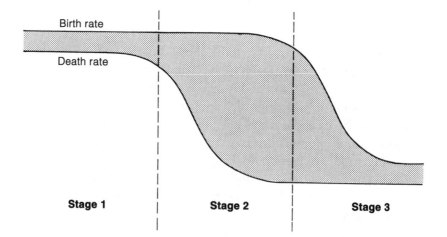

Figure 5.2   The demographic transition from high birth and death rates to low birth and death rates

populations are much higher). Countries across the planet are at different stages of the demographic transition, with some already with stable and even declining populations, while others are still in the stages where birth rates outpace death rates. The acceleration of low birth and death rates is often associated with high rates of urbanization, where public health and education assist in the achievement of this transition, and where the cost/benefit of children is different than it is in rural areas (Szreter 1996). The theory of the demographic transition describes the experience of North America and Europe better than it does that of developing countries today, although the concept is still useful in thinking about the forces at play in the decline of birth and death rates. This is an area in profound need for more research to clarify how environmental variables affect fertility, mortality, and migration processes.

The current world population of some 6 billion is expected to increase to 10 billion by the year 2050, after which time it is expected to begin a steady but slow decrease, as more nations in the world begin to have below replacement fertility (Bongaarts 1998), as is the case of Italy, Spain, and Denmark (see Figure 5.3, for regional steep declines in fertility). These trend-setters in population will face challenges in the years ahead to meet the growing demand of the elderly in their societies and the falling rates of young to support through social program the aged. In countries with vigorous immigration, this may be a lesser problem as the immigrants can provide a new source of taxes and a replenished labor force but this may depend on the status they are given in each country, and whether they are allowed to be part of the formal economy or whether their activities remain largely unaccounted for in the informal economy. There are counterpressures to limit immigration in some countries on a number of grounds, some cultural, some nativistic. These anti-immigration movements confound the need for these immigrants to provide for the growing elderly with concepts of cultural purity and fear of being overrun culturally and biologically by the immigrants.

Much of the predicted increase in total population will take place in the developing countries, particularly Asia. While the population of the developed world will remain stable between now and 2050 at 1.16 billion, the population in developing countries will go from

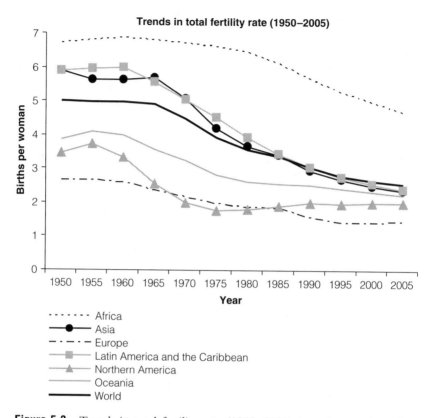

Figure 5.3   Trends in total fertility rate (1950–2000) in major continental areas. Note the general trend downwards. *Source:* Population Division of the Department of Economic and Social Affairs of the United Nations Secretariat, World Population Prospects: The 2004 Revision and World Urbanization Prospects: The 2003 Revision, http://esa.un.org/unpp

the current 4.6 billion to 8.20 in 2050 (Bongaarts 1998). However, the human population has surprised students of population several times in the past. In the 1950s many worried that Latin America's population was exploding and that a lack of food would characterize the future of the region. Instead, Latin American nations on the whole have had dramatic decreases in their populations as a result of urbanization, adopted contraception rapidly and sterilization to

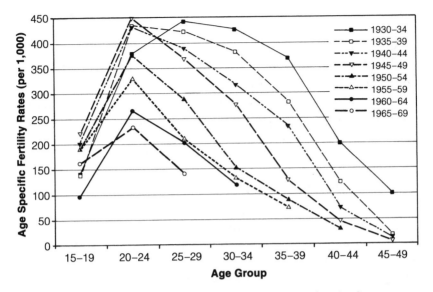

Figure 5.4 Age-specific fertility rates by birth cohort, Altamira Survey. Stephen McCracken, Anthropological Center for Training and Research on Global Environmental Change, Indiana University

reduce birth rates, and many countries export large amounts of food to other parts of the world. Figure 5.4 illustrates the rapidly declining age-specific fertility of a Brazilian population, a phenomenon happening also in a growing number of developing countries – especially those with rapid urbanization patterns and improvement in access to education and jobs for women – as is true for most of Latin America. This precipitous decline in total fertility of Brazilian women took place without any systematic government or private program to reduce population. A number of researchers are currently trying to understand the origins, and the persistence of high rates of sterilization among all social classes in Brazil (Potter 1999; VanWey and Moran, in preparation). Women in Brazil are clearly doing family planning, with 76 percent of women using some form of contraception. There is modest use of the pill between the ages of 15 and 20, followed by a period when most women have one or two children, followed by sterilization. Intrauterine devices have never been popular. Depo-provera and other injectable contraceptives have not become popular due to alleged reactions to the high levels of estrogen.

Attention to aggregate population variables, such as birth rates, death rates, and migration are not enough. One also needs to understand the population structure (age and gender), and its distribution in the landscape (settlement pattern) to understand human ecological relations. Age and gender structure influences how people use the land, by determining how much labor is available to each household, what their goals might be (e.g., how much to save to marry off daughters, or how many sons available to handle the herd – Liu et a 1999a; McCracken et al. 1999). The growing number of households, through divorce and differences in lifestyle is redefining how people are scattered on the landscape, what size of home they might choose to have, and where to locate it. Work by Liu (2001) showed that in China's Wolong Reserve, the impact of households was greater where they were located in a dispersed fashion, as compared to other parts of the Reserve, where they were settled in more concentrated nuclear villages.

The human population has a huge impact on the Earth, but what is less often considered is that it is also the world's greatest evolutionary force (Palumbi 2001), through the strong natural selection exerted by human technology upon organisms. Insects evolve resistance within a decade after introduction of a new pesticide. Weeds evolve resistance to a herbicide within 10 to 25 years. Bacterial diseases have evolved strong and devastating resistance to many antibiotics, as is the case with penicillin. The vast majority of infections today are penicillin-resistant, and 50 percent are methicillin resistant. Retroviruses with RNA genomes evolve resistance even more quickly than bacteria. Every year vaccinations against influenza must be reformulated. The virus that causes AIDS evolves so quickly that the infection within a single person becomes a quasi-species consisting of thousands of evolutionary variants. All this is to say that populations, even human ones, respond sometimes very quickly to external constraints. The move of people from rural areas to cities resulted in surprising declines in total fertility. Africa is currently viewed, as Latin America a couple of generations ago, as a "basket case" with regards to population. The still high rates of mortality, the low levels of education of women, the rurality of much of the population, and the threat of AIDS tend to support a choice for more children rather than less. As these change, we can expect Africa too to see a demographic transition to low fertility.

A number of issues are particularly timely on matters of population: how people make decisions on childbearing, household formation, residential location, and what factors affect these decisions; how people adjust their reproductive behavior in light of changing environments particularly degraded environments and urban crowding; how people gauge the impact of their behavior upon the resources they draw from. Crucial in this whole area is whether one can begin to construct sustainable communities. This means not only designing residential patterns that are ecologically low in their impact, but also that facilitate reduction in the use of cars to achieve normal day-to-day tasks (e.g., getting groceries, going to the doctor, picking up kids at school or taking them to activities, buying flowers). This model is still found in some places in Europe, where public transportation drops people off at villages with everything within a block or two before heading home from work (or on the way to work). I had the pleasure to live in Kew, U.K. where one could find next to the train station that took one to London and elsewhere, the butcher, the flower shop, the small general grocer, the bread shop, cafes, pubs, real estate offices, the dentists and doctors, all within a two block distance of the train station and within walking distance of most homes of the town (or biking distance). Some left their cars near the train station if their homes were too far to bike but the latter seemed to be preferred and most common. A car was virtually unnecessary given the connectedness of the rail system, and the proximity of most needs to home and transport. What is needed is a restoration of sustainable communities like these where they have been lost, or where they could be planned in the future. Ex-urban and peri-urban development in the United States is not planned with these kinds of amenities within walking distance, but are designed, instead, with the car in mind.

The question has to be asked, if we pretend to be serious about caring for this Earth: are our current strategies putting at risk millions of years of biological evolution? In a series of provocative novels, Daniel Quinn, in *Ishmael* (1992) and then in *The Story of B* (1996), presents a stark narrative for what has gone wrong with the way we carry out business-as-usual. In these books he argues, in a manner not dissimilar from some environmentalists, that until about 10,000 years ago humans co-existed with the planet in a way similar to other species. People used what they needed and no more. They did not accumulate possessions because they had to be on the move to harvest the fruits that the land provided and chase the game that supplemented their diet. They lived in small groups and their footprint on the planet was light.

In *The Story of B* he points out that for much of human evolution, *Homo sapiens* populations grew glacially slow: doubling only every 19,000 years. Then all began to change with the development of agriculture. Over the past 10,000 years this doubling time has been getting smaller and smaller so that now it takes only 32 years for the human population to double! In a manner not unlike the theories laid out earlier, Quinn argues that as population grows we must grow more food, but he lays out a scenario not as clearly laid out in the theories of Boserup or Malthus. He argues that producing more food results in more people and that this feedback process unless stopped will go on unimpeded resulting in the destruction of our own species. In other words, "intensification of production to feed an increased population invariably leads to a still greater increase in population" (Quinn 1996:296). His argument that we need to stop producing more food if we are to stabilize population is anathema in most quarters, as this would imply that people could starve. But Quinn argues that they starve now, not because there is a lack of food but because of problems of distribution. In fact, we know all too well that there is plenty of food, that some people have too much of it (e.g., the obesity problem in some nations like the United States), and others don't have enough of it due to poverty, war, and other disruptions in the food distribution system. Quinn's analysis lays the blame squarely on food production as the cause of population growth.

This somewhat radical picture of our current situation deserves some thought, even if the details in the novels are not accurate. He argues that we have constructed a myth in which people are the end of creation (patently not true, but one which we rarely question in our day-to-day thinking), and that we are meant to control all of creation since we are its apex. As our needs increase, we feel justified in continuing to increase our control over nature even when such control destroys the sustainability of those systems. Over time, as our population grows beyond the current 6 billion, it continues to move into increasingly marginal habitats to make them produce whatever they can for our benefit – and in many cases to detribalize the people in those heretofore marginal areas by taking the land that had been theirs. Thus, did Bali expand into the outer islands as the Balinese population exploded (Geertz 1963), and so did Indonesians through resettlement schemes move into the low population islands taking over the land of these "ethnic minorities." Human history is replete with these cases of dominant agricultural peoples taking over the land of hunter-gatherers and extensive cultivators. Quinn argues that our only hope is to reject our contemporary myth of how things are, and to remember how things were, when we knew that we are just one species among millions of species on the planet, that we belong to the world and are content to belong to it, and respect it – not control it and in so doing, destroy it. One way in which human populations have been very successful in living on this planet has been through their social interactions, the building of robust social institutions, and creating ways by which to set boundaries to resource use, and enforcement of community-based agreements, the subject we take up in the next chapter.

6
Rebuilding Communities and Institutions

Community in Human Evolution

Human beings are social animals and from the early hominids to the present, our strength has come from our capacity to live together in groups seeking to provision ourselves with adequate food, shelter, and mates. Insofar as people used pastures, woodlands, fisheries, and other resources for millennia without degrading them, it was because they shared an understanding of their rights, responsibilities, and other means to guarantee that the resource would be available to them and to their children. However, we know that this balance between common goods and human communities is not a given. It is something that results from the coevolution of systems of management tied to an understanding of the resilience or vulnerability of the resources being used and the need to conserve them in the face of the need to survive. In the distant past, it may have been possible for people to use resources carelessly, and they could always move a short distance to have some unexploited area still rich in those resources. But those days are long gone. A confluence of factors are now operative that change the impact of communities on the planet: rapid rates of population growth in a world of several billion people; increasing rates of per capita consumption; growing emphasis on materialism, individualism and competition; growing differences between the haves and the have nots; greater differences between those with access to technology and capital and those who lack it; greater difficulty in foreseeing the impacts of new technologies on ecosystems; and greater cumulative impact of human activities on an increasingly coupled human–environment system (Burger et al. 2001:2).

One of the challenges of having effective management of resources has been connected by some scholars to whether as communities grow larger in size, they become less capable of managing resources (e.g., Olson 1965). Certainly, results coming from game theory show that cooperative strategies are more likely to emerge and be sustained in smaller than in larger groups (Baland and Platteau 1996). Studies of irrigation and forestry institutions have shown, time and again, that success is more frequent in smaller groups (Barker et al. 1984; Cernea 1989). Under some conditions, however, it has been shown that small groups do not do as well. If the costs of providing a public good remains relatively constant as group size increases, then it may be advantageous to draw on a larger group as this would decrease the costs per capita to members of the group (Isaac et al. 1994).

One tends to think of ownership of resources in rather simplistic terms – as involving either private holdings, or communal holdings. In reality, one finds nearly every possible combination and permutation in human history. For example, Netting (1976) pointed out that in the alpine communities of Western Europe both types of landholding persisted for centuries in stable association. He notes that, in the absence of external powerful legal or military controls, the system of property rights in local peasant communities will be geared directly at the management of resources to be exploited. When these are complexly distributed along an altitudinal gradient, as they are in alpine regions, they will be comparably complex in this case combining elements of communal management, and private ownership. One finds this type of combination also in areas with contrasting resources as in a part of the Amazon where summer pastures dry, but floodplain pastures become available as the water recedes. In such areas we find private holdings in the uplands, but communal ownership in the floodplain (Futemma et al. 2002).

Another important factor in group resource management is the homogeneity or heterogeneity of the population. It is generally understood that coming up with common rules for managing resources in a community is easier if the members of the group are relatively homogenous in ethnicity, culture, and wealth. The smaller the group, the more likely it is that the group will be homogeneous, and thus that it will be able to arrive at consensus on rules for accessing resources promptly and to more effectively be able to enforce the wishes of the group. When the interests of those using the resources differ, achieving a self-governing solution to a common resource may be quite challenging.

The existence of community is constantly challenged by the tendency of people to seek their narrow self-interest (i.e., when self-interest turns into greed), and this struggle between narrow self-interest and the common good has enormous consequence to the fate of our planet, and to what happens to local resources from place to place. If narrow self-interest wins out, we have outcomes such as "the tragedy of the commons" in which individuals who share a common resource seek their individual advantage even when they see evidence that the resource is collapsing (Hardin 1968). This is a view with strong support all the way from Adam Smith (1977 [1804]:446) to the present. Hardin went even so far as to suggest that having an interest in "the group" was self-eliminating and that evolutionary processes would select for those who exercised self-interest over those who did not (Hardin 1968:1244). However, other scholars point to the many cases when individuals take into account the interests of the group in making decisions (Sober and Wilson 1998; Rappaport 1968; Vayda and Rappaport 1968), and that this results in better decisions for the community.

What is Sacred in Human Evolution?

Rappaport, in the *Annual Review of Ecology and Systematics* (1971), proposed that ritual played a key evolutionary role for our species. He suggested that through ritual, individuals in human communities became "as one" in common purpose, and through participation in ritual they were socialized into the value of the common good, the value of sharing, and subordinated themselves to the forces embodied in ritual's sacred texts and music. In fact, whether we are speaking of an animistic ritual in New Guinea, or the precepts of the Roman Catholic Church, they share one thing in common: the rituals and messages emphasize that members are part of a community of faith, a community of sharing, and of being one with spiritual forces. These spiritual forces, being non-material, do not value the material but only what is of the spirit. Thus, ritual leads individuals in the community to question their attachment to the material, proposes that some of those material goods be shared with the less fortunate in the community, and that in sharing those things individuals achieve one-ness with the spiritual world. In other words, the very early development of ritual, and of the notion of the sacred, in human evolution was keyed to addressing that most fundamental flaw in the human character — the tendency to seek narrow self-interest, and to accumulate material possessions without regard for the needs of others in the community. Each society that has had any longevity has come up with ways to socialize its members to their obligations to kin, to family, to the social group, and to the various other groups to which it relates. Cultural rules are devised to define the boundaries of reciprocity, the expected ways of sharing with others, and the benefits that accrue from that generosity. In Highland Papua New Guinea "Big Men" achieve that status by being productive in their gardens, and then sharing their wealth with others in the community. The cargo cults of Mesoamerica give individuals who share their wealth with the community "cargos" or important ritual and social leadership (Cancian 1972). Even in our own materialistic society, there is social pressure on the wealthy to become philanthropists, thereby sharing some of their accumulated wealth in worthwhile causes. There was considerable pressure on Bill Gates some years ago to start sharing the wealth he had accumulated as the head of Microsoft, and the world's wealthiest individual. Eventually he created a foundation that has since then engaged causes such as educational needs in this country, and health problems in the Third World.

Some religions have gone further by developing sects in which members give up all they own, and live from alms and donations, "like lilies in the field," — as in the Franciscan ideal or as Buddhist monks of some sects do. Only some rare sects, and largely in the present, advocate wealth and accumulation as a good thing. These are viewed by the great majority of the world's religions as aberrant, and as sects driven by secular values, rather than by the great traditions of faith. Whether Christian, Moslem, Jewish, Hindu, or Buddhist, the great religions share a common concern with the needs of the poor, the importance of charity by all but especially by those who have material goods to help those who are in need, and giving great value to being a part of a community of faith. The latter is important, according to Rappaport (1971), because a community of faith is not bound by the logic of reason, or the logic of self-interest. On the contrary, such a community is asked to put aside that logic in favor of the logic of faith – a logic of other-interest – just as families practice within the confines of the home.

Another way to think about this is in terms of the linear logic of self-interest vis-à-vis the circular logic of other-interest. One leads us away from the needs of others, while the other brings us back to them and builds a community of shared values, shared wealth, and common purpose. For much of human history, communities have given considerable value to leveling mechanisms that reduce disparities between community members. From the bosom of the family, to the small hunting-gathering band, the logic was one of reciprocity. In small villages built with shared ethnicity and religion, the logic continued to be one in which those who were more productive could achieve status as "big men" but only if they shared their success in material accumulation by sharing it with others in the community. Those who did not share were distrusted and could not receive the public recognition of being "big men." This process was constantly challenged by individuals throughout human history, but it is clear that leaders were expected to embody the generosity that lay behind the social contract. It is only as communities grew large, and more complex and having many specialists that we begin to see persistent social differentiation in wealth and material goods – not just in status as before. As control over land increased, and became a source of wealth that could be inherited and controlled from generation to generation, accumulation of wealth took off and the struggle between community and individual grew.

It is from this ever expanding differentiation in wealth that we have become what we are today – a population with great material wealth, concentrated in the hands of fewer and fewer families, with very little sense of community and common purpose. Those who have material wealth fear for the loss of it, or their lives, and put into place ever more ominous systems of social control to protect themselves from those who lack access to resources or wealth. Indeed, despite the large participation by Americans in church going, the values of individuals are ever more secular, and less and less driven by reciprocity and the logic of sharing at the center of the major religions. Even the secular forms of sharing, such as a progressive income tax, which take a greater share of the accumulated wealth of the rich to give to the poor through social services is under attack by political parties bent on appealing to the linear thinking of their constituents rather than to their common purpose as members of one society.

Tragedies of the Commons

When individuals seek their narrow self-interest by the millions, we have the world we live in today – one in which we have more total wealth, but which is poorly distributed and where those who are wealthy do not show signs of greater happiness because of it. In small-scale relatively egalitarian societies, individuals had consider-able autonomy, considerable voice in community affairs, and could enforce fair, responsive, even generous behavior from their leaders (Boehm 1999; Richerson et al. 2002). Legitimacy of leadership came from expressing the will of the community, not from imposing one's will upon it. Even today, leaders require legitimacy, except that the considerable power of the media can be brought to bear upon the dissemination of information so that individuals are led by those stories rather than by personal experience of the events and persons. One of the key issues here is **trust**. Trust and how to get it, varies a great deal between complex societies, and it is very hard to obtain and even harder to keep. Even the most efficient and legitimate institutions can be prey to manipulation by small-scale organizations, cabals, and special interests. When institutions fall prey to special interests, a loss of trust ensues by members of the society who feel that the institutions are only serving special inter-ests rather than the common good (Richerson et al. 2002:424).

Thus, a fundamental characteristic of successful communities is that they share common goals and that they are built on trust and cooperation. When such common objectives are present, members of the community are likely to have a shared understanding of the take-out rates that are consistent with the productivity of the resource, as overexploitation would affect everyone. Of course, there is a temptation in any commons for free-riders to take advantage. In traditional, small-scale societies this is addressed by fairly immediate feedback from others, and by the fact that the impact of small-scale societies on the environment tends to be light rather than heavy.

The problem really begins when small-scale societies grow in size. As communities grow larger, it becomes increasingly difficult to prevent individuals from pursuing their narrow self-interest, because of the higher value of present benefits of using resources as compared with future benefits which may be compromised by the interim use of resources by others (Aristotle, *Politics*, Book II, chapter 3; Marcet 1819 cited in Baumol and Oates, 1988; Lloyd 1977; Dietz et al. 2002:8). These early views laid the foundations for Hardin's conclusion that "freedom in a commons brings ruin to all" (1968:1244). His views have been, and continue to be, influential in how we view common resources such as air, water, and ocean fisheries. He saw no way out of this road to ruin − except through government intervention and ownership of the resources. Hardin did not seem to believe that trust, cooperation, and common goals are sufficiently robust in human communities to lead to self-regulation in access to common resources. This view assumes that internalized norms emerging from members of communities cannot be effective, and that only externally enforced, and coercive controls can be effective (Gibson 2001).

Differences of opinion over Hardin's dismal view of the future of the commons are rooted in one important, and apparently overlooked distinction between common access and common property resources. In open access conditions there are no rules to limit entry and use − whereas in common property situations there are owners who share a resource but who are likely to limit entry and use to those who are co-owners. While not all common property regimes optimally managed their resources, there were many which developed rich systems of use rights that sought to ensure long-term usability of the resources for those who had a common interest in it (Dietz et al. 2002). Moreover, Hardin's formulation not only forgets the vested interest of co-owners of common property but also the fact that in many cases these actors are also families living in the same villages where their families have lived for generations, and where they intend to live for generations to come (Runge 1981, 1984). Under these conditions, it is not very likely that individuals will choose to regularly free-ride, as this would undermine community solidarity and even bonds of kinship and marriage. Instead, the situation is rather a challenge of coordination, and how multiple users can arrive at agreements within the village context that assure each of them that others are conforming to a shared understanding of what is the fair share that each can extract from the resource held in common.

Netting (1976, 1981) laid out a set of conditions that seem to explain where and under what conditions we might find common property institutions. He predicted that:

- when the value of per unit production was low
- when the frequency and dependability of yield was also low
- when the possibility of improvement was low
- when the area required to effectively use the resource was large and
- when the size of the group needed to make adequate capital and labor investments to make the area productive was large

then one would see the emergence of common property institutions as an effective way to meet these conditions of production. Netting also provided evidence that when opposite conditions were present, then one would see the emergence of private property as a more effective way to meeting the needs of the population. In other words, common-pool, i.e., common access, resources, and common property institutions tend to emerge in already marginal areas with pre-existing limitations. When such areas are exploited without rules to limit access, as in common pool resources, there is a high probability of environmental destruction given the marginality of the area in the first place. When common property institutions emerge, in long-lived communities, there is a much higher probability of resource sustainability evident, for example in the occupation of East African grasslands by pastoral populations for millennia (Little and Leslie 1999; McCabe 2004).

The effectiveness of institutions in regulating common pool resources is partially dependent on the characteristics of the resource, and on the technology that might be applied to its extraction. Prior to the introduction of barbed wire it was very costly to exclude potential users from a rangeland, whereas thereafter it became more feasible. However, the larger the area of rangeland the more costly it becomes to exclude others and in many parts of the world affected by unpredictable rainfall and its location, fencing remains a seldom used strategy of exclusion given its high cost, given the low productivity of such habitats. Because these characteristics are not fully known to all users, and access to technology can be variable, over time it is likely that users will fight over the fair distribution of common resources. It is from these fights that communities construct rules that specify the do's and don'ts related to a particular resource use situation. Such rules need to take into account realities such as the renewability of the resource, the spatial extent of the resource, and the costs of monitoring the use rate of the resource. For example, fish that travel in schools are more likely to be negatively impacted by modern techniques capable of identifying their location, than are those species which spread out over a larger area and cannot be detected by modern satellites. The costs of monitoring vary a great deal: it is very difficult and costly to know exactly the impact of use on wildlife numbers, as compared say with the stock of water in a dam. On the latter it is far easier to arrive at rules and regulations to account for the condition of the resource, whereas the mobility of wildlife and its often cryptic character make such monitoring difficult and it is harder to get members of communities to agree on the need to regulate use of these species.

In short, sustainable management of common pool resources depends on the characteristics of the resource and on the characteristics of the users. For institutions to be robust, they must be locally well-informed about the resource and the users, and they must be able to mobilize enough of the members' time to be able to monitor and evaluate the condition of the resource as a basis for the emergence of effective rules. They will need to be continually modified and adjusted as population and resource change in magnitudes and rates of change. These transactional costs of monitoring, evaluating, meeting, and deciding on what rules will assure the sustainability of the resource, its equitable distribution, and its efficient use are an important reason why, in so many cases, communities are unable to adequately protect the environment – particularly when rates of change are fast, either on the human or the resource side. In a world wherein climate change, rapid population, and governments and the global economy reach into even the most isolated places, the challenge to communities to prevent a tragedy of the global, and local, commons is ever greater (Ostrom et al. 1999). In a complex international and interconnected world having institutional diversity will be important to the survival of the planet.

Institutions and Self-Organization

So, what are the requirements for successful institutions? Scholars do not agree on this, but an examination of major efforts begins to approximate the conditions that underlie successful institutions. One of the most frequently overlooked conditions are the characteristics of the resource itself. This set of conditions remains underspecified in existing research. The best syntheses on the topic by Wade (1988), Ostrom (1990), Baland and Platteau (1996) and the review by Agrawal (2002) scarcely get into the environmental characteristics that shape what institutions must address to achieve sustainable resource use. Obviously the climatic and edaphic characteristics that affect rates of regeneration are crucial. Whether a resource is highly mobile or not affects what sorts of rules, and what the transaction costs might be. Ocean fisheries are a particularly good example in that efforts to develop sustainable rates keep running into the difficulty that so little is known of what is happening in the ocean and where populations might go and hide to survive high take out rates. One of the particularly interesting questions about institutions and sustainability is what is different between the cases where a resource is driven to extinction, and those in which there is a retreat from the brink of extinction resulting in regeneration of the populations. What is it about the resource, or about the flow of information, or the rate of decline that might explain one case or the other?

Obviously, mobility makes a resource more difficult to manage and to develop effective institutions to sustain it, but it also is less likely to be an easy prey to overexploitation since it can escape out of reach in many cases. A resource which is stationary and storable, such as water in a dam, or a rangeland, are easier to assess in their amount or quality and probably easier to arrive at a way to manage them. But in the case of rangelands, the animals that graze on it are mobile and the impacts can be highly variable from place to place. Most resources include characteristics of stationarity and mobility and of storability or not. Also involved are variables such as population growth and markets. The debate on population is highly polarized, with some arguing that population pressures have enormous impacts (Ehrlich and Ehrlich 1991; Myers 1991) and others who argue that other factors are more likely to be responsible particularly at local scales of analysis (Simon 1990; Varughese and Ostrom 1998). With regards to markets there is a lot more agreement: increasing integration of local communities to external markets tends to have an adverse effect on the management of common pool resources (Chomitz 1995; Young 1994; Agrawal 2002). Connectedness to external markets results in increasing harvesting rates permitted by the cash returns possible from sales to the outside (Colchester 1994; Carrier 1987). Above all, markets have tended to undermine local institutions for resolving common pool resource problems by offering alternatives for gaining prestige (rather than generosity and reciprocity), for providing security (through credit, rather than migrating or using exchange between members of the community), and for reducing risk (through insurance, rather than by resource pooling and cooperation).

The arrival of external markets and technology not only undermines the operation of local institutions to manage common pool resources but it also changes local power relations. One of the particularly damaging effects is the rise of some individuals, or elites, who gain an upper hand on the market and/or technology and then seek to privatize or make permanent their gains vis-à-vis the rest of the community (Fernandes et al. 1988; Peluso 1992; Ascher and Healy 1990). As this process plays itself out, it is possible for common pool resources to be privatized and concentrated in the hands of a few, while the majority of previously common pool resource users become impoverished through exclusion from what were commonly used resources before.

We have already seen that small size and low levels of mobility facilitate the management of a resource. Also implicated are the clarity or boundedness of the system that is being managed, the potential for storing the resource, and the predictability of its presence. All these conditions make a resource more amenable to the design of rules that facilitate the development of strategies for sustainability and for effective institutions. The characteristics of the human population go along with those of the physical environmental system. Small size, clear boundaries, shared cultural norms, and a common shared experience in the past that has resulted in the accumulation of social capital facilitate the ability of group members to work together for common purpose. The greater the interdependence of group members the more they see this commonality and the more likely they are to select for leadership positions people who embody those values and are capable of helping all of them achieve them. It is fairly well-known that extreme poverty can result in environmental degradation, so that more equitable distribution of income and the absence of extreme degrees of poverty tend to facilitate more thoughtful and restrained use of resources with a longer time horizon. When the environment is richly endowed, or variable in endowments, it facilitates the arrival at strategies of resource use that can circulate among resources over time, rather than depend on one resource for group survival, thereby assisting with the time needed for restoration and regeneration following resource use.

Since one of the greatest obstacles to the effective operation of institutions are the transaction costs involved, institutions operate best when the rules they develop are simple to understand, are easily enforced, result from local needs, are graduated in their sanctioning, and are relatively easy to adjudicate. None of this would work unless the monitors appointed by the community are accountable to the larger community and trust is maintained. One of the most common failures of institutions is when monitors are corrupted by special interests, thereby undermining the very foundations of trust and enforcement of local institutions. In order to successfully gain approval and maintenance of rules, the rates of resource extraction and penalties must be carefully graduated to the regeneration of the resources. Without assurance of an acceptable rate of use, and regeneration, members of the community are unlikely to agree to exercise sanctioning and restrictions on their use of resources.

Restricting access to a common pool resource, while at the same time creating incentives for users to invest in the resource instead of overexploiting it is a way to begin to solve the puzzle posed by Hardin. Limiting access alone will not work because users will compete for shares and the resource can become depleted through overexploitation. Assigning shares of the resource to users can lead to investing in the resource so that there is more for everyone to share, rather than less (Ostrom et al. 1999). Research over the past 30 years has shown that tragedies of the commons are real, but not inevitable. The resources must be valuable to the users and frequently used by them, they must have good knowledge of the resource and constraints to its use, and the flow of the resource must be relatively predictable. If users depend on the resource for a major portion of their livelihood, they will more likely be interested in making rules of access that include sanctioning for violations. They must be interested in the sustainability of the resource well into the future so that current costs are not the only consideration. For all this to happen there must be trust between users based on common values and shared access to the resource.

Local institutions do not operate in a vacuum. The external environment impacts what they can do, and how they do it. The larger state and government can undermine local authority and institutions by passing regulations contrary to those that local populations have agreed on, or it can be supportive of those same institutions and encourage their proliferation. Markets, as we have noted earlier, can be devastating to local institutions particularly when their arrival is sudden and the rate of change is rapid. Low levels of articulation with external markets and/or gradual integration into markets also seems to facilitate the effective evolution of local institutions of resource use. Similarly, when the technology available does not exclude users with ease (through high cost or complexity) and when its diffusion is gradual and allows for adaptation of local institutions to a changing system of production, it is easier for institutions to adjust and take these new factors of production into account in the design of rules-of-use.

Bioregionalism, Deep Ecology, and Embedding People In Nature

The deep ecology movement has developed over the past four decades and has taken a variety of forms. The movement is born from conservation activists such as Alan Watts and Rachel Carson among others. In turn, these writers can be connected to a tradition going back to Thoreau, and pre-Socratic philosophers. Arne Naess distinguishes between "shallow" and "deep" ecology, considering the former as concerned with the fight against pollution and resource depletion, while the latter went beyond by including concepts such as ecocentrism, sustainability, and to new ways of conceiving the human–nature relationship (Naess 1974, 1979, 1989). They advocated a paradigm-shift in the face of a planetary scale ecological crisis (Catton and Dunlap 1980; Drengson 1980; Naess 1979), a need for each person to define their own ecosophy, or philosophy directed at ecological harmony.

The practice of deep ecology, according to some of its theorists, includes change in personal lifestyles and community lifestyles (Devall 1993). These lifestyles come from deep experiences with free nature, or what some call wild nature (rather than managed nature, as is often the case in some national parks). This emphasis on personal lifestyle has made progress in some quarters, however, there has been less success in having this view of nature impact public policy. In part this may come from its tendency to use not only practical arguments or empirically based arguments, but to rely heavily on deep ecocentrism which does not always resonate well politically. For example, anthropological research in the United States found widespread acceptance of major principles in the platform of deep ecology across a wide spectrum of the population, from labor union members to rural residents (Kempton et al. 1995). However, they differed widely in their view of ecosophy as to what needs to be done and their degree of willingness to do it.

Environmentalism has become part and parcel of every nation's discourse, and it is part of the political agenda. Politicians promise in their campaigns to protect the environment. Governments work with each other to carry out debt-for-nature swaps that allow areas to be protected in exchange for discounting accumulated external debt of Third World countries. The major religions' leaders have presented statements affirming the value of conservation and that people have no right to destroy the integrity of natural systems (Oelschlaeger 1994). In 1982, the UN general assembly passed the World Charter for Nature, which contains several deep ecology statements: that nature must be respected; that species must be preserved; that special care must be taken with rare and endangered species and habitats; and that nature must be secured against degradation. The World Summit on Ecology and Development Conference in Rio in 1992, and the Kyoto Conference on Global Warming in 1998, added to these views, but some governments retreated from some of the commitments sought at these meetings. These documents retreated from a deep ecology perspective into a more shallow ecology approach that did not challenge the current paradigm of trade liberalization and industrial development.

Deep ecologists, nevertheless, seem to take an optimistic view of the future. The twenty-first century is a moment of grace, according to some, enabling humanity to turn around and be one with the planet (Berry 1999). Others go further and argue that Gaia herself, a concept that argues for the earth as a conscious and self-organizing system, will regulate even an unruly species such as *Homo sapiens*. They foresee gains as the world population recognizes the folly of the current model of development, and the need to develop a deeply ecocentric philosophy driven by sustainability of the planet (Sessions 1995a).

A spin-off from the deep ecology movement is the resurgence of bioregionalism, restoration ecology, and locally based agriculture (Pretty 2002, 1998). These are locally based approaches to developing ecocentrism that focus on changing local communities as living units through mutual dependence at local level. In some cases they involve linking western populations with tribal groups to protect both culture and wildness (Devall 2001; Sponsel 1995, 2000). These efforts are challenged by the dominant view of a consumer-oriented society, which is a subject taken up in the next chapter.

7

Can We Learn When We Have Enough?

Material Boys and Material Girls

The question of how many people the Earth can support is often asked. Estimates have varied from 1.5 billion to 1 trillion. The differences are clearly tied to the assumptions made about available technology, but perhaps most importantly, to assumptions about standards of living and consumption patterns. Efforts are made politically and economically, more often than not, to keep consumption levels stable, or rising, and in hardly any case found in the literature, is the case made for the need to significantly reduce the consumption levels of Euro-American society. Instead, we seem to offer our consumption levels as models to strive for to the rest of the developing world – a Brave New World made possible by trade liberalization and economic development.

At a meeting of the Ecological Society of America in 1996 several scholars debated these issues (reported in Moffat 1996). Joel Cohen argued that estimates of carrying capacity depend on standards of living, a point that others agreed with. William Rees of the University of British Columbia added that bringing the developing world up to the living standard of Canada would require the resources of two more planet Earths. The choice of standard of living includes many elements but can be considered in terms of broad categories such as the difference in land needed to supply a billion beef-eaters vis-à-vis a billion vegetarians, a billion people wearing cotton clothing vis-à-vis a billion people wearing wool clothing (because of the larger area needed to raise sheep). Even this does not begin to touch important elements such as the forms of transportation and energy depended upon, the volume of water per capita used, the number of vehicles and their fuel efficiency, and the square footage of homes requiring differences of heating and cooling that can vary by several orders of magnitude (Moffat 1996).

Patterns of Consumption in Developed Countries

The patterns of consumption in developed countries today are very different from what they were before World War II. As noted in chapter 1, the global picture of human impact on the Earth takes a very different, and exponential, shape beginning around 1950. Before that, even in developed countries the size of homes was modest. Cooling through air conditioning makes its coming only after 1950. Heating was with coal, and accounted for heavy pollution in large cities like London, Pittsburgh, Hong Kong, and St. Louis (see Figure 3.3). The size of the middle class was modest and their wants were equally modest. They were noted in the sociological literature to be interested in thrift, and in hard work, and while they accumulated capital they did not consume personally at a high level. Instead, their savings made possible capital investment in industry, railroads, and other infrastructure that gradually transformed urban industrial societies (see Figure 7.1).

Following World War II, there was an enormous investment in reconstruction in war ravaged countries, and the enormous war effort which had limited access to consumer goods of even the most modest kind, was turned to the production of consumer goods, snapped up by an eager population. The ad industry went into action impressing the post-war population with all the appliances that could release them from "the tedium of manual labor," and products from all over the world with which the soldiers had come into contact with during their time overseas. A global taste for consumer goods began and expanded. The allure of the foreign did not begin after World War II, but is long-standing but had been restricted before 1950 to a very select elite (Orlove 1997). What is new since 1950 is the effort to convince the entire population that they can access these foreign goods, even if it means serious personal indebtedness.

a)

b)

Figure 7.1   Comparison of a) 1950s homes and b) 2000 homes.
Photos by William J. McConnell

Returning soldiers received assistance to attend college, and many turned to business and the professions. Women had grown accustomed during the war to working full time on behalf of the war effort and, while there were efforts to return them to the home, many had grown appreciative of the freedoms that working outside the home gave them, and the benefits of having their own income. As a result, household income began to grow as more and more households had more than one adult working. This income was not invested in savings as in the past, but began to be spent on homes: the American dream. From that day to today, the American economy's well-being is largely a function of the well-being of the real estate market, especially the construction of new homes. The dream of owning one's home, with yard, garage and other amenities grew and was facilitated by Congress through legislation that allowed interest for home mortgages to be deducted from personal income taxes. This subsidy to the home construction industry, and to increasing jobs, also made home ownership more viable than it had been before. The movement out of apartments into single family homes increased the land area devoted to housing, particularly when such homes had significantly sized yards.

A look around the country at homes built in the early 1950s suggests that the middle class still remained modest in its dreams (see Figure 7.1). Homes were small, with footprints of 1,200 to 1,600 square feet, even for families with a substantial number of children. Children shared rooms, bathrooms were few and small. These, often ranch homes, were built quickly but provided a major change from the pre-war period when home ownership was far more rare and life was in rented apartments, even more crowded than these modest homes.

The depression was long past, and the boom in the U.S. economy spurred by the war effort, and then the production of goods for the rest of the world through reconstruction efforts spurred the entire economy. The automobile industry released from the shackles of production for the war effort, innovated and came out with spectacular vehicles produced on state-of-the-art assembly lines to a public suddenly with jobs, security, and high aspirations. The returning soldiers formed new families and were eager to provide for and please family members. The purveyors of consumption began their campaign to convince these young families that they could be happy by consuming every kind of consumer product, and their lives would be enriched and happier thereby.

During the 1950s and 1960s this process went on, unabated and largely unquestioned, except in some academic circles which began to note the shift in values that seemed to pass unnoticed in society at large. This was a period of "good feeling" following the horrors of World War II, where families grew, the economy grew alongside with them, and there was plenty for everyone. But was there? By the 1960s a number of overlooked problems began to be noticed more: the inequalities present in American society, especially for "people of color"; and the continued engagement of America's military overseas in activities which did not seem to be consistent with traditional views of security stood out. The civil rights movement highlighted the fact that since the abolition of slavery in the nineteenth century, African-Americans had not had equal access to jobs, schools, and not even to public places and transportation. They had remained a poorly paid labor force in an economy that was booming. The growing inequities in housing, schools, churches, and public transportation were particularly grating – and thus the peace of the 1950s ended and an awareness that just having more of everything did not ensure that all benefited – unless provision was made to ensure equal access.

Even more connected to the current crisis was the continued military investments that did not end in 1945. Indeed, one could argue that the boom in industry created by the war had made many industries addicted to war materiel production. The Cold War following World War II, and the confrontation between the Soviet Union and the United States and Western Europe drove the war industries to new heights of innovation, and expenditures. It drove the Soviet Union out of business eventually by the last decade of the twentieth century, until it became the Former Soviet Union (FSU), its empire spent on an ever expanding drive to win the arms race. It has driven the United States now into an economic situation where it is the world's largest debtor, with external debt in excess of 7.6 trillion dollars by 2005 and rising at the rate of 2 billion per day. Even after the end of the Cold War, the war industries continue to insist that the danger is not over, and that continued investment in state-of-the-art weapons is essential to national security.

Following 1950, as noted in an earlier chapter, there was a growing number of armed conflicts worldwide, which demanded weapons, which our industry, our World War II allies, the Soviet Union, and now the FSU are happy to provide. Thus, while it is not in the interest of people or the environment to have chronic armed conflict, industrial nations continue to produce armaments that in a few years come back to be used against our own soldiers and people. The argument is made that if we did not sell those weapons, our competitors would. This is fallacious in that the number of producers is limited, and in most cases, act as multinationals. They act purely in the interest of their companies, not of any one national interest, as multinationals have done and continue to do. Those who worry about being elected care about the jobs produced by this very large industry segment, and thus are reluctant to challenge their role in society, afraid to be accused of being unpatriotic and not caring for jobs in their home states.

The armed conflicts took more concrete form first in the Korean Conflict, as it was called, and then further in the Vietnam War. The latter, in particular, proved to be very divisive. Many young people began to challenge the reasons for being there, and reasons that had not been mentioned by press releases, such as the interest of the United States in Vietnam's offshore oil resources, began to be seen as compromising our motives for the war. The carnage of war, the use of air drops of chemicals that charred everything below including women and children (e.g., Agent Orange) left a bad taste in even patriotic citizens' mouths. Young people also began to note that the Earth was in crisis, that there were many environmental issues that were being overlooked, and that priorities were skewed in favor of the war, rather than in saving the planet. By 1968, students worldwide exploded into the streets demanding a change in society, in its priorities, and in a commitment to a simpler life. Roy Rappaport, author of *Pigs for the Ancestors* (1968) confessed to me once, that he thought his book had been so successful since its release because young people were looking for models of a simple life, where people were close to the Earth, and did not consume more than what they needed. His book on how Highland New

Guinea people relied on ritual to preserve their ecology proved inspiring, as well as other books such as Barry Commoner's *The Closing Circle* (1971) and Rachel Carson's *Silent Spring* (1962). Even today, but perhaps less than in that period, we see efforts by scientists to remind us that tribal knowledge is fast disappearing, and with it many of the finest adaptations of people to the environment, knowledge of rare botanicals with curative powers, and a more holistic understanding of how the Earth system works (Cox 2000; Posey and Balée 1989; Sponsel 2000).

During the late 1960s and early 1970s a vibrant environmental movement arose, many young people went into academic programs to study ecology and environmental science, and ecosystem ecology thrived as a new field of study, linking ecology and systems theory with cybernetics, taking advantage of the growing computing power of technology. Activist groups produced books on how to get back to a simple life, (e.g., *The Whole Earth Catalog* – Brand 1969), that provided access to simpler ways to survive and make a living than those purveyed by the ads from industry. Throughout the country communes were created in which people strove to live simply and protecting the environment. Some of those communities continue to exist today.

However, something surprising happened towards the end of the 1970s and in the 1980s, another great forgetting took place, and a vast number of those same young warriors who seemed to resist the seductiveness of the new consumerism, with its high environmental and armed conflict costs, settled into the new middle class – now more wealthy than ever, and ever more inclined to consume more. The 1980s were a period characterized by a self-centered approach to living unmatched probably in the history of the Western World, except perhaps for a brief period in the late stages of the Roman Empire. Environmental programs languished, funding receded, and societal interest in the environment seemed to evaporate – but not for long. In 1985, an article in the *New York Times* featured Tom Lovejoy, then with the World Wide Fund for Nature, who showed the devastation of the Amazon and the potential for species extinctions in that richest realm of nature. It was a moving account, and this story and a host of other ones revived interest in the price paid by economic expansion. Then in 1988, just as Congress was about to cut off funding for global change research, we had the simultaneous floods in the Mississippi and the hottest temperatures in Washington D.C. ever recorded. Congress, aware of the growing evidence for global warming swallowed hard and passed increased funding for global environmental change research, and accepted with some reluctance that there was some credible evidence for climate change and that this could have adverse consequences to human health, and to human communities, particularly along our coastlines where a substantial portion of our economy is located.

Since then, the story has continued to unfold with ever stronger evidence for deleterious impacts on the environment of our current patterns of energy use, consumption behavior, and population growth. The story is quite different in the developing countries, but not entirely so.

Patterns of Consumption in Developing Countries

Telling the story of changing consumption patterns in developing countries is an ever more complex endeavor. The gloss "developing countries" includes countries where populations may still be mostly rural and with per capita incomes of less than US$300 annually, and countries like Brazil where per capita national income is US$7,100, and is considered the eighth largest economy in the world. One of the problems is that national per capita income hides the disparities present within each country. In the case of Brazil, considered one of the countries with the most wide disparities, the population of the southeast of the country are far above the national average and are close to that of several developed countries, with highly industrialized sectors and export markets, and metropolises like Rio de Janeiro and São Paulo. At the same time, rural areas of Northeast Brazil remain to this day with levels of poverty that one can only find in the most destitute parts of Africa.

Nevertheless, the story in developing countries, while highly uneven, parallels what happened in the developed countries. The pace of change from the initial conditions before World War II accelerated after 1950. In many parts of Africa and in India this process was further accelerated by the transition from colonialism to national independence. While the colonial powers left, they remained present through the profound trade dependencies that had been created by the long colonial period. With independence, the influence shifted from political to economic domination, and the countries faced a comparable barrage of advertising encouraging them to join the new freedom that independence brought – by buying products that they had had restricted access to during the colonial period.

The pace of change was not as fast as in the developing countries because levels of investment were slow at first. The cost of labor in developing countries while rapidly rising, was still relatively low and productive capacity was still concentrated in the developed countries. Beginning in the 1970s and accelerating in the 1980s one sees the migration of industries from their home bases in the developed countries to developing countries, as companies sought to reduce the costs of labor to manufacture products in a global economy. It had become cheaper to rebuild facilities in developing countries, send most of the parts or materials from the United States or elsewhere, and assemble them in these countries, and then ship them back than produce them at home where labor unions had gained considerable concessions in salaries and benefits that made the costs of production high and profit margins lower. To seek higher profit margins, companies began to leave and have continued to leave until the present, where what had been a local series of crises, is now considered a major problem: not only has blue collar and manufacturing jobs gone overseas, but so have white collar jobs in high tech industries, services, and management begun to go overseas. The advent of the internet and other forms of very fast global communication have made it possible to have telemarketers and tech support for computer companies locate their people in India – and customers think that it is a call or a response from a nearby state or city.

The more advanced developing countries, from an income and industrialization perspective, began soon after the war to engage in what was then called import-substitution industrialization by economists. Developed country economists advocated that countries needed to substitute high priced imports with locally produced manufactured goods. One way, and the most common way, to achieve the levels of investment to do so was to divert funds from the dominant agricultural sectors in each of these countries and invest the gains in developing the industrial park. Additional funds were obtained by providing subsidies to the industrial sector, and by making imported industrial goods more dear by placing higher tariffs upon them. This had two important results: it prevented the technical development of small-scale agriculture in many countries, which suddenly found the tractors and other agricultural inputs beyond their reach; and it led to rural to urban migration, as the impoverished farmers left for the cities where the emerging jobs in industry were clamoring for cheap labor. Another, and very important, environmental consequence of these policies was to increase the dependence of many of these countries on imported agricultural products due to the stagnant productivity of agriculture through the reduced availability of machinery and inputs at prices farmers could afford.

Associated with this, was a push to increase yields in agriculture in developing countries through new varieties and a growing amount of chemical inputs. A vast set of resources was spent at international agricultural centers such as CIMMYT in Mexico, CIAT in Colombia, and IRRI in the Philippines and indeed breakthroughs were achieved. Out of CIMMYT and IRRI, in particular, came the high yielding varieties of maize and rice that were to revolutionize agriculture and which was dubbed the Green Revolution. But the change was not just in breeding for better varieties; rather it required that farmers also buy into a considerable package of inputs to achieve the greater yields: higher inputs of water, fertilizers, pesticides and herbicides. As we have seen above, these advances, allegedly to stave off the threat of world famine and to feed the fast growing populations of developing countries, came out at a time when the economic policies advocated by the developed countries, and followed by developing countries' economic planners, raised the cost of inputs to the average farmer, but not to the large-scale farmer. The Green Revolution package, probably unintentionally, favored the larger agricultural operators and thus during the heyday of the adoption of the new high yielding varieties critics were quick to point out that while agricultural output was increasing, this increase was also associated in many countries with land concentration in the hands of fewer and fewer farmers, and the marginalization of most small farmers unable to apply the package required to achieve those yields. In short, the new varieties required substantial amounts of capital up front to apply the technological requirements, and the benefits were measurably higher at larger scales of operation. The distance in yield between small farmers and large farmers grew rapidly and resulted in the loss of land for many and their exit to the cities in hopes of employment (Dahlberg 1979).

In some places, this rural to urban migration had positive results environmentally. In Puerto Rico, scholars had predicted in the 1970s that most of the island would be deforested by the year 2000 (Lugo 2002). Instead, in 2003 a re-analysis of land cover in Puerto Rico shows not only a reduction in deforestation, but a rapidly growing secondary forest returning–largely because of so many farmers leaving the countryside for the urban and industrial way of life – and considerable outmigration to the United States. An examination of how widespread this process may be remains to be done to understand when and under what distinct set of conditions this rural-to-urban migration results in environmental restoration of initial land cover. It has happened, of course, throughout the forested regions of the eastern United States and in parts of Western Europe beginning in the first two decades of the twentieth century. Declining prices for agricultural products, and a growing industrial sector in cities, resulted in depressed farms, land abandonment, and rural to urban migration in states such as Indiana, Ohio, Michigan, Pennsylvania, New York, and Massachusetts. Where else might this have happened? It has not yet happened in Brazil in any noticeable scale, despite very large rates of land abandonment and rural to urban migration. The high rates of natural increase seem to have more than made up for the losses through outmigration.

The process of land concentration in many developing countries, and the rapid rate of urbanization and industrialization, has led to huge changes in developing countries. Politically, agricultural policies often favored control of prices of staple foods to reduce the incidence of foot riots in cities, and to obtain favorable votes from the growing urban masses who were more prone to vote in elections. This control over the prices of basic food commodities further hurt the small farmers who were more likely than large scale farmers to produce staple foods. Large scale farmers more often produce for export, since they, and national policy makers, need the foreign exchange to keep up the capacity to pay for imports – sometimes the very food that could be produced by smallholders if they had adequate prices for inputs and price incentives. In a study area in the Brazilian Amazon where I work, fully one third of our small farmer sample disappeared between October 2002 and June 2003, as large-scale farmers bought up smallholders to create large mechanized farms to grow soybeans for export. This process of land concentration has repeated itself for years throughout the Earth.

At present, we see a rapidly growing urban population world-wide, but especially in developing countries, where the countryside is being depopulated by both push and pull forces. The forces mentioned above have pushed smallholders into cities in ever growing numbers, and they have been pulled by the education, health, and other services available in urban areas – but often absent from the rural countryside. As with food prices, policy makers in developing countries have opted to focus their scarce resources in these services in the cities where great human concentrations are present, and where political mobilization near the capital is always a threat to political stability. The growing availability of media to rural people makes them ever more aware of the disparities in access to basic services, and pulls them towards the city as they naturally wish access to these resources. The promise of those services is often a mirage, as urban areas are stretched very thin in providing services for these rapidly growing urban poor, but limited as they may be, they are still greater than they are in many rural areas. A reversal in investment in the service sectors of rural areas, which would ensure access to these basic human needs for education and health and infrastructure, would reverse the process within a short period. The security that land provided, in terms of food and shelter, was traded for hopeful access to education and jobs in the expanding urban-industrial sector.

A Feeding Frenzy and a Crisis in Public Health

The emphasis on convenience provided by labor-saving devices, and cars, has changed much of the activity patterns of people in the

United States. The growing girth of people in developed countries, and increasingly in developing countries as well – particularly among the well to do – is a crisis that only in the past couple of years has begun to receive public attention. It is not surprising in itself that as individuals and households achieve greater income security that their diet changes, sometimes in favor of more animal protein. It is also not surprising that with technological advances to make hard work easier that the amount of effort and calories burnt to do work declines. But we have a crisis of epidemic proportions in obesity – and associated with a rise in adult onset diabetes, or diabetes type II; in cardiovascular disease; hypertension; and a host of other ills resulting from excessive weight gain or over-consumption of food.

It is a complex epidemic, compounded not only by an abundance of food, but by constant consumption of sugar-rich carbonated beverages, by extended periods of inactivity (often associated with extensive television watching), by reduced amounts of walking as a result of reliance on motorized transportation to even short distances, and by a growing reliance on fast-foods and eating out. The latter for the most part tends to have higher fat content than meals at home and is carbohydrate rich for the most part. What is interesting about this set of causes of the growing girth of the population is that many of them are associated with growing passivity and less engagement in taking care of one's basic needs. This passivity has grown steadily in a number of ways, through the professionalization of sports from an early age so that many kids give up on sports participation early as standards are set high as early as grade school and high school. In college, only a few participate in the competitive teams, and amateur leagues are relatively rare. It has grown through the increasing hours per day that children and adults spend watching television and playing virtual games (rather than going out to play them physically). While television has the potential to serve people and society, the amount of useful information is swamped by the mostly vacuous entertainment offered as an interim to the real purpose of the TV medium which is to commercialize commodities and encourage consumption. At a time when fewer and fewer Americans cook at home, we see a growing number of cooking shows that provide the audience – probably eating fast food such as pizza while they watch – with virtual cooking experiences. It just so happens that most cooking shows spawn lines of cooking pots, knives, and all sorts of other products which are bought by that same audience even though they are seldom used because "they have so little time to cook."

This passivity encouraged by television viewing, now with cable and satellite technology offering hundreds of optional channels, saps the willingness of most households to engage in their own food preparation from scratch. Meals can be prepared from scratch by a knowledgeable person in 20 to 45 minutes – a shorter time than one single sitcom or news program. And this without even the use of a microwave! In a household where everyone learns to function in the kitchen from an early age, as a basic skill for life, it makes little difference who gets home first and who gets home last, meals can be prepared that are attractive enough to bring a family together to interact and know how each is doing with their lives. Interestingly, it is claimed that the lack of attention to home cooked meals is a result of lives that are too busy, too filled with activities. Yet, if that is so, how come this frenzy of activities burns so few calories and fails to keep us in good shape physically? Many of the activities that fill people's lives are, again, rather passive meetings to which one goes and comes back from by car, and which involve very little physical activity. Even young people are encouraged to fill their lives with activities that they can list on their resumes when they apply to college, even though the most selective schools (e.g., Harvard) often mention that one or two long-term activities that engage the student deeply are more valuable than a long list of memberships in organizations that meet irregularly. Scheduling one or two activities, is not difficult and permit a family to be together for cooking and meals, thereby improving their nutrition and their social relations with each other at the same time. Another benefit from preparing one's own food is that one begins to pay close attention to nutritional value, taste, and controls for high salt, high carbohydrate fillers used to increase the profit margins for fast food outlets. Bigger is better has also gotten Americans into deep trouble. Hamburgers, French fries, soft drinks, chocolate bars and movie popcorn now come in sizes often twice those of just 50 years ago. They appear to be bargains to the pocketbook but they inflict serious damage to health.

Burning Fossil Fuels instead of Calories

We have seen above that contemporary lifestyles in developed countries, and in some social classes of developing countries, have resulted in a decreased amount of calories burnt by walking, and other physical activities such as gardening, cooking, and exercising. This has contributed to our growing epidemic of obesity. Alongside this reduction in calories burnt, one sees an ever expanding rate of burning of fossil fuels not only by industry but by each person as they transport themselves everywhere by car. It is not an uncommon site in neighborhoods across America to see people leave their home in their SUV and drive a block or half a block, even in perfectly good weather, to get the mail from the mailboxes clustered nearby. Or to drive to a neighbor's party two or three blocks away. The list could go on. Yes, there are the legions of walkers, who each day vigorously walk around their neighborhoods in exercise. Some are regulars, and these are mostly in good shape physically. Most are occasional walkers only, and it shows. Walking, without a host of other elements, such as a healthy diet, and higher engagement in activities throughout the day is unlikely to keep at bay flaccidity.

The real culprit is the overuse of the motor car to get everywhere, aided by the suburbanization of America and the distance to be traveled to even the most basic services such as a vegetable stand, a flower shop, a butcher, or a coffee shop. In England, for example, many communities throughout the country are not only linked by rail to other ones, making travel easier than having to face congested highways, but upon stepping out of the train, there is usually a town square with all the basic shops within a block or two: bread shops, butchers, flowers, small general food market, liquor store, barber, and even pre-prepared food to take home in a pinch – usually prepared fresh that day with superior ingredients. Customers develop a personal relationship to these small shop owners, who in turn look out to have the items that customers prefer and who take orders for special wishes. This type of arrangement is rarely found in American cities outside of the cosmopolitan boroughs of New York and Boston.

Thus, to overcome our dependence on the motor car one must begin to re-imagine the American city or town, to re-build neighborhoods that are diverse in every way, and that purposefully reduce the need to go to mega-stores to meet one's needs. In mega-stores, food and most items are pre-packaged into large sets so that customers buy much more than they would otherwise buy, because "it is such a bargain." But is it? Are we not likely to consume a lot more of a soft drink if we have a package of 24 around the house than if we have only a six-pack or a dozen? Are we not likely to take larger servings of ravioli if the bags are two pound bags, if we feed a family of only four? We know from consumer behavior studies that one's propensity to consume increases with availability of product, a fact that has not gone unnoticed among the purveyors of consumption to promote purchase in ever larger and larger quantities. Purchasing what one needs is viewed as a thing of the past, and freezers across America are chockfull of every kind of product, often there for very long periods, losing their flavor and even their identity to most in the household in due time.

So, the alleged economies of buying in bulk propel us to buy larger amounts, to eat more, and to drive farther to get them (because these mega-stores can only locate themselves at the edge of cities to reduce the cost of their large buildings to the company and to provide "easy" parking). Thus, along the edge of communities, often near interstate highways, one finds clusters of these mega-stores for food, for household products, for pet products, and every imaginable fast food franchise catering to the appetites and thirst of the mega-shoppers. I would hazard to guess that households that shop in this manner, which is increasingly a majority of the American public, spends more time shopping than those who shop in those places where the so-called mom-and-pop stores are still vibrant, and that they are heavier and at the end of the day have enjoyed it less than those who walk on a regular basis to chat and who buy just what they need. Economists would argue that products are more expensive at these small stores, and that the public is right to choose the greater savings from mega-stores. But price per item is not the only criteria. There are many other things left out of the usual economic analysis: the gasoline used to get on the interstate to shop at those distant locations, the lack of exercise that results from that approach to shopping vis-à-vis shopping on a more regular basis by walking to a local small store, the social satisfaction that comes from having a person who knows one's taste and knows one's name, the fewer calories consumed because there was probably little need to stop at a fast food franchise because the trip was short, and it was easy to go home and prepare the fresh food right away. We discussed earlier the growing movement in Japan, Europe, and in small pockets of the United States that is working towards regenerating sustainable agriculture and providing a direct connection between consumers and producers of food (Pretty 2002, 1998, 1995).

None of this is nirvana, nor difficult. It requires a new way of scheduling one's life, of setting priorities so that one is in charge of what one wants to do – presumably, to take better care of one's health, to have a better set of social relations and friends across all walks of life, to feel more energetic and vibrant physically instead of lethargic. Obviously, any one can choose lethargy, passivity, and lack of social engagement. That is their right, but I wonder whether the mass of people leading passive lives and feeling lethargic have chosen that as a better way to live over the alternative. I suspect that they have fallen into habits that are encouraged daily by television, by putting an emphasis on consumption and convenience rather than meeting one's needs in satisfying engagement with the production of what one is about to consume (the same can be said of engagement in real physical exercise rather than virtual games).

Do We Have Enough Material Goods Now?

Clearly not everyone has enough material goods. The President of the World Bank has said that 1.3 billion human beings today live on less than a dollar a day, and that 3 billion live on less than three! This is fully one-half of the world's current population. Most of the world's population lacks even the most basic human needs of adequate food, water, access to health and education, and other services. It is this disparity between the world's teeming billions who lack even their most basic needs, alongside substantial populations who seek to satisfy wants created by the global economy that is a threat to the well-being of all. For the poor, because they lack even the most basic things: education, health, and enough food to stave off hunger. For the wealthy, the excess of consumption and passive lifestyles has resulted in unhealthy lives due to lack of physical activity and unbalanced diets. For the planet, because the burning of fossil fuels, and the transformation of the Earth for the production of consumer goods which are less needed than other needs results in the growing pollution of the planet, and the destruction of habitats.

The goal of rethinking patterns of consumption is not to bring the engine of industry to a halt. Rather, it is to reflect upon the needs of people in various parts of the globe, to reflect upon new ways to produce those needs in ways that have a lesser impact on the environment, to reflect on how one can engage more people in both the developed and the developing world in the process of meeting their needs by recognizing that they share the same planet and resources. Just as Denmark became the world leader in wind energy production through its leadership in addressing energy needs in renewable form, each country could become a leader in one aspect of how to produce the needs of people at low cost to the environment. Japan invested in hybrid cars over a decade ago, and it now leads and is so far ahead that Ford, for one, was forced to buy that technology from Toyota. Ford bet its future on being able to delay the implementation of more fuel efficient standards, but doing so simply postpones the day when more efficient ways for getting around are required. The result has been erosion of market share and drop in share price for Ford – and the opposite for Toyota. Environmental leadership and stewardship can be very rewarding – and will be increasingly so in the future as our natural resources decline and go up in price. The current addiction to fossil fuels has a price: not only the pollution of the planet, global warming, and climate change – but a price in human lives as powerful countries act militarily, politically, and economically to protect their access to oil supplies. We can expect these conflicts to continue and to expand if we continue our current dependence on fossil fuels.

One of the harsh realities that needs to be confronted is that "the environmental movement is very middle class . . . and its organizations do not challenge middle class values" (Conca et al. 2001). This means that "the environmental problems" are seen as a production problem that must be solved technically, rather than confront it as a consumption problem, thereby avoiding the uncomfortable considerations of re-thinking consumption values. In the next two decades a major shift in consumption orientation may occur, and students of consumption are lining up trying to predict its direction (Wilk 1998). Some predict emulation by developing countries of the consumerist patterns of the developed countries. Others see a divergent pattern wherein local values resist cultural homogenization. Wilk (1998) sees it as a hybrid, with acceptance of some basic consumer items (like refrigerators) but the choice of many other consumption items being highly selective and diverse across the developing world. In the final chapter we explore some ways in which we can begin to re-think our priorities and to move towards a bio-centric set of values.

8
Quality of Life:
When Less Is More

The world provides enough to satisfy everyman's need, but not
enough for everyman's greed.

Gandhi

Resource Abundance versus Resource Scarcity

Asked many years ago whether newly independent India would
follow the British pattern of development, Gandhi replied, "It took
Britain half the resources of the planet to achieve this prosperity.
How many planets will a country like India require?" Indeed, estimates in recent years calculate that it would take two additional
planets to support the world at the standards of the industrialized
world, three if population doubled as expected it will do, and 12 if
standards of living doubled (Wackenagel and Rees 1995). In short,
we must reject the cruel and misleading message of those who
advocate business-as-usual, and an ever faster push towards a world
based on the current model of development. The current model
of development is not sustainable in environmental terms.

In the first seven chapters of this book, I have laid out a picture
of our changing ways of interacting with the environment, and how
our focus on local environment has not prepared us to think or act
in ways that are consistent with our current global impact. In this
final chapter, I am shifting my discourse into what many will call a
more subjective mode. I think I have laid out in this book, through
the use of substantive scientific sources, the evidence for the urgency
of the environmental crisis we face, and the need to change course

now. I trust readers will view the plea in this chapter as part and parcel of bringing passion to our actions if we are to change from comfortable business-as-usual to the discomfort of thinking anew how we might re-organize our lives in a manner more consistent with the need to protect the planet we call our home. I offer no global solutions but a set of considerations for reflection so that each of us, following our own ethics, and conscience, can begin to construct a set of human ecological relations that is consistent with the sustainability of people in nature. I trust that scholarship, and passion, are not seen as incompatible but, rather, as necessary to living unified rather than divided lives. Readers will find in the recent book by Jared Diamond, *Collapse: How Societies Choose to Fail or Succeed* (2005), further evidence along the lines of what I have presented in this book – and further arguments about why we need to act now.

John Muir and Aldo Leopold urged us to take action many decades ago. We have little time left to address what is becoming a globally scaled disaster. At the 2005 Annual Meeting of the American Association for the Advancement of Science, an expert panel of scientists showed convincingly that if we stopped CO_2 emissions at 2005 levels, that the predicted temperature increase resulting from these levels already doomed the coral reefs within 20 years (in other words, it is already too late to save the coral reefs! See also Sheppard 2003 and Hoegh-Guldberg 1999); that if we let CO_2 emissions continue to rise at current levels for another 20 years, resulting in an increase of 2.5 degrees centigrade in temperature, we should expect a collapse of the West Antarctic Ice Sheet in less than 40 years, and a resulting rise in sea level of 6 to 10 meters – enough to put half of the state of Florida under water (see also International Climate Change Taskforce 2005). Lack of action for another 4 decades could turn off the conveyor belt that regulates global climate (cf. Cox et al. 2000; and International Climate Change Taskforce, 2005). These predictions are based on very careful scientific research and conservative quantitative modeling. There is considerable agreement that the economy has to be "decarbonized" or changed from its current addiction to the use of fossil fuels to other forms of energy production, reduction of consumption levels, and re-examination of every bit of the use of our resources. Business-as-usual will result in the above disasters with consequences that we cannot imagine.

There are a number of movements trying to develop ways to reconcile "development" with the Earth's environmental limits (i.e., to think in terms of sustainable development). These movements recognize the complexity of the task, and they can be found from august bodies such as the National Research Council's work on Sustainability Science, to NGOs mobilizing local populations to develop ways to meet basic needs while reducing their impact in their communities. An idea of the enormous level of interest can be found in the virtual Forum on Science and Technology for Sustainability http://sustainabilityscience.org. It is recognized that what remains is to move from diagnosing the problem to practical solutions for the current crisis, through a practical dialogue between scientists and stakeholders to ensure that the Earth's life support system is preserved, and that human needs are met.

Intensive agriculture has been a bonanza for human populations, providing vast amounts of grain to societies and has allowed us to support billions of people. However, when our economic activities destroy the capacity of our biological world to function and for the Earth's species to survive, we must question our direction. The draining of the Aral Sea in the former Soviet Union is a classic case of misplaced priorities and environmental degradation, and the arid lands of the world are littered with the ghosts of failed irrigation projects (Redman 1999). More and more forested land is being converted into grasslands to feed animals at the top of the food chain. As incomes rise in many parts of the developing world, food preferences shift away from vegetable and grain diets to a larger proportion of animal protein that we know can increase the risk of heart disease, unless accompanied by a comparable increase in physical activity.

After World War II, the United States and Europe undertook an unprecedented intensification of agriculture. Compared with the 1940s, we now produce three times the amount of wheat and barley per hectare, and more than twice as much potatoes and sugar beets. Cows produce twice the amount of milk per lactation (Pretty 1998:4). But this growth came at a huge cost that has accumulated each decade: ponds and woodlands have disappeared; water has become both eutrophied and polluted from pesticides and fertilizers; biodiversity has declined; farms have become fewer and larger; and we see a growing loss of trust in our food system. This is particularly true for health threats coming from industrial scale production: bovine spongiform encephalopathy (mad cow disease); poisonous strains of bacteria such as Salmonella in eggs, Listeria in soft cheeses, and E. Coli in meats; residues of pesticides in our food and drinking water (Pretty 1998:5). The list can go on and on. And it is increasingly difficult to be able to choose food that is safe and that has been produced by farmers using organic methods. The farming industry is so dominant that small farmers have difficulty in marketing their produce except in alternative places such as farmers' markets.

It has been estimated that there are some 2,400 farmers' markets in the United States (Pretty 1998:21). Each one is unique but they offer a broad array of farm-fresh and often organic produce, flowers, cheese, baked goods and sometimes even fresh fish and seafood in areas near the coast. Each week during the growing season, about one million people visit these markets, 90 percent of whom live within 11 km of the location of the market. These markets have a social as well as an economic function since they help people to develop skills, to work together in producing and marketing food, and builds community and trust among collaborating farmers and consumers. Community supported agriculture is another arrangement that has developed that brings together producers and consumers. It works by committing consumers to buy a portion of the produce in exchange for a regular provisioning of food of guaranteed quantity and quality. Consumers visit the farms and farmers and a link is created that can last a lifetime, based upon mutual dependence and trust. In Britain, by 1997, 25,000 households were being served by farmers marketing directly to these households, thereby deriving greater returns for their efforts, and consumers having both convenience and quality delivered to their door. This has encouraged diversified production on farms which benefits the land through a more rich set of plants and nutrient use. Direct links between consumers and farmers has been a spectacular success in Japan through consumer cooperatives, direct from the place of production groups, and mutual commitment schemes that connect consumers to producers. There were 11 million people spending over US$15 billion in Japan in 1998 in these cooperative food production and consumption schemes, and they are based on face-to-face contact, and have benefited farmers and the environment (Pretty 1998:22).

Whereas industrial farming seeks to hide the source of their produce by creating a limited number of bulking locations (e.g., as in having a few places that process most of the ground beef, making tracing of the source of *E. coli* very difficult), sustainable agriculture can provide a winning alternative for the consumer by emphasizing traceability. This would allow any food product to be traced back to the individual farm from which it came. This should increase consumer confidence in the food supply, and make it much easier to control health outbreaks. We see this already in the social relations built in farmers' markets where customers gravitate to given producers with whom they develop trust in how they go about farming. This trust comes from conversations between farmers and consumers about values, methods, and care taken in managing the farm.

Our growing individuality, worldwide, promoted by the very corporations which benefit from the consumerist mantra that the individual's choice is all-important, leads us away from public transportation and walking as inconvenient and inefficient choices. Inefficient for whom? Certainly not for the planet. Our hunger for cars consumes huge resources through the use of fossil fuels and materials. Whereas walking and using public transportation preserves these same resources. Convenience is one of the high pitched messages used to promote consumption. However, when we all begin to seek those same conveniences we have . . . huge inconvenience. Recently, it took me two and a half hours to get from the international airport in São Paulo, Brazil into the center of town – and it was not even rush hour! The ride when not impeded by gridlock – as it is for most of the day now – takes no more than 20 minutes, as it did a few days later – on a Sunday at 6 am!

Our conveniences have become very inconvenient. But perhaps that has always been the case? The inconvenience of public transportation results in more walking (which is healthy for our body), and in conservation of fuel and materials (which is healthy for the planet) – and it turns out to also be a faster way to get where you are going in some of our mega-cities. In European and Japanese cities, for example, trains run right up to the international airports, and shuttle passengers efficiently and rapidly from the distant airport in a matter of minutes, rather than hours as would be the case on the clogged roads. I reflected upon this as I sat for those two and a half hours in the road to the center of São Paulo, as compared to the fast train ride into town in London, Tokyo, and Amsterdam from their distant international airports. Brazil, like the United States, opted for the automobile, rather than efficient public transportation. The cost to both of them to convert to train-based public transportation now will be very high.

After much hesitation, we now have a clear consensus among scientists that we are experiencing unprecedented global warming, manifested not so much in higher temperatures everywhere, but in very unstable and variable differences throughout the planet: some places being much warmer, others being cooler, and most of them experiencing unusual degrees of variability from year to year (IPCC 2000). There is enough warming, per se, to know that our long-standing glaciers like Kilimanjaro are melting away and will soon no longer be snow capped year round (Thompson et al. 1994; see Figure 8.1). We see evidence in parts of the arctic of the melting of the ice caps, and while sea level rise will not be dramatic, for many places already at or below sea level, the slight shift could result in disastrous flooding. We see clear evidence for more destructive storms and more frequent occurrence of El Niño climate events that result in drought in some places, while others experience unusually heavy precipitation and flooding. This is the shape of the future and it will take considerable effort to reverse it even if we begin now. As with trying to shift the course of an ocean liner or a large tanker, it takes quite a bit of time to change the forward momentum of a ship. Given our large population, and the lags in bringing about a change in our patterns of production and consumption, we can expect things to get quite a bit worse, before we can start restoring the Earth to the degree we need to. But we need to begin now if we are to succeed at all.

A new report, *Meeting the Climate Challenge*, was released in January of 2005, by an international panel of scholars, government representatives, and NGOs (International Climate Change Taskforce 2005), with many of them having participated earlier in the IPCC report discussed earlier (2000). For the first time it lays out a timetable: in

Figure 8.1 Changes over time to Mt. Kilimanjaro. © Courtesy of Lonnie Thompson, Ohio State University

as little as ten years, the report indicates, the point of no return with global warming may be reached. Once this tipping point or threshold is reached we can expect the loss of the West Antarctic and Greenland Ice Sheets which could raise sea levels, and shutdown of the Thermohaline Ocean Circulation could occur (see chapter 1 and Figure 1.5), and agricultural failures would become common place (International Climate Change Taskforce 2005). This report is consistent with the IPCC, the report of 63 national academies of science and other recent reports that consider doubling of CO_2 as a watershed threshold in the conditions of the planet, a level that is now expected to be reached in ten years.

Perhaps one of the most significant changes we can make is to wean ourselves as rapidly as we can from our fossil fuel dependence. We know, and have known for some time, that fossil fuels are non-renewable resources that in time will grow scarce and expensive – and that their emission since the industrial revolution accounts for the bulk of the global warming, particularly CO_2 increases. Instead of making fossil fuels as inexpensive as possible to keep us addicted to them, as seems to be current policy particularly in the United States, we need to raise the price of these fossil fuels steadily year after year, investing the funds thus obtained in research and development in alternative sources of energy and using the higher prices to push consumers towards more efficient vehicles and public transportation. Instead of viewing this development as worrisome, society and the energy companies need to embrace this shift as an appropriate turning of our vision from today to the future. Instead of business as usual, we need a radically different foundation for our society, based on sustainable and renewable resources (Diamond 2005).

If we do not move in this direction consciously, we will be forced to make these changes, but it will be far more painful to more people because the conditions will be less favorable than they are now and resources even more scarce. We already see greater and greater wealth concentration resulting in growing anger by people left behind by the promised "development" and the barrage of ads promoting consumption of goods that only a few can actually buy. Already even First World citizens are drowning in credit card debt as they desperately try to consume what they cannot in fact afford, becoming trapped in having to work to pay debts for things they do not need. The gasoline will become more scarce and expensive, but if we have allowed the corporations to continually resist targets for fuel efficiency, we will not have options for transportation, and no public transport to take us where we want to go without even more costly investments by society.

The choice may really amount to either a conscious deflation of the global economic bubble, built on ever growing consumption or facing a growing number of global disasters. Countries are acting now through cooperation and international agreements to keep the bubble from bursting, through food aid, through moving industries into Third World countries, through carbon trading, and other actions. But these actions do not bring into question the economic model itself which is based on an unsustainable view of life.

When Less Is More

What to do? What must be done is perhaps the most difficult thing of all, especially for those addicted to high levels of consumption and unfettered individualism: they must choose to consume a lot less and become models of a new biocentric model of production and consumption. Is this unlikely? Perhaps. The good news is that it is precisely in these countries that resides a substantial number of people who have begun to question our current economic model as an environmental and social disaster, and who long for greater simplicity (see Figure 8.2). It is from a growing awareness that our well-being is threatened by these myriad and interconnected insults against the functioning of the planet that such a shift may occur. We already have a growing number of people who are choosing to move out of mega-cities to smaller towns where a closer relationship can be built between people and the physical environment that supports them. It is there that it is possible to begin to reconnect to the challenges of production in a given growing zone, and to make do with what the land can produce sustainably.

Without those who currently consume the bulk of the world's resources in a very public and convincing way giving up their current patterns of consumption, we cannot hope to turn around

Figure 8.2   "Someday I want to be rich enough to get rid of everything and live like a monk" © Cartoon Bank / David Sipress

what is now a global consumerism that threatens us all. Like anything else, what seems pretty good when done by a few people, is a disaster when it becomes a global phenomenon. In small villages it is ok to throw one's mostly organic garbage in the street because there are plenty of scavenging animals loose to clean it up and recycle. When everyone does that in a mega-city, or even a modestly sized city, it is completely untenable. A sophisticated system of garbage cans, daily clean up of streets, and penalties for littering must come into place to keep the city livable. All it takes is for the Garbage Workers to go on strike for a few days, to see a city like New York, or São Paulo come to its knees in a few days and concede. Likewise, the use of private cars offers unparalleled convenience. As a complement to public transportation it is a useful convenience. But when it dominates as a mode of transportation, it is an unmitigated disaster to the health of people and the planet.

Figure 8.3 The new American standard home, with a three-car garage, and soon to be four-car garage. Photo by William J. McConnell

Since the 1960s we have gone from the one-car garage to the two- and three-car garage as standards of the middle-class home (see Figure 8.3), and we are inching towards the 4-car garage. The multicar family in the United States hardly walks and thus grows yearly more obese and unhealthy.

What sorts of action might be needed to change from our current unsustainable development path? There are probably several paths, some more unpleasant than others, none easy.

If we choose not to change our entire political and economic system, which presumably would be the choice of most people, then we need to use our very institutions to bring about change – but we must insist that they be truthful, which currently they are not. By truthful institutions I mean institutions that do complete accounting of costs, rather than leave out the costs to the environment (e.g., air, water) of their resource use and the costs of degradation which are passed on to citizens and taxpayers rather than incorporated into the price of the products sold. Oystein Dahle, former Vice President of Exxon for Norway and the North Sea, said once that "Socialism collapsed because it did not allow the market to tell the economic truth. Capitalism may collapse because it does not allow the market to tell the ecological truth" (quoted in Brown 2001).

We can begin to tell the truth by asking some questions from our current price system, which is supposed to be very wise, through the "invisible hand of the market." However, we know that prices are not set really by supply and demand, as the theory would have it, but by what the market will carry. Thus, advertising creates demand for things that we do not need a supply of and prices it by characteristics that they can manage to make consumers want. Let's take the rise of the luxury SUV, for example. The SUV in its first generation was a convenient vehicle for those living in mountainous areas who needed some carrying capability, serious four-wheel drive to climb rough terrain, and high enough to clear obstacles such as rocks on that terrain. However, it became evident to a number of marketing experts that it could be marketed with other appealing characteristics: safety in traffic, higher visual perspective in traffic jams, a sense of power, and eventually for the luxury versions it became a clear sign of being wealthy enough to be able to afford it. For the companies which made them, it was also a way to get around regulations put into place to improve personal car mileage, by getting the SUVs considered as "trucks" and thus not subject to the regulations. However, is it not reasonable to expect civil society (i.e., all of us) to demand vehicles that are not an insult to the health of others on the road, and that those vehicles be priced and taxed so as to ensure that society can have some of those funds to heal those wounded by those vehicles because they are able to ride above the bumpers of smaller cars, and that we can invest in research on more efficient cars. That idea was suggested after some rather grisly car accidents but fought immediately by the attorneys for the auto companies. The outcome was a modest move to have a few SUVs which are built on a car platform, rather than a truck platform and thus less likely to ride over the bumper and hood of cars.

The now old debate over whether it is population or consumption which threatens us must be replaced with the more nuanced recognition that both are a part of the problem – and the solution. Already some 36 countries have stabilized their population, but these same countries have growing levels of consumption which threatens us all. The great majority of countries have not stabilized their population, but their per capita footprint on the planet is still small. The key is to move the 36 countries with a large footprint on the planet to reduce their per capita footprint significantly while maintaining their populations stable or even falling further, as is already the case for Italy, Spain, and a couple of other countries that are below replacement level fertility. This is not to mean that we advocate leaving the great majority of countries in poverty. Rather, it means that we must begin to value their cultures and to value their less materialistic goals. In other words, instead of developing countries emulating our consumption behaviors, seeking to value and emulate the more modest consumption behavior of developing countries, their values of family, hearth, and other components of social socidarity where they still are present. Anthropology, geography and the other social sciences have a role to play in valuing local cultures and in showing how those ways of relating to nature are more attuned to the needs of our place within nature. The current economic model undervalues what people worldwide do, because much of it does not enter the market which is how our economy counts value. Thus, if I bake my own bread, its retail value for an equivalent loaf would be $3.20, but all that is accounted in our system is the price of the flour and yeast, which might be a mere $0.40. Thus by baking my own bread I have reduced by $2.80 the economic value calculated in total gross domestic product. Thus, worldwide the work of households at home is simply undervalued, and they are encouraged to give it up in favor of working harder on the street, to buy goods which in some cases they could make themselves, and this is what we call having a higher standard of living as measured by national accounts. The current development model values only what enters the market, and devalues what happens at home. This is patently wrong and sends all the wrong signals to households and encourages the breakdown of all that families are capable of doing together for themselves.

One step away from this folly is to begin to value self-reliance, community activities, and more time to share those values. Whether it is gardening, baking bread, or cooking one's meals, each of these activities promote more active participation by family members in a life together. Even in urban blighted cities, there is an emerging urban gardening movement that is converting abandoned areas into food gardens that can result in a change in activity patterns towards a more productive attitude towards life and better nutrition. Taking care of plants is a healthy antidote to urban myopias, and helps develop a consciousness of the Earth that cannot occur in its absence – not to speak of the nutritional benefits and the reduction in despair. Cities like Curitiba in Brazil have become models, through neighborhood recycling programs that are driven not just by the need to recycle but also by the need to involve people in the process thereby providing jobs, teaching responsibility, and teaching the young generation about the cycle of materials.

Another activity is to ensure that health and education are provided to these heretofore neglected world citizens. Instead of bombarding them with soft drinks, candies, sugar, and flour, and many other unhealthy consumer goods, we need to ensure first that they have access to health and schools attuned to their values so that they can make choices informed by their own cultures, and an awareness of how things really work on the planet, so they can make informed choices instead of simply seeking to imitate what they presume must be the ideal model, driven by high levels of consumption of whatever one can afford. Many societies still retain many of their values of home, family and ethnic community, and the effort should be to keep these from being overwhelmed in the decades ahead by the forces of the global economy and consumption. Students of consumption believe that citizens of developing countries are developing a critical viewpoint on emulating developed countries and that they are quite selective in what they choose to buy (Wilk 2002).

Such a strategy would lead to a smaller footprint by the North, and an improvement in quality of life things like health and education without increasing significantly the ecological footprint. Some might argue that this is classic North-talk, trying to keep the South from developing. This is not the case, at all. Such a path is not acceptable unless the North undertakes a massive and significant reduction in its consumption behavior first. To date, the United States, the largest consumer nation of all, has refused efforts to reduce energy consumption, to reduce carbon emissions as per the Kyoto Protocol, and a host of other efforts by the international community to move towards moderation in consumption patterns. Our leaders claim that we must refuse to be part of the Kyoto Protocol to stay competitive in the global economy. The United States and Japan claim that Kyoto, by exempting China from the carbon emissions standards put them at a disadvantage in economic competitiveness. But, who buys most of what China is producing? Much of it goes now to the United States and Japan, the very countries who claim are losing competitiveness to China. It is the United States and Japan who moved and continues to move their factories to China! It was done, allegedly, to get a foothold in the future consumption market of China but to date the bulk of this production has been exported to the USA and Japan. A significant portion of that production is coming out of factories built by multinational corporations based in the United States and Japan. American and Japanese consumers snap up the cheaper goods coming out of China because they can take advantage of cheaper labor there, and thereby can consume more than they could if the same goods were produced in their home country, where the costs of production would reflect the higher standards of living there. In other words, the United States and Japan are losing jobs to China, increasing their external debt by consuming more than they are able to export (especially the United States), and buying goods from China (often thinking that they are from Japan or the United States because the companies are based in the United States and Japan). This rapid development is incorporating China into the global economy at a very fast speed, and resulting in huge disparities in Chinese society. India is rapidly entering this same pathway with the added burden that unlike China – that has managed to control population growth – India's population is still growing rapidly. India is expected to pass China in population in the next two decades. The dual burden of fast population growth and the expected high consumption demanded by that vast population will be hard for the planet to bear. But it need not be the case.

India is a society with religions strong in their anti-materialism. Hinduism and Buddhism both advocate a life wherein nature is valued, where the human connection to all living things is intimate and deeply felt. Thus, if Indian society is able to preserve its traditional values and religions as effective restraints on the behavior of its citizens, we may see India as a leader of a New Biocentric World. A lot will depend on how India develops in the next 40 years. It is the influence of these eastern religions which underlies some of the best thinking about how to re-connect with nature. They provide an intellectual link between the East and the West, around a set of values that is consistent in its worldview and which is consistent with what we know of the ecology of the planet.

Currently in the West, we are crawling our way out of the crisis faced by our Earth system: Denmark and Germany are developing vast wind turbines that generate substantial renewable energy. Denmark already gets 19 percent of its energy from this source. The Netherlands has advocated the bicycle as an alternative to the car, and already 40 percent of trips are taken on a bicycle. This has been possible by giving bicycle riders some preferential treatment in traffic, such as getting to go first when the light changes. The Canadian province of Ontario is moving away from coal towards gas, wind, and other sources of energy, closing coal powered plants beginning in 2005 and hoping to close the last one by 2015. Setting tough but clear goals is one way to plan strategically so that adjustments can be made but wherein foot dragging is not acceptable, as with the fuel efficiency standards in the USA (Brown 2001).

The kind of conversion needed to move from our unsustainable consumerism to a sustainable society will not be easy, but it can be done. Witness the rapid conversion of the United States manufacturing economy from consumer goods to the war effort in 1940–45. In a matter of a couple of years, under strong urging from Franklin D. Roosevelt, the automobile industry shifted its production on existing plants, production and sale of cars and trucks for private use was prohibited, residential and highway construction was stopped, and driving for pleasure was banned – all in the name of the war effort and defeating the enemy. A country, and the world, can restructure its economy quickly if it is convinced of the need to do so – but it needs to recognize that it has no time to lose.

The Scale of the Problem and the Scale of the Solution

As we have seen in the pages before, the scale of the problem is global – and we feel it at local, regional, national, and international scale. We see it in the polluted air and streams in our communities, we see it in the degraded areas that have been exploited with virtually no effort at restoration, we see it in the efforts of lobbying groups to scare people over the loss of jobs if environmental concerns are taken into account, and we see it in the struggle for control of energy resources globally, particularly the struggle for the oil fields of the Middle East.

The solution to these environmental problems lies within us and is closely tied to our choices. The solution must begin with the individual and a commitment to resist the forces of global consumerism in favor of a concern with the planet as our home – now at risk due to policies that fail to give value to environmental goods and services. From the very first chapter of this book I have emphasized the importance of human agents, i.e., individuals, in making a difference through their choices. But the individual alone cannot adequately win this battle with the well-organized interests that have since World War II led us in an unsustainable path (see chapter 1). Individuals and organizations must come together to bring about institutional change through changes in priorities, in how we set prices and assign value, and in building a society where trust and community are more important than having a larger vehicle or a larger home.

Moving in this direction is not easy for a single individual, who often feels alone in having values different from the neighbors. Yet, that is what must be done. The appearance of being alone is a mirage, because what gives an appearance of inevitability to global consumerism is the barrage of advertising that creates a demand for what we do not need. One of the first steps is to disconnect as much as possible from this barrage of ads, and from a substantial portion of television viewing to begin to reconnect to what the individual and the family need (not want). Turning off the television set is a revolutionary act but one that breaks no windows and does not threaten the existence of the state. Rather, it is a revolutionary act of empowerment permitting members of households to talk to each other, to explore what it is that is valuable, how they can do more things together to lead a richer life with their friends and neighbors – in short, how they can re-build community and trust. At present community and trust are undermined by the media and advertising through their emphasis on consumption and on satisfaction of individual wants. The result, in more homes than we care to acknowledge, is a television set in each major room, and even in each bedroom, where each person connects more with the wants created by the industry, than with members of their family who are alien in their priorities and tastes.

Industry is particularly effective in convincing the very young of the importance of consuming what they see advertised and to demand it from their parents as a way of expressing love and affection. Disconnecting television will be no less hard than it is for an addict to give up a drug. We are hooked to the images of television and we have become uncritical of those images and messages. Television could be an excellent medium for ideas, for knowing the richness of life, and the beauty of art. There is such programming available and it should be watched, appreciated, and supported financially. However, the global consumer industry pays a substantial portion of the bill for commercial television and the price is that the content of television is geared as much at the ads as it is at the content programming. Not content with the ads themselves, they even place the products in the hands of the actors so that even during the content programming the advertising and brand name recognition is still at play. In short, there is no break from the pressure of advertising. The only short term solution is to disconnect long enough to break the addiction, to reflect on how much more time we suddenly have for others in our family and community, and for thinking about what we truly value.

Having undergone this difficult transition, and even as one is going through it, it is important to use the very market forces that overwhelm us with consumerism to change the way they do business. It is important not only to resist buying what we don't need, but to let the companies know what we need and what we expect in terms of responsible standards for making those goods through truth in labeling, accountability in labor standards for workers, and the use of raw materials that are renewable – i.e., "green" consumerism. In short, this is an opportunity to have the real laws of supply and demand that have long been subverted by the global economy become accountable. If the theory is right, if we demand goods of a certain quality, with given environmental standards accounted for, and can make this demand substantial enough then the supply will come to meet the demand. This process will not be any easier than the turning off of the televisions. No, it will be even harder because it will be resisted by the forces of global capital which have operated on an entirely different set of standards: lower the price of goods by moving industry to lower waged areas, to areas where environmental standards are more lax, and where taxes are lower (thereby undermining the communities into which they move by costing them the cost of roads and infrastructure, without paying for them with taxes, and by polluting the environment into which they move through the lax enforcement).

But it will work. Why? Because the **consumer is powerful**. That much the global economy knows is true. The difference is that they have worked hard to make the consumer want what they wish to sell, by appealing to that side of each person that always wants more, our greedy side. As Gandhi noted, in the quote at the beginning of this chapter, the Earth has plenty to meet all our wants, but not everyman's greed. As with Gandhi's nativistic movement which succeeded in bringing the then all-powerful British empire to concede and liberate India, the refusal to consume can work in changing the economy. This we must do if we are to regain our liberty as individuals, and as communities who wish to stay in this planet beyond the end of this century. The prospects are not good unless we take environmentally significant actions.

So far, we have turned off our televisions, and we have reconnected with members of our families and communities, and begun to buy only what we really need, and to demand that the products that we are provided are environmentally–responsible. What next? There is a lot more to be done. We need to examine what is happening in our schools, in our churches, and in our daily lives. Have these places too been overtaken by the forces of the consumerist global economy? Evidence suggests that more and more schools have given up their own food programs and turned over the concessions to the major purveyors of fast food. Why? Because "that is what the students want," we are told by school administrators. One more victory for the forces of consumerism, but they can be defeated through the actions taken earlier. One critical way to approach this is simply through concern with one's health. The evidence is abundant that the food served as these facilities is unhealthy and accounts for the growing girth of Americans, and now reaching other shores. Exponential rates of obesity, diabetes and even high blood pressure are now found among the young. If education means anything, it means that this is the place where we learn about what is good, how to live healthy lives, and how to learn for a lifetime ahead. Schools can insist that they will only carry what is healthy for their students, using rigorous nutritionists' standards.

One of the great battles is to uncover the true face of "convenience" in product marketing. No one in their right mind would oppose convenience in the face of it, however, it is usually a cover for products that remove the consumer from the action of producing the item consumed. This has the benefit of increasing income for the industries, and of increasing GDP because each item that has a higher market value increases GDP because it is in the market. But if one reflects upon family rituals, is not one of the special things about holidays like Christmas and Thanksgiving that we make things from scratch? Actually bake a turkey and prepare filling, mash the potatoes, boil those yams or sweet potatoes, make those pies from scratch, etc. That is the sort of thing we know, as making family special, the investment in taking care of our own, and our friends. In our ever busier lives, we have given up on that for the sake of convenience foods that require a few minutes in the microwave and pronto! But if we take the time to look at the ingredients in most pre-prepared foods we find huge amounts of sodium salt, high fat, and other not so healthy components. They contribute to the contemporary rash of obesity and high blood pressure. We can transform our lives, our bodies, and our communities and families by taking over the kitchen again and learning to prepare foods regularly that are good for you, and that engage members of the family in its production, thereby re-enforcing opportunities for interaction and the re-building of trust. Parents teaching their kids to make bread, to make pasta, to make pies, to make cakes, and to stir fry. None of it is difficult in itself, and when done regularly it is supremely easy and satisfying. There are few better moments that when family members construct a meal together that is delicious but also has brought them together in conversation and in knowing what each one is about. These are moments for trust, between mothers and daughters, between fathers and sons, and across the gender and age gap.

Restoring Our Balance: Valuing Community and Trust, Rather Than More "Stuff"

Are we convinced yet? Citizens worldwide are being barraged with advertisements making them want more and more of the consumer goods produced by the global economy. In contrast, the message of the state-of-the-Earth is hardly heard over the loud advertisements on TV, magazines, highway posters, and radio. A few years ago some Buddhist monks were jailed simply for advocating being content with one's life and possessions, at a time when the Thai government wanted a Plan for Economic Development to be accepted and implemented – and the government feared that the monks could block their efforts. Ordinary citizens can expect little help from governments where those in power are at the service of the global economy and the multinational corporations.

As deep ecologists, Buddhists and other activists would suggest, the change must begin with us, and from there to our families, our communities, our regions and on upwards. No one has to consume what the ads sell. True, their barrage creates a demand but only in those with uncertain values or with an uncritical view of the world. Thus, by strengthening one's personal values and seeing the folly of consuming more than one really needs, the process of building a sustainable society can begin. Another pair of jeans? I have plenty, thank you. A bigger SUV? No thanks, I am getting a more efficient hydrogen or hybrid vehicle, and will start using public transportation as soon as we can lobby the city to put more bus routes in town. A larger house? Are you kidding? my family is smaller, the cost of energy will keep going up, and I would hate to leave my friends and neighbors and the community I have lived in and has nurtured my family.

Is this hard? A little, but a lot less hard than most of us think, if we think through our values, and the implications of each of those little choices that we make often out of habit and without forethought. Look at those closets. How often do you use most of those clothing items? Do they even fit anymore? Why 12 pairs of jeans? Why 8 pairs of sneakers? Why 7 winter coats? How many pens are in the drawers of the house? I have asked several friends and they have counted never less than 45 and often as many as 210! Do they even work? Why pick up a pen because it is free? It is not free from an ecological perspective. It required energy to produce, plastic, some metals, ink, advertising in magazines, etc. By not consuming it (even if free) one is reducing one's consumption. There is no such thing as a free item of material goods. They all require substantial costs in terms of both matter and energy. The cost are simply passed on to users and consumers through the price of other things such as the cost of the hotel room, the cost of the car, or whatever is the business that had the pen made to give away as advertisement.

An unexamined life is not worth living, is an ancient quote that is particularly true when it comes to fending off the forces of consumption. Developing a mantra such as "no thanks, I have plenty" can be very effective in having a quick response to the fast firing ads trying to get us to do their will. The trick is not to do without, but to do without what we don't need. It is natural to always want more, but it is neither morally good, nor environmentally sustainable to be greedy. We should demand what we need – but have we reflected upon our need? Upon reflection, many consumption decisions would never be made.

Would this be bad for the global economy? Yes, but only in the sense that the global economy as currently operating is unsustainable and destroying the planet's future productive capacity by exhausting its fisheries, its water, its soils, and a host of other resources. So, yes, it would be very bad for the business-as-usual global economy, but very good for the planet and the resurgence of local economies and, perhaps for a more biocentric global economy. Why? Because the result would be people conscious of their values, of the value of their own local labor (no need to buy/sell in the market to have it "count"), of the value of life itself as the most valuable thing we have and that we are ensuring by our actions, of the value of spending more time with our fellows having a sense of community, instead of rushing to the mall to buy more stuff.

Restoring our choices to what we need, and not just what we want, would put us more in parity with the rest of the planet which does not have the luxury to have what it wants. Remember, two thirds of the people on the planet today live on less than US$2 per day. Reducing our wants to our needs would bring us in harmony with others. The excessive displays of wealth of our super-rich are a disgrace, not only morally, but also in what it does in creating models that are simply wrong.

One concept which bears a close resemblance to the ecological principles we have been discussing is the Buddhist conception that we "co-arise," that each of us arises in conjunction with others, and that we are dependent and inseparable from those others. We are composed of stuff that we share with everyone and everything. We are created from spare parts scavenged from the same cosmic junk heap – we are made of parts that could have been part of Peter the Great, a wooly mammoth, a komodo dragon, a pine tree, or who knows what. Everything comes into being and everything gets recycled back into the planet making its appearance in unknown ways later on. Traditional Tibetan Buddhists repeat over and over, that all things have at some time been our mothers, just as we have at some time been theirs. So, our existence is not distinct and separable, as we would like to have it. We are interconnected, inseparable, part of never ending food webs, trophic levels, community interactions, and so on. We used to study the spotted owl and the bison, but now we study the bison–prairie system, and the owl–coniferous forest system. We have moved from studying ecosystems to studying complex systems which include all the interconnected parts including humans (who were left out of many ecological studies because they were inconvenient and unpredictable! – Barash 2001).

The implications of ecology, as of Buddhism, can be subversive in a materialistic consumerist world. Shortly after the First National Economic Development Plan was drafted by Thailand, the Bangkok government imprisoned many Buddhist monks for teaching *santutthi* (contentment with what one has – Naess 1989). The authorities feared that this Buddhist ideal would interfere with their plans for economic development schemes in the Plan – which it would do, and did (Barash 2001). There is deep fear in the centers of the new global economy for the subversive science of ecology and for subversive religions that remind their believers of what are true, core values to guide one's life. Being content with less, sharing with others, seeing clearly how our consumption wounds other living things on the planet, and our interconnectedness is a major paradigm shift but one that is required to restore the balance of people in nature.

This balance is currently absent. Nature is seen as a provider of raw materials priced without sufficient valuation for their non-renewability, as with fossil fuels or minerals. Renewable resources are treated in the same fashion, with little investment made in ensuring their long term productivity and their rate of restoration to initial conditions. When loggers cut a piece of rain forest, they extract the value of sometimes hundreds of years of growth – and they sell the wood at prices that do not include the value of all those goods and services provided by all those trees. In places like the Amazon, they do not even bother replanting. Where they replant, it is often with tree species of much lower value, often in homogenous plantations of fast growing species. The real costs are not put into the accounting. Instead, those costs are borne by citizens who justifiably protest when the deforestation gets to be extreme. Would they consume those resources in the first place if they were priced at their real long-term cost? Probably not, which is why corporations do not tell the truth of what the cost of those forests would be if they were logged and the cost of their restoration was included in the harvest cost. We need to account for the direct and the indirect costs: the costs to society of pollution, global warming, respiratory illnesses, etc. The precedent now exists for charging corporations for the costs of respiratory illness from smoking cigarettes. This cost is staggering, which is why they fought against accepting responsibility, and for years claimed there was no credible evidence. They knew there was, as memoranda have shown during recent trials. The same can be said to be true for the costs of over-exploiting resources worldwide. They know that their actions are destroying the productivity of that area. In fact, this overexploitation simply makes the cost per unit lower so that consumers avidly snap it up, rather than thoughtfully reflect at the staggering price tag and consider more carefully whether they really needed that object.

Tax shifting has begun in some countries as a way of telling the truth. A tax on carbon emission adopted in Finland in 1990 lowered emissions by 7 percent in only 6 years. A trash tax of $1.20 per bag in British Columbia reduced daily trash flow by 18 percent in the first year. The $8 charged to motorists driving into central London since early 2003 immediately reduced the number of vehicles by 24 percent, permitting traffic to flow more easily and cutting pollution and noise (Brown 2001:211). Tax shifting can further stimulate economies to become leaders in a new generation of technologies. The incentives of the Danish government for wind-generated electricity led to that country becoming the world's leading manufacturer of wind turbines (ibid. 212).

While some countries subsidize gasoline to keep its price below its world price, others price it at or above the world price through the use of taxes to encourage shifts in use. Iran subsidizes its gasoline at the tune of $3.6 billion annually, an amount that would resolve many social needs in that society, and its elimination is estimated would reduce carbon emissions by 49 percent. Venezuela, Russian, Indonesia, and India also subsidize it. *The Economist* noted, America taxes gasoline too lightly, and that a significant tax on carbon emissions would be feasible and desirable (Brown 2001:214).

Business-as-usual is no longer a viable option if we are to avoid economic and environmental ruin. Instead of demeaning the long-standing cultural traditions throughout the world that live modestly and with respect for the environment, we need to encourage them, strengthen them by ensuring that health and education are available to the people in those countries, in terms consistent with their values. If First World countries work towards strengthening developing countries, show a real shift in values towards greater biocentricity, steps can be taken towards convincing developing countries that we in developed countries truly have rejected the failed model of more-is-better. The choice is ours. It does not depend on any external force. In democratic societies we have the further capability to elect leaders who will lead us away from business as usual towards a more sustainable society. Check out http://www.newdream.org a web site from the Center for a New

American Dream, full of ideas for how we can begin to disengage from consumerism and to value rich experiences, community, and each other more.

Are We Happier When We Have More?

The correlation between income and happiness is surprisingly weak, observed University of Michigan researcher Ronald Inglehart in a 16 nation study of 170,000 people. Once comfortable, more money provides diminishing returns. Lottery winners and the 100 wealthiest Americans listed in Forbes express only slighter greater happiness than the average American. While the average American made only $8,700 in today's dollars in 1957, and today he or she makes $20,000, over this period the number of Americans who say they are very happy has declined from 35 to 32 percent. Meanwhile, the divorce rate has doubled, teen suicide rates have tripled, violent crime has quadrupled, and more people are depressed. Today, more than ever before, we have big houses and broken homes, high incomes and low morale, secure rights and diminishing civility. We celebrate our prosperity, but yearn for a sense of purpose. In an age of plenty we are hungry for what money cannot buy. Having secured human rights and affluence, we seek purpose. One first step is to have less, and changing the world into a sustainable one (Myers 2000).

The basic conditions for change must come from within us: we need new ways of thinking about our place in the world, and the ways in which we relate to natural systems in order to be able to develop a sustainable world for our children and grandchildren. In fact, we need to rediscover and redevelop for ourselves what so many peoples throughout the world have long known: that we are one with nature, and that we must nurture it if it is to sustain us.

As I have tried to suggest throughout this book, continuing to operate under business-as-usual procedures just will not do. Our history on the planet is a recent one, one filled with remarkable successes – and catastrophic local failures. What is new is that our population in the last 50 years has reached numbers that are unsustainable, particularly at the levels of consumption of the Earth's resources promoted by a global economy. The Earth and our very own existence is threatened with a breakdown of proportions that we cannot imagine – e.g., modeling exercises offer a number of scenarios for what might happen if CO_2 doubles, but no reasonable scientist has offered any scenarios for a tripling of CO_2, which is quite possible given current trends. It is so far from anything we can imagine biophysically, that scenario building cannot be realistic. We have managed to bring these changes about gradually, but mostly in the past 50 years.

There is still time, but we probably have not more than another 50–60 years to turn our production and consumption behavior around, and our view of our place in nature. A report released in January 2005 presents evidence that the tipping point will come sooner, as soon as 2015, because of the speed with which we are reaching 400 ppm of CO_2!

In his analysis of the changes brought about by the Industrial Revolution, Landes (1969:555) concluded by saying: "the Industrial Revolution and the subsequent marriage of science and technology are the climax of millennia of intellectual advance. They have also been an enormous force for good and evil. Still, the march of knowledge and technique continues, and with it the social and moral travail. No one can be sure that mankind will survive this painful course, especially in an age when man's knowledge of nature has far outstripped his knowledge of himself. Yet, we can be sure that man will take this road and not forsake it; for although he has fears, he also has eternal hope. This, it will be remembered, was the last item in Pandora's box of gifts." Indeed, the worries at the end of the 1960s when Landes wrote this have only grown in the past four decades, as our technology has made possible the doubling of population in this period, and changes in the physical conditions on the planet that give scientists reason to worry.

In 1992, the Union of Concerned Scientists, an alliance of over 1,700 scientists, including 104 Nobel laureates, signed a declaration that stated that "Human beings and the natural world are on a collision course . . . a great change in our stewardship of the Earth and the life on it is required, if vast misery is to be avoided and our global home on the planet is not to be irretrievably mutilated . . . no more than . . . a few decades remain before the chance to avert the threats we now confront will be lost" (quoted in Ehrlich and Ehrlich 1996, appendix B).

To find balance on a very populated planet, connected by tele-communications into a global village, will require rethinking what we value. We have learned in this book that when resources are abundant, we squander them. We value them when they become scarce. That day is rapidly approaching, but we seem to pretend and act as if that day will never come. To regain our balance as a species, we need to reconnect to our human evolution and to our place in nature – the value to the human species of trust, community, shared values, and reciprocity. We need to restore the value of people in the environment, and of our obligation to future genera-tions. We commonly say in anthropology that human communities are all about production and reproduction, and that these processes explain how we make decisions. What has been missing from this equation is the importance of having that production and reproduc-tion take into account the ecological processes within which it takes place. The social sciences together with the biophysical sciences have a role to play in alerting us to the seriousness of the crisis, and through engagement with civil society and policy makers bring about necessary changes in how we use the Earth's resources. It is really a matter of human agency – of choosing to act with urgency and a sense of commitment. We have brought about these problems. We can also bring about solutions. In our contemporary scene we sometimes comment that the more we have, the less happy we seem to be. To regain our balance as a species may mean to recognize that less may be more, that the awesomeness of the natural world around us trumps most of our constructions, and that the human spirit is richer when there is more trust, reciprocity, and community.

We have not a moment to lose. . . .

References

Abbitt, R., Scott, J. & Wilcove, D. (2000) The geography of vulnerability: Incorporating species geography and human development patterns into conservation planning. *Biological Conservation* **96**, 169–175.

Achard, F., Eva, H., Stibig, H., et al. (2002) Determination of deforestation rates of the world's humid tropical forests. *Science* **297**, 999–1002.

Adams, R.M. (1966) *The Evolution of Urban Society*. Aldine Publishing Company, Chicago.

Adams, R.N. (1974) *Energy and Structure*. University of Texas Press, Austin.

Agrawal, A. (2002) Commons resources and institutional sustainability. In Ostrom, L. et al. (eds.) *The Drama of the Commons*. National Academies Press, Washington, DC, pp. 41–85.

Agrawal, A. (2005) Environmentality: Community, Intimate Government, and the Making of Environmental Subjects in Kumaon, India. *Current Anthropology* **46** (2), 161–190.

Alavi, S. (1965) *Arab Geography in the 9th and 10th Centuries*. Dept. of Geography, Aligarth Muslim University, Aligarth.

Alland, A. (1975) Adaptation. *Annual Review of Anthropology* **4**, 59–73.

Alvard, M. (1993) Testing the ecologically noble savage hypothesis: Interspecific prey choice by Piro hunters of Amazonian Peru. *Human Ecology* **21**, 355–387.

Andersson, K. (2003) Can Decentralization Save Bolivia's Forests: An Institutional Analysis of Municipal Forest Governance. Ph.D. Dissertation, Political Science Dept., Indiana University, Bloomington.

Andersson, K. (2004) Who talks with whom? The role of repeated interactions in decentralized forest governance. *World Development* **32** (2), 233–249.

Aristotle. (350 B.C.E.) *Politics*, Book II.

Ascher, W. & Healy, R. (1990) *Natural Resource Policy–making in Developing Countries.* Duke University Press, Durham.

Atran, S. (2002) *In Gods we Trust: The Evolutionary Landscape of Religion.* Oxford University Press, New York.

Atran, S. & Medin, D. (1997) Knowledge and action: Cultural models of nature and resource management in Mesoamerica. In Bazerman, M. et al. (eds.) *Environment, Ethics and Behavior: The Psychology of Environmental Valuation and Degradation.* New Lexington Press, San Francisco, pp. 171–208.

Atran, S., Medin, D., Ross, N., et al. (2002) Folkecology, cultural epidemiology, and the spirit of the commons: A garden experiment in the Maya Lowlands, 1991–2001. *Current Anthropology* **43**, 421–450.

Axelrod, R. (1984) *The Evolution of Cooperation.* Basic Books, New York.

Bahn, P. & Flenley, J. (1992) *Easter Island, Earth Island.* Thames and Hudson, London.

Baker, P. & Little, M. (eds.) (1976) *Man in the Andes: A Multidisciplinary Study of High Altitude Quechua.* Dowden, Hutchinson, and Ross, Stroudsburg.

Baland, J. & Platteau, J. (1996) *Halting Degradation of Natural Resources: Is There a Role for Rural Communities?* Clarendon Press, Oxford.

Balée, W. (1989) The culture of Amazonian forests. *Advances in Economic Botany* **7**, 1–21.

Balée, W. (ed.) (1998) *Advances in Historical Ecology.* Columbia University Press, New York.

Barash, D.P. (2001) Buddhism and the subversive science. *Chronicle of Higher Education*, Section 2, pp. B13–14.

Barker, R., Coward, Jr., E., Levine, G. & Small L. (1984) *Irrigation Development in Asia: Past Trends and Future Directions.* Cornell University Press, Ithaca.

Barth, F. (1956) Ecologic relationships of ethnic groups in Swat, North Pakistan. *American Anthropologist* **58**, 1079–89.

Barth, F. (1961) *Nomads of S. Persia*: Little, Brown, Boston.

Bates, D.G. (2001) *Human Adaptive Strategies: Ecology, Culture, and Politics.* 2nd Edn. Allyn and Bacon, Boston.

Bateson, G. (1972) *Steps to an Ecology of Mind.* Ballantine Books, New York.

Batistella, M. (2001) *Landscape change and Land-Use/Land-Cover dynamics in Rondônia, Brazilian Amazon.* Ph.D. dissertation, School of Public and Environmental Affairs, Indiana University, Bloomington.

Baumol, W.J. & Oates, W.E. (1988) *The Theory of Environmental Policy.* Cambridge University Press, Cambridge.

Bebbington, A. (2004) NGOs and uneven development: geographies of development intervention. *Progress in Human Geography* **28** (6), 725–745.

Beckerman, S. (1994) Hunting and fishing in Amazonia: Hold the answers, what are the questions? In Roosevelt, A. (ed.) *Amazonian Indians from Prehistory to the Present: Anthropological Perspectives.* University of Arizona Press, Tucson, pp. 177–200.

Begossi, A. (2001) Cooperative and territorial resources: Brazilian artisanal fisheries. In Burger, J. et al. (eds.) *Protecting the Commons: A Framework for Resource Management in the Americas.* Island Press, Washington, DC, pp. 109–130.

Bellah, R.N., Madsen, R., Sullivan, W.M., Swidler, A. & Tipton, S.M. (1986) *Habits of the Heart: Individualism and Commitment in American Life.* Updated 1996. University of California Press, Berkeley.

Bennett, J. (1969) *Northern Plainsmen.* Aldine: Chicago.

Berlin, B. (1976) The concept of rank in ethnobiological classification. *American Ethnologist* **3**, 381–399.

Berlin, B. (1992) *Ethnobiological Classification: Principles of Categorization of Plants and Animals in Traditional Societies.* Princeton University Press: Princeton.

Berlin, B., Breedlove, D.E. & Raven, P.H. (1973) General principles of classification and nomenclature in folk biology. *American Anthropologist* **75**, 214–42.

Berry, T. (1999) *The Great Work: Our Way into the Future.* Bell Tower, New York.

Bicchieri, M.G. (ed.) (1972) *Hunters and Gatherers Today.* Holt, Rinehart and Winston, New York.

Bilsborrow, R.E. (1987) Population pressure and agricultural development in developing countries: A conceptual framework and recent evidence. *World Development* **15**, 183–203.

Bilsborrow, R.E. & Carr, D. (2001) Population, agricultural land use and the environment in developing countries. In Lee, D.R. & Barrett, C.B. (eds.) *Tradeoffs or Synergies? Agricultural Intensification, Economic Development, and the Environment.* CABI Publishing, Cambridge.

Bilsborrow, R.E. & Ogendo, H.W. (1992) Population-driven changes in land use in developing countries. *Ambio* **21**, 37–45.

Bird-David, N. (1996) Hunter-gatherer research and cultural diversity. In S. Kent ed. *Cultural Diversity among Twentieth-century foragers: an African Perspective.* Cambridge University Press, New York, pp. 297–304.

Boas, F. (1910) Changes in bodily form of descendants of migrants. Senate Document 208, 61st Congress, 2nd session, Washington, DC.

Boas, F. (1912) Changes in bodily form of descendants of immigrants. *American Anthropologist* **14**, 530–562.

Bodley, J.H. (1996) *Anthropology and Contemporary Human Problems*, 3rd Edn. Mayfield Publishing, Mountain View.

Boehm, C. (1999) *Hierarchy in the Forest: The Evolution of Egalitarian Behavior.* Harvard University Press, Cambridge.

Boff, L. & Berryman, P. (1997) *Cry of the Earth, Cry of the Poor.* Orbis Books, Maryknoll, NY.

Boischio, A.A. & Henshel, D. (2000) Linear regression models of methyl mercury exposure during prenatal and early postnatal life among riverside people along the Upper Madeira River, Amazon. *Environmental Research, Section A*, **83** (2), 150–161.

Bongaarts, J. (1998) Demographic consequences of declining fertility. *Science* **282**, 419–420.

Boserup, E. (1965) *The Conditions of Agricultural Growth.* Aldine, Chicago.

Boserup, E. (1981) *Population and Technological Change.* University of Chicago Press, Chicago.

Boyd, R. & Richerson, P.J. (2005) The Origin and Evolution of Cultures. Oxford University Press, New York.

Brand, S. (1969) *Whole Earth Catalog.* 30th Anniversary Celebration, 1998. Whole Earth, Denville, NJ.

Braudel, F. (1972) *The Mediterranean and the Mediterranean World in the Age of Phillip II.* Vol. 1. Harper and Row, New York.

Broecker, W.S. (1991) The Great Ocean Conveyor Belt. *Oceanography* **4**, 79.

Brondizio, E. (1996) *Forest Farmers: Human and Landscape Ecology of Caboblo Populations in the Amazon Estuary.* Ph. D. dissertation, School of Public and Environmental Affairs. Indiana University, Bloomington.

Brondizio, E. (In press) *Forest Farmers of the Amazon estuary: Commodity markets, Land Use, and the Identity of Amazonian Caboclos.* Advances in Economic Botany Series. The New York Botanical Garden Press, New York.

Brondizio, E., Moran, E.F., Mausel, P. & Wu, Y. (1996) Land cover in the Amazon estuary: Linking of thematic with historical and botanical data. *Photogrammetric Engineering and Remote Sensing* **62**, 921–929.

Brondizio, E., McCracken, S., Moran, E.F., Siqiera, A.D., Nelson, D. & Rodriguez-Pedraza, C. (2002) The colonist footprint: Toward a conceptual framework of land use and deforestation trajectories among small farmers in the Amazonian frontier. In Wood, C.H. & Porro, R. (eds.) *Deforestation and Land Use in the Amazon.* University Press of Florida, Gainesville, pp. 133–161.

Brosius, P. (1999) Green dots, pink hearts: Displacing politics from the Malaysian rain forest. *American Anthropologist* **101** (1), 36–57.

Brown, L. (2001) *Plan B: Rescuing a Planet under Stress and a Civilization in Trouble.* Earth Policy Institute, Washington, DC.

Brumfiel, E. (1992) Distinguished lecture in archeology: Breaking and entering the Ecosystem – Gender, class, and faction steal the show. *American Anthropologist* **94** (3), 551–568.

Burger, J., Ostrom, E., Norgaard, R., Policansky, D. & Goldstein, B. (eds.) (2001) *Protecting the Commons: A Framework for Resource Management in the Americas.* Island Press, Washington DC.

Butzer, K. (1971) *Environment and Archeology: An Ecological Approach to Prehistory.* 2nd Edn. Aldine-Atherton, New York.

Butzer, K. (1976) *Early Hydraulic Civilization in Egypt: A Study in Cultural Ecology.* University of Chicago Press, Chicago.

Butzer, K. (1990) A human ecosystem framework for archeology. In Moran, E.F. (ed.) *The Ecosystem Approach in Anthropology: From Concept to Practice.* University of Michigan Press, Ann Arbor, pp. 91–130.

Butzer, K. (1996) Ecology in the long view: Settlement, agroecosystem strategies, and ecological performance. *Journal of Field Archeology* **23** (2), 141–150.

Camerer, C. (1998) Bounded rationality in individual decision-making. *Experimental Economics* **1**, 163–183.

Camerer, C. (2003) *Behavioral Game Theory: Experiments in Strategic Interaction.* Princeton University Press, Princeton.

Cancian, F. (1972) *Change and Uncertainty in a Peasant Economy.* Stanford University Press, Stanford.

Carrier, J.G. (1987) Marine tenure and conservation in Papua New Guinea: Problems in interpretation. In McCay, B.M. & Acheson, J.M. (eds.) *The Question of the Commons.* University of Arizona Press, Tucson, pp. 142–167.

Carson, R. (1962) *Silent Spring.* Houghton Mifflin, Boston.

Castaglioni, A. (1958) *A History of Medicine.* 2nd Edn. Alfred Knopf: New York.

Catton, W. & Dunlap, W. (1980) A new ecological paradigm for post-exuberant sociology. *American Behavioral Scientist* **24** (1), 15–47.

Caviedes, C. (2001) *El Niño in History: Storming Through the Ages.* University Press of Florida, Gainesville.

Central Arizona – Phoenix Ecological Research (CAP LTER) Project (Nancy B Grimm and Charles L Redman, Project Co-Directors).

Cernea, M. (1989) User groups as producers in participatory afforestation strategies. *World Bank Discussion Papers No. 70.* World Bank: Washington, DC.

Chagnon, N. (1968) *Yanomamo: The Fierce People.* Holt, Rinehart and Winston, New York.

Chernela, J. (1987) Endangered ideologies: Tukano fishing taboos. *Cultural Survival Quarterly* **11** (2), 50–52.

Childs, G. (1998) *A Cultural and Historical Analysis of Demographic Trends and Family Management Strategies among the Tibetans of Nubri, Nepal.* PhD dissertation. Dept of Anthropology, Indiana University, Bloomington.

Childs, G. (2004) *Tibetan Diary.* University of California Press, Berkeley.

Chomitz, K. (1995) Roads, Land, Markets and Deforestation. Paper presented at Open Meeting of Human Dimensions of Global Change. Duke University, June 1–3.

Chomitz, K. & Gray, D. (1996) Roads, land use, and deforestation: A spatial model applied to Belize. *World Bank Economic Review* **10** (3), 487–512.

Clark, J.D. (1960) Human ecology during the Pleistocene and later times in Africa south of the Sahara. *Current Anthropology* **1**, 307–324.

Clarke, W.C. (1966) From extensive to intensive shifting cultivation: a succession from New Guinea. *Ethnology* **5**, 347–359.

Clarke, W.C. (1971) *Place and People: An Ecology of a New Guinean Community.* University of California Press, Berkeley.

Cochrane, M. & Schulze, M. (1998) Fire as a recurrent event in tropical forests of the Eastern Amazon. *Biotropica* **31**, 2–16.

Cochrane, M., Alencar, A., Schulze, M. & Souza Jr., C. (1999) Positive feedbacks in the fire dynamics of closed canopy tropical forests. *Science* **284**, 1832–1835.

Cohen, M. & Murphy, J. (2001) *Exploring Sustainable Consumption.* Pergamon, Amsterdam.

Coimbra, C., Flowers, N., Salzano, F. & Santos, R. (2002) *The Xavante in Transition: Health, Ecology, and Bioanthropology in Central Brazil.* University of Michigan Press, Ann Arbor.

Colchester, M. (1994) Sustaining the forests: The community-based approach in southeast Asia. *Development and Change* **25** (1), 69–100.

Collins, J. (1986) Smallholder settlement of tropical South America: The social causes of ecological destruction. *Human Organization* **45**, 1–10.

Commoner, B. (1971) *The Closing Circle: Nature, Man and Technology.* Random House, New York.

Conca, K., Princen, T. & Maniates, M. (2001) Confronting consumption. *Global Environmental Politics* **1** (3), 1–10.

Conklin, H.C. (1954) An ethnoecological approach to shifting agriculture. *Transactions of the New York Academy of Sciences* **17** (2), 133–142.

Conklin, H.C. (1957) *Hanunoo Agriculture.* Yale University Press, New Haven.

Constanza, R., d'Arge, R., de Groot, R., et al. (1997) The value of the World's ecosystem services and natural capital. *Nature* **387**, 253–260.

Coughenour, M., Ellis, J., Swift, D., et al. (1985) Energy extraction and use in a nomadic pastoral system. *Science* **230**, 619–625.

Cox, P. (2000) Will tribal knowledge survive the millennium? *Science* **287**, 44–45.

Cox, P., Betts, R., Jones, C., Spalls, S. & Totterdell, I. (2000) Acceleration of global warming due to carbon cycle feedbacks in a coupled climate model. *Nature* **408**, 184–187.

Cronon, W. (1983) *Changes in the Land*. Hill and Wang, New York.

Cronon, W. (ed.) (1996) *Uncommon Ground: Rethinking the Human Place in Nature*. Norton, New York.

Cropper, M. & Oates, W. (1992) Environmental Economics: A survey. *Journal of Economic Literature* **30**, 675–704.

Crosby, A. (1986) *Ecological Imperialism: The Biological Expansion of Europe, 900–1900*. Cambridge University Press, Cambridge.

Crown, P. & Judge, J. (eds.) (1991) *Chaco and Hokokam: Prehistoric Regional Systems in the American Southwest*. School of American Research Press, Santa Fe.

Crumley, C. (ed.) (1994) *Historical Ecology: Cultural Knowledge and Changing Landscapes*. School of American Research Press, Santa Fe.

Crumley, C. (ed.) (2001) *New Directions in Anthropology and Environment*. Altamira Press, Walnut Creek.

Crutzen, P. (2002) Geology of mankind. *Nature* **415**, 23.

Cutter, S., Mitchell, J. & Scott, M. (2000) Revealing the vulnerability of people and places: A case study of Georgetown County, South Carolina. *Annals of the Association of American Geographers* **90** (4), 713–737.

Cyert, R.M. & March, J.G. (1963) *A Behavioral Theory of the Firm*. Prentice-Hall, Englewood Cliffs.

Dahlberg, K.A. (1979) *Beyond the Green Revolution: The Ecology and Politics of Global Agricultural Development*. Plenum, New York.

Daily, G. & Ellison, K. (2002) *The New Economy of Nature*. Island Press, Washington DC.

Daily, G., Alexander, S., Ehrlich, P., et al. (1997) Ecosystem services: Benefits supplied to human societies by natural ecosystems. *Issues in Ecology* **2**, 1–16.

Dales, J.H. (1968) *Pollution, Property and Prices: An Essay in Policy-Making and Economics*. University of Toronto Press, Toronto.

Damas, D. (1969) The study of cultural ecology and the ecology conference. In Damas, D. (ed.) Contributions to Anthropology: Ecological

Essays. *National Museum of Canada Bulletin 230*, Anthropological Series **86**, 1–12.

daMatta, R. (1985) *A Casa e a Rua*. Brasiliense, São Paulo.

Darwin, C. (1859) *On the Origin of Species by Means of Natural Selection*. Murray, London.

Dasgupta, P. & Heal, G. (1979) *Economic Theory and Exhaustible Resources*. Cambridge University Press, Cambridge.

Davis, K. (1963) The theory of change and response in modern demographic history. *Population Index* **29**, 345–366.

Deagan, K. (1996) Environmental archeology and historical archeology. In Reitz, E.J. et al. (eds.) *Case Studies in Environmental Archaeology*. Plenum, New York, pp. 359–3776.

Demarest, A. (2004) *The Maya: The Rise and Fall of a Rain Forest Civilization*. Cambridge University Press, Cambridge.

Descola, P. (1994) *In the Society of Nature: a native ecology in Amazonia*. Cambridge University Press, Cambridge.

Descola, P. & Palsson, G. (eds.) (1996) *Nature and Society:Anthropological Perspectives*. Routledge, London.

Devall, B. (1993) *Living Richly in an Age of Limits*. Peregrine Smith Books, Salt Lake City.

Devall, B. (2001) The deep, long-range ecology movement, 1960–2000: A review. *Ethics and the Environment* **6** (1), 18–41.

Diamond, J. (1995) Easter's End. *Discovery* **16** (5), 62–69.

Diamond, J. (1997) *Guns, Germs, and Steel: The Fate of Human Societies*. Norton, New York.

Diamond, J. (2005) *Collapse: How Societies Choose to Fail or Succeed*. Viking, New York.

Dietz, T., Ostrom, E. & Stern, P. (2003) The struggle to govern the commons. *Science* **302**, 1907–1912.

Dietz, N., Dolsak, P., Ostrom, E. & Stern, P. (2002) The drama of the commons. In E. Ostrom, et al. *The Drama of the Commons*. National Academies Press, Washington, DC, pp. 1–36.

Dove, M.R. (1985) *Swidden Agriculture in Indonesia: the subsistence strategies of the Kalimantan Kantu*. Mouton, New York.

Dove, M.R. (ed.) (1988) *The Real and Imagined Role of Culture in Development*. University of Hawaii Press, Honolulu.

Dow, K. (1992) Exploring differences in our common future(s): The meaning of vulnerability to global environmental change. *Geoforum* **23**, 417–436.

Drengson, A. (1980) Shifting paradigms: From the technocrats to the person-planetary. *Environmental Ethics* **3**, 221–240.

Durham, W. (1991) *Co-evolution: Genes, Culture, and Human Diversity.* Stanford University Press, Stanford.

Economic and Social Affairs of the United Nations Secretariat, Population Division (2005) World Population Prospects: The 2004 Revision; and World Urbanization Prospects: The 2003 Revision. http://esa.un.org/unpp/

Edgerton, R.B. (1971) *The Individual in Cultural Adaptation: A Study of Four East African Peoples.* University of California Press, Berkeley.

Ehrlich, P. & Ehrlich, A. (1991) *The Population Explosion.* Simon and Schuster, New York.

Ehrlich, P. & Ehrlich, A. (1996) *Betrayal of Science and Reason: How Anti-Environment Rhetoric Threatens our Future.* Island Press, Washington, DC.

Ellen, R. (2002) Modes of Subsistence: hunting and gathering to agriculture and pastoralism. In T. Ingold (ed.) *Companion Encyclopedia of Anthropology.* Routledge, New York, pp. 197–225.

Ellen, R., Parkes, P. & Bicker, A. (eds.) (2000) *Indigenous Environmental Knowledge and its Transformations.* Harwood Academic Publishers, Amsterdam.

Epoch Times (2004) Acid Rain Pollution Causes Huge Losses in China. May 19.

Evenari, M., Shanan, L. & Tadmor, D. (eds.) (1971) *The Negev: The Challenge of a Desert.* Harvard University Press, Cambridge.

Fang, J., Chen, A., Peng, C., Zhao, S. & Ci, L. (2001) Changes in forest biomass carbon storage in China between 1949 and 1998. *Science* **292**, 2320–2322.

Fearnside, P. (1986) *Human Carrying Capacity of the Brazilian Rainforest.* Columbia University Press, New York.

Fearnside, P. (2001) Soybean cultivation as a threat to the environment in Brazil. *Environmental Conservation* **28**, 23–38.

Fearnside, P. & Guimarães, W.M. (1996) Carbon uptake by secondary forests in Brazilian Amazonia. *Forest Ecology and Management* **80**, 35–46.

Fernandes, W., Menon, G. & Viegas, P. (1988) *Forests, Environment and Tribal Economy.* Indian Social Institute, New Delhi.

Fish, P. & Fish, S. (1992) Prehistoric landscapes of the Sonoran Desert Hohokam. *Population and Environment* **13**, 269–283.

Fiske, S. (1990) Resource management as people management: Anthropology and renewable resources. *Renewable Resources Journal*, Winter, pp. 16–20.

Flannery, K. (1968) Archeological systems theory and early Mesoamerica. In Meggers, B. (ed.) *Anthropological Archeology in the Americas.* Anthropological Society of Washington, Washington, DC, pp. 67–87.

Folke, C., Jansson, J. & Constanza, R. (1997) Ecosystem appropriation by cities. *Ambio* **26**, 167–172.

Forde, C.D. (1934) *Habitat, Economy and Society.* Dutton, New York.

Foster, D. (1995) Land use history and 400 years of vegetation change in New England. In Turner, B.L., II, et al. (eds.) *Global Land Use Change: A Perspective from the Columbian Encounter.* Consejo Superior de Investigaciones Científicas, Madrid, pp. 253–319.

Foster, D. & Aber, J. (eds.) (2004) *Forests in Time: The Environmental Consequences of 1,000 years of change in New England.* Yale University Press, New Haven.

Foster, D., Knight, D. & Franklin, J. (1998a) Landscape patterns and legacies resulting from large, infrequent forest disturbances. *Ecosystems* **1**, 497–510.

Foster, D., Motzkin, G. & Slater, B. (1998b) Land use history as long-term broad-scale disturbance: Regional forest dynamics in central New England. *Ecosystems* **1**, 96–119.

Fowler, D. (1987) Uses of the past: Archeology in the service of the state. *American Antiquity* **52** (2), 229–248.

Fowler, D. (1993) Hermes Trismegustus in Eden: Praxis, process and postmodern archeology. *Society for California Archeology Proceedings* **6**, 1–14.

Fowler, D. & Hardesty, D. (2001) Archeology and environmental change. In Crumley, C. (ed.) *New Directions in Anthropology and Environment.* Altamira Press, Walnut Creek. pp. 72–89.

Fricke, T. (1986) *Himalayan Households: Tamang Demography and Domestic Processes.* University of Michigan Press, Ann Arbor.

Futemma, C., Castro, F., Silva-Forsberg, M.C. & Ostrom, E. (2002) The emergence and outcomes of collective action: An institutional and ecosystem approach. *Society and Natural Resources* **15**, 503–522.

Galloway, J.N., Aber, J.D., Erisman, J.W., Seitzinger, S.P., Howarth, R.W., Cowling, E.B. & Cosby, B.J. (2003) The nitrogen cascade. *BioScience* **53** (4), 341–356.

Geertz, C. (1963) *Agricultural Involution: The Process of Ecological Change in Indonesia.* University of California Press, Berkeley.

Geist, H. & Lambin, E. (2001) *What Drives Tropical Deforestation?* Land Use Cover Change Report Series No. 4, Louvain-la-Neuve.

Geist, H. & Lambin, E. (2002) Proximate causes and underlying driving forces of tropical deforestation. *BioScience* **52**, 143–150.

Gibson, C. (2001) Forest resources: Institutions for local governance in Guatemala. In J. Berger, et al. (eds.) *Protecting the Commons: A Framework for Resource Management in the Americas.* Island Press, Washington, DC.

Gibson, C. & Becker, C.D. (2000) A lack of institutional demand: Why a strong local community in western Ecuador fails to protect its forest. In Gibson, C. et al. (eds.) *People and Forests*. MIT Press, Cambridge.

Gibson, C., McKean, M. & Ostrom, E. (eds.) (2000) *People and Forests: Communities, Institutions, and Governance*. MIT Press, Cambridge.

Giorgi, F., Mearns, L., Shields, C. & McDaniels, L. (1998) Regional nested model simulations of present day and two times CO_2 climate over the central plains of the US. *Climatic Change* **40**, 457–493.

Glacken, C. (1967) *Traces on a Rhodian Shore*. University of California Press, Berkeley.

Goldstein, M. (1943) *Demographic and Bodily Changes in Descendants of Mexican Immigrants*. Institute of Latin American Studies, University of Texas, Austin.

Goodchild, M. & Janelle, D. (eds.) (2004) *Spatially Integrated Social Science*. Oxford University Press, New York.

Goodman, B. (1993) Drugs and people threaten diversity in Andean forests. *Science* **261**, 293.

Goodman, A. & Leatherman, T. (eds.) (1998) *Building a New Biocultural Synthesis: Political-economic perspectives in Human Biology*. University of Michigan Press, Ann Arbor.

Granados, J. & Korner, C. (2002) In deep shade, elevated CO_2 increases the vigor of tropical climbing plants. *Global Change Biology* **8**, 1109–1117.

Gross, D., Eiten, N., Flowers, N., Leoi, F., Ritter, M. & Werner, D. (1978) Ecology and acculturation among native peoples of central Brazil. *Science* **206**, 1043–1050.

Grove, M. & Burch, W., Jr. (1997) A social ecology approach and applications of urban ecosystem and landscape analyses: A case study of Baltimore, Maryland. *Urban Ecosystems* **1**, 259–275.

Guillet, D. (1987) Terracing and irrigation in the Peruvian highlands. *Current Anthropology* **24**, 561–574.

Guillet, D. (1992) *Covering Ground: Communal Water Management and the State in the Peruvian Highlands*. University of Michigan Press, Ann Arbor.

Gunderson, L. & Holling, C.S. (eds.) (2002) *Panarchy: Understanding Transformations in Human and Natural Systems*. Island Press, Washington, DC.

Gutman, G., Janetos, T., Justice, C., et al. (2004) *Land Change Science: Observing, Monitoring and Understanding Trajectories of Change on the Earth's Surface*. Springer-Verlag, Berlin.

Guyer, J. & Lambin, E. (1993) Land use in an urban hinterland – ethnography and remote sensing in the study of African intensification. *American Anthropologist* **95**, 839–859.

Hardesty, D. (1977) *Ecological Anthropology.* Wiley, New York.

Hardin, G. (1968) The tragedy of the commons. *Science* **162**, 1243–1248.

Harvell, C.D., Mitchell, C., Ward, J., et al. (2002) Climate warming and disease risks for terrestrial and marine biota. *Science* **296**, 2158–2162.

Heijnen, L. & Kates, R.W. (1974) Northeast Tanzania: Comparative observations along a moisture gradient. In White, G. (ed.) *Natural Hazards.* Oxford University Press, New York.

Helm, J. (1962) The ecological approach in anthropology. *American Journal of Sociology* **17**, 630–639.

Hodell, D., Brenner, M., Curtis, J. & Guilderson, T. (2001) Solar forcing of drought frequency in the Maya lowlands. *Science* **292**, 1367–1373.

Hoegh-Guldberb, O. (1999) Climate change, coral bleaching, and the future of the world's coral reefs. *Marine and Freshwater Research* **50** (8), 839–866.

Holling, C.S. (2001) Understanding the complexity of economic, ecological, and social systems. *Ecosystems* **4**, 390–405.

Hurrell, J., Kushnir, Y. & Visbeck, M. (2001) The North Atlantic oscillation. *Science* **291**, 603–605.

Ingold, T. (1986) *Evolution and Social Life.* Cambridge University Press, New York.

Ingold, T. (2000) *The Perception of the Environment.* Routledge, London.

Ingold, T., Riches, D. & Woodburn, J. (eds.) (1991) *Hunters and Gatherers: Property, Power and Ideology.* Berg, New York.

Interacademies (2000) *Transition to Sustainability in the 21st Century: The Contribution of Science and Technology.* National Academies Press, Washington, DC.

Intergovernmental Panel on Climate Change (IPCC) (2000) *Climate Change 2001: The Scientific Basis.* Cambridge University Press, Cambridge.

International Climate Change Taskforce (2005) *Meeting the Climate Challenge.* Institute for Public Policy Research, London; Center for American Progress, Washington DC; and Australia Institute, Canberra.

Isaac, R., Walker, J. & Williams, A. (1994) Group size and the voluntary provision of public goods. *Journal of Public Economics* **54** (1), 1–36.

Johnson, C.M., Vieira, I.C.G., Zarin, D.J., Frizano, J. & Johnson, A.H. (2001) Carbon and nutrient storage in primary and secondary forests in eastern Amazônia. *Forest Ecology and Management* **147**, 245–252.

Johnson, J. (1971) *Sharecroppers of the Sertão.* Stanford University Press, Stanford.

Johnston, B.R. (2001) Anthropology and environmental justice: Analysts, advocates, mediators, and troublemakers. In C. Crumley (ed.) *New*

Directions in Anthropology and Environment. Altamira Press, Walnut Creek, CA, pp. 132–149.

Justice, C. & Desanker, P. (2001) Africa and global climate change. *Climate Research* **17**, 93–103.

Kaimowitz, D. & Angelsen, A. (1998) *Economic Models of Tropical Deforestation: A Review.* Center for International Forestry Research, Bogor.

Kaplan, H. & Hill, K. (1985) Food sharing among Aché foragers: Tests of an explanatory hypothesis. *Current Anthropology* **26** (2), 223–246.

Kasperson, J. & Kasperson, R. (2001) *International Workshop on Vulnerability and Global Environmental Change.* Programme Report. Stockholm Environmental Institute, Stockholm.

Kates, R. & Parris, T. (2003) Long-term trends and a sustainability transition. *Proceedings of the National Academy of Sciences* **10** (14), 8062–8067.

Keeling, C.D. & Whorf, T.P. (2000) Atmospheric CO_2 records from sites in the SIO air sampling network. In U.S. Department of Energy (ed.) *Trends: A Compendium of Data on Global Change.* Carbon Dioxide Information Analysis Center, Oak Ridge National Laboratory, U.S. Department of Energy, Oak Ridge, TN.

Keller, M., Clark, D.A., Clark, D.B., Weitz, A.M. & Veldkamp, E. (1996) If a tree falls in the forest . . . *Science* **273**, 201.

Kempton, W. (1991) Lay perspectives on global climate change. *Global Environmental Change* **1**, 183–208.

Kempton, W. (2001) Cognitive anthropology and the environment. In Crumley, C. (ed.) *New Directions in Anthropology and Environment.* Altamira Press. Walnut Creek.

Kempton, W., Boster, J. & Hartley, J. (1995) *Environmental Values in American Culture.* MIT Press, Cambridge.

Kertzer, D. & Fricke, T. (eds.) *Anthropological Demography: Towards a Synthesis.* University of Chicago Press, Chicago.

Kirch, P. (1992) The archeology of history. In Kirch, P. & Sahlins, M. (eds.) *Anahulu: The Anthropology of History in the Kingdom of Hawaii.* Vol. 2. University of Chicago Press, Chicago.

Kirk, D. (1996) Demographic transition theory. *Population Studies* **50**, 361–387.

Klein Goldwijk, C.G.M. & Battjes, J.J. (1997) *One Hundred Year Database for Integrated Environmental Assessments.* National Institute for Public Health and Environment (RIVM), Bilthoven.

Knapp, G. (1982) Prehistoric flood management on the Peruvian coast: Reinterpreting the "sunken fields" of Chilca. *American Antiquity* **47**, 144–154.

Kohler, T. (1992) Prehistoric human impact on the environment in upland North American southwest. *Population and Environment* **13** (4), 255–268.

Kormondy, E.J. & Brown, D.E. (1998) Evolution: then and now. *Fundamentals of Human Ecology*. Prentice Hall, Upper Saddle River, N.J.

Kroeber, A. (1939) *Cultural and Natural Areas of Native North America*. University of California Press, Berkeley.

Kummer, D.M. & Turner, II, B.L. (1994) The human causes of deforestation in southeast Asia. *BioScience* **44**, 323–328.

Lambin, E.F., Turner, B.L., Geist, H.J., et al. (2001) The causes of land-use and land-cover change: Moving beyond the myths. *Global Environmental Change: Human and Policy Dimensions* **11** (4), 261–269.

Lambin, E.F., Geist, H. & Lepers, E. (2003) Dynamics of land-use and land cover change in tropical regions. *Annual Review of Environment and Resources* **28**, 205–241.

Landes, D.S. (1969) *The Unbound Prometheus: Technological Change and Industrial Development in Western Europe from 1750 to the Present*. (2nd Edn. published 2003). Cambridge University Press, Cambridge.

Lansing, J.S. (1991) *Priests and Programmers: Technologies of Power in the Engineered Landscape of Bali*. Princeton University Press, Princeton.

Lasker, G. (1952) Environmental growth factors and selective migration. *Human Biology* **24**, 52–58.

Lasker, G. & Mascie-Taylor, C.G.N. (1988) The framework of migration studies. In Mascie-Taylor C.G.N. & Lasker G.W. (eds.) *Biological Aspects of Human Migration*. Cambridge University Press. Cambridge, pp. 1–13.

Laurence, W., Cochrane, M., Bergen, S., et al. (2001) The future of the Brazilian Amazon. *Science* **291**, 438–442.

Laurence, W.R., Lovejoy, T.E., Vasconcelos, H.L., et al. (2002) Ecosystem decay of Amazonian forest fragments: A 22-year investigation. *Conservation Biology* **16**, 605–618.

Lee, R.B. (1979) *The !Kung San: Men, Women, and Work in a Foraging Society*. Cambridge University Press, Cambridge.

Lee, R.B. & DeVore, I. (eds.) (1968) *Man, the Hunter*. Aldine, Chicago.

Lee, R.B. & DeVore, I. (eds.) (1976) *Kalahari Hunter-gatherers*. Harvard University Press, Cambridge.

Leemans, R. & Zuidema, G. (1995) Evaluating changes in land cover and their importance for global change. *Tree* **10**, 76–81.

Lees, S. & Bates, D. (1977) The role of exchange in productive specialization. *American Anthropologist* **79**, 824–841.

Leibenstein, H. (1976) *Beyond Economic Man*. Harvard University Press, Cambridge.

Levin, R.I. & Kirkpatrick, C.A. (1975) *Quantitative Approaches to Management*. 3rd Edn. McGraw-Hill, New York.

Levine, J.M. (2000) Species diversity and biological invasions: Relating local process to community pattern. *Science* **288**, 852–854.

Levins, R. (1968) *Evolution in Changing Environments*. Princeton University Press, Princeton.

Libecap, G. (1989) *Contracting for Property Rights*. Cambridge University Press, New York.

Libecap, G. (1995) The conditions for successful collective action. In Keohane, R. & Ostrom, E. (eds) *Local Commons and Global Interdependence: Heterogeneity and Cooperation in Two Domains*. Sage, London, pp. 161–190.

Lindblom, C. (1964) The science of muddling through. In Gore, W.J. & Dyson, J.W. (eds.) *The Making of Decisions*. Free Press, New York.

Little, M.A. & Leslie, P.W. (eds.) (1999) *Turkana Herders of the Dry Savana: Ecology and Biobehavioral Response of Nomads to an Uncertain Environment*. Oxford University Press, New York.

Liu, J. (2001) Integrating ecology with human demography, behavior, and socioeconomics: Needs and approaches. *Ecological Modelling* **140**, 1–8.

Liu, J., Ouyang, Z., Taylor, W., Groop, R., Tan, Y. & Zhang, H. (1999) A framework for evaluating effects of human factors on wildlife habitat: The case of the giant pandas. *Conservation Biology* **13** (6), 1360–1370.

Liu, J., Daily, G.C., Ehrlich, P.R. & Luck G.W. (2003) Effects of household dynamics on resource consumption and biodiversity. *Nature* **421** (6922), 530–533.

Liverman, D.M. (1994) Vulnerability to global environmental change. In Cutter, S. (ed.) *Environmental Risks and Hazards*. Prentice Hall, New York, pp. 326–342.

Liverman, D.M. & O'Brien, K.L. (2001) Southern skies: International environmental policy in Mexico. In The Social Learning Group (eds.) *Learning to Manage Global Environmental Risks: A Comparative History of Social Responses to Climate Change, Ozone Depletion and Acid Rain*. Vol. 1. MIT Press, Cambridge.

Liverman, D.M., Moran, E.F., Rindfuss, R. & Stern, P. (eds.) (1998) *People and Pixels: Linking Remote Sensing and Social Science*. National Academies Press, Washington, DC.

Lloyd, W. (1977) On the checks to population. In Hardin, F.V. & Baden, J. (eds.) *Managing the Commons*. (Originally published in 1833). W.H. Freeman, San Francisco, pp. 8–15.

Losey, J.S., Rayor, L.S. & Carter, M. (1999) Transgenic pollen harms monarch larvae. *Nature* **399**, 214.

Loucks, C., Lu, Z., Dinerstein, E., et al. (2001) Giant pandas in a changing landscape. *Science* **294**, 1465.

Lu, D., Mausel, P., Brondizio, E. & Moran, E.F. (2003) Classification of the successional forest stages in the Brazilian Amazon basin. *Forest Ecology and Management* **181**, 301–312.

Lugo, A. (2002) Can we manage tropical landscapes? An answer from the Caribbean perspective. *Landscape Ecology* **17** (7), 601–615.

Lugo, A. & Brown, S. (1992) Tropical forests as sinks of atmospheric carbon. *Forest Ecology and Management* **54**, 239–255.

Lutz, W., Sanderson, W. & Scherbov, S. (2001) The end of world population growth. *Nature* **412**, 543–545.

Lutz, W., Prskawetz, A. & Sanderson, W. (eds.) (2002) Population and environment: Methods of analysis. *Supplement to Population and Development Review* **28**, 1–250.

Lyell, C. (1830–1833) *Principles of Geology*. John Murray, London.

Mackay, D.M. (1968a) The informational analysis of questions and commands. In Buckley, W. (ed.) *Modern Systems Research for the Behavioral Scientist*. Aldine, Chicago, pp. 204–209.

Mackay, D.M. (1968b) Towards an information flow model of human behavior. In Buckley, W. (ed.) *Modern Systems Research for the Behavioral Scientist*. Aldine, Chicago, pp. 359–368.

Malthus, T.R. (1803) *An Essay on the Principle of Population*. Reprinted in 1989, University Press, Cambridge.

Mann, M.E., Bradley, R.S. & Hughes, M.K. (1999) Northern Hemisphere temperatures during the past millennium: inferences, uncertainties, and limitations. *Geophysical Research Letters* **26** (6), 759–762.

March, J.G. & Simon, H.A. (1958) *Organizations*. Wiley, New York.

Martin, C. (2004) Landscape Water Use in a Desert Metropolis, Phoenix, Arizona. Vignette. Center for Environmental Studies Research.

Martin, P. (1972) The discovery of America. *Science* **179**, 969–974.

Martin, P. (1984) Prehistoric overkill: the global model. In Martin, P. & Klein, R. (eds.) *Quaternary Extinctions*. University of Arizona Press, Tucson, pp. 354–403.

Martin, P. & Szuter, C. (2004) Revising the Wild West: Big game meets the ultimate keystone species. In Redman, C. et al. (eds.) *The Archeology of Global Change: The Impact of Humans on their Environment*. Smithsonian Books, Washington, DC.

Marvier, M. (2001) Ecology of transgenic crops. *American Scientist* **89**, 160–167.

McCabe, T. (2004) *Cattle Bring Us to Our Enemies: Turkana Ecology, History, and Raiding in a Disequilibrium System*. University of Michigan Press, Ann Arbor.

McConnell, W.J. & Keys, E. (2005) Meta-analysis of agricultural change. In Moran, E.F. & Ostrom, E. (eds.) *Seeing the Forest and the Trees: Human-Environment Interactions in Forest Ecosystems.* MIT Press, Cambridge, pp. 325–353.

McCracken, S., Brondizio, E., Nelson, D., Moran, E. & Siqueira, A., Rodrigues-Pedraza, C. (1999) Remote Sensing and GIS at Farm Property Level: Demography and Deforestation in the Brazilian Amazon. *Photogrammetric Engineering and Remote Sensing* **65**, 1311–1320.

McCracken, S., Boucek, B. & Moran, E.F. (2002) Deforestation trajectories in a frontier region of the Brazilian Amazon. In Walsh, S.J. & Crews-Meyer, K. (eds.) *Linking People, Place, and Policy: A GIScience Approach.* Kluwer Academic Publishers, Boston, pp. 215–234.

McGovern, T., Bigelow, G., Amorosi, T. & Russell, D. (1988) Northern islands, human error, and environmental degradation: A view of social and ecological change in the medieval North Atlantic. *Human Ecology* **16** (3), 225–270.

Mead, J. & Steadman, D. (eds.) (1995) *Late Quaternary Environments and Deep History: A Tribute to Paul Martin.* Scientific Papers **3**, The Mammoth Site, Hot Springs.

Meggers, B.J. (1971) *Amazonia, Man and Culture in a Counterfeit Paradise.* Aldine, Chicago.

Mesquita, R.C.G., Ickes, K., Ganade, G. & Williamson, G.B. (2001) Alternative successional pathways in the Amazon Basin. *Journal of Ecology* **89**, 528–537.

Meyer, W. & Turner II, B.L. (1994) *Changes in Land Use and Land Cover: A Global Perspective.* Cambridge University Press, Cambridge.

Miller, G., Jr. (1975) *Living in the Environment.* Wadsworth, Belmont, CA.

Moffat, A.S. (1996) Ecologists look at the big picture. *Science* **273**, 1490.

Moran, E.F. (1976) *Agricultural Development in the Transamazon Highway.* Indiana University Latin American Studies Center, Bloomington.

Moran, E.F. (1979a) *Human Adaptability.* Duxbury Press, N. Scituate.

Moran, E.F. (1979b) Criteria for choosing successful homesteaders in Brazil. *Research in Economic Anthropology* **2**, 339–359.

Moran, E.F. (1981) *Developing the Amazon.* Indiana University Press, Bloomington.

Moran, E.F. (1988) Social reproduction in agricultural frontiers. In Bennett, J. & Bowen, J. (eds.) *Production and Autonomy: Anthropological Studies and Critiques of Development.* University Press of America, Society for Economic Anthropology, Washington, DC, pp. 199–212.

Moran, E.F. (ed.) (1990) *The Ecosystem Approach in Anthropology: From Concept to Practice.* University of Michigan Press, Ann Arbor.

Moran, E.F. (1993) Deforestation and land use in the Brazilian Amazon. *Human Ecology* **21**, 1–21.

Moran, E.F. (2000) *Human Adaptability: An Introduction to Ecological Anthropology.* 2nd Edn. Westview Press, Boulder.

Moran, E.F. & Brondizio, E.S. (1998) Land use change after deforestation in Amazonia. In Liverman, et al. (eds.) *People and Pixels: Linking Remote Sensing and Social Science.* National Academies Press, Washington DC, pp. 94–120.

Moran, E.F. & Brondizio, E.S. (2001) Human ecology from space: Ecological anthropology engages the study of global environmental change. In Messner, E. & Lambeck, M. (eds.) *Ecology and the Sacred: Engaging the Anthropology of Roy A. Rappaport.* University of Michigan Press, Ann Arbor, pp. 64–87.

Moran, E.F. & Ostrom, E. (eds.) (2005) *Seeing the Forest and the Trees: Human-Environment Interactions in Forest Ecosystems.* MIT Press, Cambridge.

Moran, E.F., Brondizio, E.S., Mausel, P. & Wu, Y. (1994) Integrating Amazonian vegetation, land use, and satellite data. *Bioscience* **44** (5), 329–338.

Moran, E.F., Packer, A., Brondizio, E.S. & Tucker, J. (1996) Restoration of vegetation cover in the eastern Amazon. *Ecological Economics* **18**, 41–54.

Moran, E.F., Brondizio, E., Tucker, J., da Silva-Forsberg, M.C., McCracken, S. & Falesi, I. (2000a) Effects of soil fertility and land-use on forest succession in Amazonia. *Forest Ecology and Management* **139**, 93–108.

Moran, E.F., Brondizio, E.S., Tucker, J., Silva-Forsberg, M.C., Falesi, I. & McCracken S. (2000b) Strategies for Amazonian forest restoration: Evidence for afforestation in five regions of the Brazilian Amazon. In A. Hall (ed.) *Amazonia at the Crossroads: The Challenge of Sustainable Development.* Institute of Latin American Studies, London. pp. 129–149.

Moran, E.F., Brondizio, E.S. & McCracken, S. (2002) Trajectories of land use: soils, succession, and crop choice. In Wood, C.H. & Porro, R. (eds.) *Deforestation and Land Use in the Amazon.* University Press of Florida, Gainesville, pp. 193–217.

Moran, E.F., Siqueira, A. & Brondizio, E. (2003) Household demographic structure and its relationship to Deforestation in the Amazon Basin. In Fox, J. et al. (eds.) *People and the Environment: Approaches to Linking Household and Community Surveys to Remote Sensing and GIS.* Kluwer Academic Publishers, Boston, pp. 61–89.

Myers, D. (2000) *Wealth, Well-Being, and the New American Dream.* Column No. 2, Center for a New American Dream. http://www.newdream.org/

Myers, T. (1991) The world's forests and human populations: The environmental interconnections. In Davis, K. & Bernstam, M. (eds.) *Resources, Environment and Population.* Oxford University Press, New York, pp. 237–251.

Naess, A. (1974) *Gandhi and Group Conflict: An Exploration of Satyagraha.* University of Oslo Press, Oslo.

Naess, A. (1979) Modesty and the Conquest of Mountains. In Tobias, M. (ed.) *The Mountain Spirit.* Overlook Press, Woodstock.

Naess, A. (1989) *Ecology, Community and Lifestyle: Outline of an Ecosophy.* Cambridge University Press, Cambridge.

National Research Council (1989) *Alternative Agriculture.* National Academies Press, Washington, DC.

National Research Council (1992) *Global Environmental Change: Understanding the Human Dimensions.* National Academies Press, Washington, DC.

National Research Council (1994) *Science and Judgment in Risk Assessment.* National Academies Press, Washington, DC.

National Research Council (1996) *Understanding Risk: Informing Decisions in a Democratic Society.* National Academies Press, Washington, DC.

National Research Council (1997) *Environmentally Significant Consumption.* National Academies Press, Washington, DC.

National Research Council (1999a) *Human Dimensions of Global Environmental Change: Research Pathways for the Next Decade.* National Academies Press, Washington, DC.

National Research Council (1999b) *Making Climate Forecasts Matter.* National Academies Press, Washington, DC.

National Research Council (2001) *Grand Challenges in the Environmental Sciences.* National Academies Press, Washington, DC.

Nepstad, D., Moreira, A. & Alencar, A. (1999) *Flames in the Rainforest: Origins, Impacts, and Alternatives to Amazonian Fire.* World Bank, Washington, DC.

Nepstad, D., McGrath, D., Alencar, A., et al. (2002) Frontier governance in Amazonia. *Science* **295**, 629–631.

Netting, R.M. (1968) *Hill Farmers of Nigeria; Cultural Ecology of the Kofyar of the Jos Plateau.* University of Washington Press, Seattle.

Netting, R.M. (1971) The ecological approach in cultural study. *Addison-Wesley Module in Anthropology* **6**.

Netting, R.M. (1972) Of men and meadows: Strategies of alpine land use. *Anthropological Quarterly* **45**, 132–144.

Netting, R.M. (1974) Agrarian ecology. *Annual Review of Anthropology* **3**, 21–56.

Netting, R.M. (1976) What alpine peasants have in common: Observations on communal tenure in a Swiss village. *Human Ecology* **4** (2), 135–146.

Netting, R.M. (1977) *Cultural Ecology*. Cummings, Menlo Park.

Netting, R.M. (1981) *Balancing on an Alp*. Cambridge University Press, Cambridge.

Netting, R.M. (1986) Cultural Ecology. 2nd Edn. Waveland, Project Heights.

Netting, R.M. (1993) *Smallholders, Householders*. Stanford University Press, Stanford.

Netting, R.M., Stone, G.D. & Stone, M.P. (1995) Social organization of agrarian labor. In Moran, E. (ed.) *The Comparative Analysis of Human Societies*. L. Rienner Publisher, Boulder.

Norby, R.J., Hanson, P.J., O'Neill, E.G., et al. (2002) Net primary productivity of a CO_2-enriched deciduous forest and the implications for carbon storage. *Ecological Applications* **12**, 1261–1266.

Nordhaus, W.D. (1997) Do real-output and real-wage measures capture reality? The history of lighting suggests not. In Bresnahan, T. & Gordon, R. (eds.) *The Economics of New Goods*. University of Chicago Press, Chicago, pp. 29–66.

Norton, B.G. (1991) *Towards Unity among Environmentalists*. Oxford University Press, New York.

Odum, E. (1971) *Fundamentals of Ecology*, 3rd Edn. Saunders, Philadelphia.

Odum, H.T. (1971) *Environment, Power and Society*. Wiley-Interscience, New York.

Oelschlaeger, M. (1991) *The Idea of Wilderness: From Prehistory to the Age of Ecology*. Yale University Press, New Haven.

Oelschlaeger, M. (1994) *Caring for Creation: An Ecumenical Approach to the Environmental Crisis*. Yale University Press, New Haven.

Ogilvie, A. (1981) *Climate and Society in Iceland from the Medieval Period to the late 18th century*. Doctoral dissertation. University of East Anglia, Norwich.

Olson, M. (1965) *The Logic of Collective Action: Public Goods and the Theory of Groups*. Harvard University Press, Cambridge.

O'Neill, B. & Chen, B. (Submitted) Demographic Determinants of Household Energy Use in the U.S. *Population and Development Review*.

O'Neill, B., McKellar, L. & Lutz, W. (2004) Population, greenhouse gas emissions, and climate change. In Lutz, W. et al. (eds.) *The End of World Population Growth in the 21st Century: New Challenges for Human Capital Formation and Sustainable Development*, Earthscan, London, pp. 249–280.

Orlove, B. (1980) Ecological anthropology. *Annual Review of Anthropology* **9**, 235–273.

Orlove, B. (1997) *The Allure of the Foreign*. University of Michigan Press, Ann Arbor.

Ostrom, E. (1990) *Governing the Commons: The Evolution of Institutions for Collective Action*. Cambridge University Press, New York.

Ostrom, E. (1998) A behavioral approach to the rational choice theory of collective action. *The American Political Science Review* **92** (1), 1–22.

Ostrom, E. (1999) Self-governance and forest resources. *CIFOR Occasional Paper, no. 20*. Center for International Forestry Research, Bogor, Indonesia.

Ostrom, E., Burger, J., Field, C., Norgaard, R. & Policansky, D. (1999) Revisiting the commons: Local lessons, global challenges. *Science* **284**, 28–282.

Pacala, S., Canham, D., Saponara, J., Silander, J., Kobe, K. & Ribbens, E. (1996) Forest models defined by field measurements estimation, error analysis and dynamics. *Ecological Monographs* **66**, 1–43.

Palerm, A. (1955) The agricultural basis of urban civilization in Mesoamerica: Irrigation civilizations, a comparative study. In Steward, J. (ed.) *Social Science Monographs*, Pan American Union, No. 1, Washington, DC, pp. 28–42.

Palerm, A. (1968) The agricultural basis of urban civilization in Mesoamerica. In Cohen, Y. (ed.) *Man in Adaptation*. Aldine, Chicago, pp. 492–505.

Palumbi, S. (2001) Humans as the world's greatest evolutionary force. *Science* **293**, 1786–1790.

Parry, M. (1990) *Climate Change and World Agriculture*. EarthScan, London.

Pebley, A. (2001) Demography and the environment. *Demography* **35**, 377–389.

Peluso, N. (1992) *Rich Forests, Poor People*. University of California Press, Berkeley.

Penuelas, J. & Filella, I. (2001) Responses to a warming world. *Science* **294**, 793–795.

Petit, J.R., Jouzel, J., Raynaud, D., et al. (1999) Climate and atmospheric history of the past 420,000 years from the Vostock ice core, Antarctica. *Nature* **399**, 429–436.

Pimentel, D. & Pimentel, M. (1996) *Food, Energy, and Society*. Revised Edn. University Press of Colorado, Boulder.

Pimentel, D., Harvey, C., Resosudarmo, P., et al. (1995) Environmental and economic costs of soil erosion and conservation benefits. *Science* **267**, 1117–1123.

Polsky, C. & Easterling III, W. (2001) Adaptation to climate variability and change in the U.S. Great Plains. *Agriculture, Ecosystems and Environment* **85**, 133–144.

Posey, D.A. & Balée, W. (eds.) (1989) Resource management in Amazonia: Indigenous and folk strategies. *Advances in Economic Botany* **7**, 1–282.

Posey, D.A. & Hecht, S. (1989) Preliminary results on soil management techniques of the Kayapó Indians. *Advances in Economic Botany* **7**, 174–188.

Potter, J.E. (1999) The Persistence of Outmoded Contraceptive Regimes: The cases of Mexico and Brazil. *Population and Development Review* **25** (4), 703–739.

Potts, R. (1996) *Humanity's Descent: The Consequences of Ecological Instability.* William Morrow, New York.

Prance, G.T. (ed.) (1986) *Tropical Rain Forests and the World Atmosphere.* Westview Press, Boulder.

Pretty, J.N. (1998) *The Living Land.* Earthscan, London.

Pretty, J.N. (1995) *Regenerating Agriculture: Policies and Practice for Sustainability and Self-reliance.* Joseph Henry Press, Washington DC.

Pretty, J.N. (2002) *Agri-culture: Reconnecting People, Land, and Nature.* EarthScan, London.

Quinn, D. (1992) *Ishmael: An Adventure of the Mind and Spirit.* Bantam/Turner Books, New York.

Quinn, D. (1996) *The Story of B: An Adventure of the Mind and Spirit.* Bantam/Turner Books, New York.

Rahmstorf, S. (2002) Ocean circulation and climate during the past 120,000 years. *Nature* **419**, 207–214.

Rahmstorf, S. & Stocker, T.F. (2003) Thermohaline circulation: past changes and future surprises. In: W. Steffen et al. (eds.) *Global Change and the Earth System,* IGBP Series, Springer, 240–241.

Rappaport, R. (1968) *Pigs for the Ancestors: Ritual in the Ecology of a New Guinea People.* (New Edn. 1984) Yale University Press, New Haven.

Rappaport, R. (1971) The sacred in human evolution. *Annual Review of Ecology and Systematics* **2**, 23–44.

Rappaport, R. (1979) *Ecology, Meaning and Religion.* North Atlantic Books, Richmond.

Raven, P. (2002) Science, sustainability, and the human prospect. *Science* **297**, 954–958.

Redclift, M. (1996) *Wasted: Counting the Costs of Global Consumption.* EarthScan, London.

Redman, C. (1999) *Human Impact on Ancient Environments.* University of Arizona Press, Tucson.

Redman, C. & Kinzig, A. (2003) Resilience of past landscapes: resilience theory, society, and the Longue Durée. *Conservation Ecology* **7**, 14.

Redman, C., James, S. & Fish, P. (eds.) (2004) *The Archeology of Global Change*. Smithsonian Press, Washington, DC.

Relethford, J. (2003) *The Human Species: An Introduction to Biological Anthropology*, 5th Edn. McGraw-Hill, Boston.

Richerson, P., Boyd, R. & Paciotti, B. (2002) An evolutionary theory of commons management. In Ostrom, E. et al. (eds.) *The Drama of the Commons*. National Academies Press, Washington, DC, pp. 403–442.

Ricklefs, R. (1973) *Ecology*. 3rd Edn. Chiron Press, Portland.

Ricklefs, R. (2001) *The Economy of Nature*. 5th Edn. W.H. Freeman, New York.

Rindfuss, R., Walsh, S., Mishra, V., Fox, J. & Dolcemascolo, G. (2003) Linking household and remotely sensed data: Methodological and practical problems. In Fox, J. et al. (eds.) *People and the Environment: approaches for linking household and community surveys to remote sensing and GIS*. Kluwer, Dordrecht, pp. 1–29.

Rival, L. (ed.) (1998) *The Social Life of Trees: Anthropological Perspectives on Tree Symbolism*. Berg, New York.

Roosevelt, A. (1989) Resource management in Amazonia before the conquest: Beyond ethnographic projection. *Advances in Economic Botany* **7**, 30–62.

Roosevelt, A. (1991) *Moundbuilders of the Amazon: Geophysical Archaeology on Marajó Island, Brazil*. Academic Press, San Diego.

Roush, W. (1997) Putting a price tag on Nature. *Science* **276**, 1029.

Runge, C.F. (1981) Common property externalities: isolation, assurance and resource depletion in a traditional grazing context. *American Journal of Agricultural Economics* **63**, 595–606.

Runge, C.F. (1984) Strategic interdependence in models of property rights. *American Journal of Agricultural. Economics* **66**, 807–813.

Sanford, R., Saldarriaga, J., Clark, K., Uhl, C. & Herrera, R. (1985) Amazon rain forest fires. *Science* **227**, 53–55.

Samuelson, P. (1983) Thunen at two hundred. *Journal of Economic Literature* **21**, 1468–1488.

Santos, R., Flowers, N., Coimbra Jr., C.E.A. & Gugelmin, S. (1997) Tapirs, tractors and tapes: the changing economy and ecology of the Xavante Indians of central Brazil. *Human Ecology* **25**, 545–566.

Schick, K. & Toth, N. (1993) *Making Silent Stones Speak: Human Evolution and the Dawn of Technology*. Touchstone Publishers, New York.

Schimel, D., et al. (2001) Recent patterns and mechanisms of carbon exchange by terrestrial ecosystems. *Nature* **414**, 169–172.

Schneider, H. (1974) *Economic Man*. Free Press, New York.

Sessions, G. (ed.) (1995) *Deep Ecology for the 21st Century: Readings on the Philosophy and Practice of the New Environmentalism.* Shambhala, Boston.

Sheppard, C.R.C. (2003) Predicted recurrences of coral reef mortality in the Indian Ocean. *Nature* **425**, 294–297.

Simon, H. (1985) Human nature in politics: the dialogue of psychology with political science. *American Political Science Review* **79**, 293–304.

Simon, H. (1997) *Models of Bounded Rationality: Empirically Grounded Economic Reason.* MIT Press, Cambridge.

Simon, J. (1990) *Population Matters: People, Resources, Environment and Integration.* Transaction Publishers, New Brunswick.

Skole, D. & Tucker, C. (1993) Tropical deforestation and habitat fragmentation in the Amazon: Satellite data from 1978 to 1988. *Science* **260**, 1905–1909.

Slovic, P., Kunreuther, H. & White, G.F. (1974) Decision processes, rationality and adjustment to natural hazards. In White G.F. (ed.) *Natural Hazards, Local, National and Global.* Oxford University Press, New York, pp. 187–205.

Smith, A. (1977) *A Theory of Moral Sentiments.* (From the 1804 original.) Oxford University Press, New York.

Smith, B. (1989) Origins of agriculture in eastern North America. *Science* **246**, 1566–1571.

Smith, E.A. (1983) Anthropological applications of optimal foraging theory. *Current Anthropology* **24** (5), 625–651.

Smith, E.A. (1984) Anthropology, evolutionary ecology, and the explanatory limitations of the ecosystem concept. In E.F. Moran (ed.) *The Ecosystem Concept in Anthropology.* American Association for the Advancement of Science, Washington DC, pp. 51–86.

Smith, N.J.H. (1982) *Rainforest corridors: The Transamazon Colonization Scheme.* University of California Press, Berkeley.

Smith, N.L. (2002) Species Extinction. http://www.whole-systems.org/extinctions.html, 24 Jan 2003.

Sober, E. & Wilson, D. (1998) *Unto Others: The Evolution and Psychology of Unselfish Behavior.* Harvard University Press, Cambridge.

Sponsel, L.E. (ed.) (1995) *Indigenous Peoples and the Future of Amazonia.* University of Arizona Press, Tucson.

Sponsel, L.E. (ed.) (2000) *Endangered Peoples of Southeast and East Asia.* Greenwood Press, London.

Sponsel, L.E. (2001) Do anthropologists need religion, and vice versa? Adventures and dangers in spiritual ecology. In C. Crumley (ed.) *New Directions in Anthropology and the Environment.* Altamira Press, Walnut Creek, CA, pp. 177–200.

Spooner, B. (1972) *Population Growth: Anthropological Implications*. MIT Press, Cambridge.

Steadman, D. (1995) Prehistoric extinctions of Pacific Island birds: biodiversity meets zooarcheology. *Science* **267**, 1123–1131.

Steffen, W., Sanderson, A., Tyson, P., et al (eds.) (2003) *Global Change and the Earth System: A Planet under Pressure*. Springer-Verlag, New York.

Steininger, M.K. (1996) Tropical secondary forest regrowth in the Amazon: Age, area and change estimation with Thematic Mapper data. *International Journal of Remote Sensing* **17**, 9–27.

Stern, P. (1999) Information, incentives, and proenvironmental consumer behavior. *Journal of Consumer Policy* **22**, 461–478.

Stern, P. (2000) Psychology and the science of human–environment interactions. *American Psychologist* **55**, 523–530.

Stern, P. & Easterling, W.E., (eds.) (1999) *Making Climate Forecasts Matter*. National Academies Press, Washington, DC.

Stern, P., Aronson, E., Darley, J., et al. (1986) The effectiveness of incentives for residential energy conservation. *Evaluation Review* **10**, 147–176.

Stern, P., Dietz, T., Abel, T., Guagnano, G. & Kaloff, L. (1999) A social psychological theory of support for social movements: the case of environmentalism. *Human Ecology Review* **6**, 81–97.

Steward, J. (1938) *Basin-Plateau Aboriginal Sociopolitical Groups*. Smithsonian Institution, Bureau of American Ethnography Bulletin 120, Government Printing Office, Washington, DC.

Steward, J. (1955) *The Theory of Culture Change*. University of Illinois Press, Urbana.

Suttles, W. (1968) Coping with abundance. In Lee, R. & DeVore, I., *Man the Hunter*. Aldine, Chicago, pp. 56–68.

Szreter, S. (1996) *Fertility, Class and Gender in Britain, 1860–1940*. Cambridge University Press, New York.

Szuter, C. (1991) *Hunting by Prehistoric Horticulturalists in the American Southwest*. Garland, New York.

Thomas, F. (1925) *The Environmental Basis of Society*. Century Company, New York.

Thomas, W., Sauer, C., Bates, M. & Mumford, L. (1956) *Man's Role in Changing the Face of the Earth*. University of Chicago Press, Chicago.

Thompson, L., Davis, M. & Mosley-Thompson, E. (1994) Glacial records of global climate: A 1500-year tropical ice core record of climate. *Human Ecology* **22**, 93–96.

Thünen, J.H. von (1966) *The Isolated State* – An English Translation of *Der Isolierte Staat* (Translated by Carla M. Wartenberg). Pergamon Press, Oxford.

Tilman, D. (1999) Global environmental impacts of agricultural expansion: The need for sustainable and efficient practices. *Proceedings of the National Academy of Sciences* **96**, 5995–6000.

Tilman, D. (2001) Effects of diversity and composition on grassland stability and productivity. In Press, M. et al. (eds.) *Ecology: Achievement and Challenge*. Cambridge University Press, New York, pp. 183–207.

Tucker, J., Brondizio, E. & Moran, E.F. (1998) Rates of forest regrowth in eastern Amazônia: A comparison of Altamira and Bragantina regions, Pará state, Brazil. *Interciencia* **23** (2), 64–73.

Turgot, A.R.J. (1973 [1808]). On universal history. In *Turgot on Progress, Sociology and Economics* (translated and edited by Ronald L. Meek). Cambridge University Press, Cambridge, pp. 61–118.

Turner, II, B.L., Clark, W.C., Kates, R.W., Richards, J.F., Mathews, J.T. & Meyer, W.B. (eds.) (1990) *The Earth as Transformed by Human Action: Global and Regional Changes in the Biosphere over the Past 300 Years*. Cambridge University Press, Cambridge.

Turner, II, B.L., Hyden, G. & Kates, R. (eds.) (1993) *Population Growth and Agricultural Change in Africa: Studies from Densely Settled Areas of Sub-saharan Africa*. University Press of Florida, Gainesville.

Turner, II, B.L., Cortina Villar, S., Foster, D., et al. (2001) Deforestation and agricultural change in the Southern Yucatan Peninsular Region: Integrative land change for global change studies. *Forestry, Ecosystems, and Management* **154** (3), 343–370.

Turner, II, B.L., Geoghegan, J. & Foster, D.R. (eds.) (2004) *Integrated Land-Change Science and Tropical Deforestation in the Southern Yucatan*. Oxford University Press, Oxford.

United Nations Environment Programme (UNEP) (2000) *Global Environmental Outlook 2000*. United Nations Environment Programme.

U.S. Bureau of the Census (2000) International database. http://www.census.gov/ipc/www/Worldpop.htm, data updated 10 May 2000.

Van der Leeuw, S. (ed.) (1998) *The Archaeomedes Project: Understanding the Natural and Anthropogenic Causes of Land Degradation and Desertification in the Mediterranean Basin*. European Communities, Luxembourg.

VanWey, L. & Moran, E. (In prep) The household developmental cycle in the Amazon frontier. To be submitted to *Population and Development Review*.

Varughese, G. & Ostrom, E. (1990) The contested role of heterogeneity. Unpublished paper. Worshop in Political Theory and Policy Analysis. Indiana University, Bloomington.

Vayda, A.P. & Rappaport, R. (1968) Ecology, cultural and non-cultural. *Introduction to Cultural Anthropology*. Clifton, J. (ed.) Houghton Mifflin, Boston, pp. 477–497.

Visser, S. (1982) On agricultural location theory. *Geographical Analysis* **14**, 167–176.

Vitousek, P.M. (1994) Beyond global warming: Ecology and global change. *Ecology* **75**, 1861–1876.

Vitousek, P.M., Mooney, H.A., Lubchenco, J. & Melillo, J.M. (1997a) Human domination of Earth's ecosystems. *Science* **277** (5325), 494–499.

Vitousek, P.M., Aber, J., Howarth, R., et al. (1997b) Human alteration of the global nitrogen cycle: Sources and consequences. *Ecological Applications* **7**: 737–750.

Vorosmarty, C., Green, P., Salisbury, J. & Lammers, R. (2000) Global water resources: Vulnerability from climate change and population growth. *Science* **289**, 284–288.

Wackenagel, M. & Rees, W. (1995) *Our Ecological Footprint: Reducing Human Impact on the Earth*. New Society Publishers: Gabriola Island, BC.

Wade, R. (1988) The management of irrigation systems: How to evoke trust and avoid prisoners' dilemma. *World Development* **16** (4), 489–500.

Walker, R., Moran, E. & Anselin, L. (2000) Deforestation and cattle ranching in the Brazilian Amazon: External capital and household processes. *World Development* **28**, 4, 683–720.

Walsh, S.J. & Crews-Meyer, K.A. (eds.) (2002) *Linking People, Place, and Policy: A GIScience Approach*. Kluwer Academic Publishers, Boston.

Walsh, S.J., Evans, T., Welsh, W., Enwisle, B. & Rindfuss, R. (1999) Scale dependent relationships between population and environment in northeastern Thailand. *Photogrammetric Engineering and Remote Sensing* **65**, 97–105.

Watts, M. & Bohle, H. (1993) The space of vulnerability: The causal structure of hunger. *Progress in Human Geography* **17**, 43–67.

Webber, M. (1973) Equilibrium of location in an isolated state. *Environment and Planning* **5**, 751–759.

Wells, M.J. (1990) Mexican farm workers become strawberry farmers. *Human Organization* **49** (2), 149–156.

Wernick, I. (1997) Consuming materials: the American way. *Environmentally Significant Consumption: Research Directions*. National Academies Press, Washington, DC, pp. 29–37.

White, G. (ed.) (1974) *Natural Hazards*. Oxford University Press. New York.

Whittaker, R.H. (1970) *Communities and Ecosystems*. Macmillan Publishing Co.

Wilk, R. (1998) Emulation, imitation, and global consumerism. *Organization and Environment* **11**, 314–333.

Wilk, R. (2002) Consumption, Human Needs, and Global Environmental Change. *Global Environmental Change* **12** (1), 5–13.

Wilmsen, E.N. (1989) *Land Filled with Flies: a political economy of the Kalahari*. University of Chicago Press, Chicago.

Winterhalder, B. (1981) Foraging strategies in a Boreal environment: An analysis of Cree hunting and gathering. In Winterhalder, B. & Smith, E.A., *Hunter-Gatherer Foraging Strategies*. University of Chicago Press, Chicago, pp. 66–98.

Winterhalder, B. (1984) Reconsidering the Ecosystem Concept. *Reviews in Anthropology* **11** (4), 301–330.

Winterhalder, B. (1986) Diet choice, risk and food sharing in a stochastic environment. *Journal of Anthropological Archeology* **5**, 369–392.

Winterhalder, B. (1994) Concepts in Historical Ecology: The view from evolutionary theory. In *Historical Ecology*. C. Crumley (ed.) School of American Research Press, Santa Fe. Pp. 17–42.

Winterhalder, B., Larsen, R. & Thomas, R.B. (1974) Dung as an essential resource in a highland Peruvian community. *Human Ecology* **2**, 89–104.

Wood, C. & Skole, D. (1998) Linking satellite, census, and survey data to study deforestation in the Brazilian Amazon. In Liverman, D., et al. (eds.) *People and Pixels*. National Academies Press, Washington, DC. Pp. 70–93.

Worster, D. (1984) History as natural history: An essay on theory and method. *Pacific Historical Review* **3**, 1–19.

Worster, D. (1988) *The Ends of the Earth: Perspectives on Modern Environmental History*. Cambridge University Press, Cambridge.

Yellen, J. (1977) *Archeological Approaches to the Present: Models for Reconstructing the Past*. Academic Press, New York.

Young, K. (1994) Roads and the environmental degradation of tropical montane forests. *Conservation Biology* **8** (4), 972–976.

Zarin, D., Ducey, M.J., Tucker, J.M. & Salas, W.A. (2001) Potential biomass accumulation in Amazonian regrowth forests. *Ecosystems* **4**, 658–668.

Zarin, D., Alavapati, J., Putz, F.E. & Schmink, M. (eds.) (2002) *Working Forests in the Tropics: Conservation Through Sustainable Management?* Columbia University Press, New York.

Index

Note: page numbers in *italics* denote illustrations, tables or figures